ORFF-SCHULWERK
Applications for the Classroom

BRIGITTE WARNER
The Key-School
Annapolis, MD

PRENTICE HALL   Englewood Cliffs, New Jersey 07632

Library of Congress Cataloging-in-Publication Data

Warner, Brigitte
    Orff-Schulwerk : applications for the classroom / Brigitte Warner.
        p.   cm.
    Includes bibliographical references and index.
    ISBN 0-13-639824-3
    1. School music--Instruction and study. 2. Orff, Carl, 1895-1982
Orff-Schulwerk.   I. Title.
MT1.W33 1991
780'.7--dc20   90-40203
                                                        CIP
                                                         MN

Editorial/production supervision and
   interior design: Arthur Maisel
Cover design: Miriam Recio
Prepress buyers: Ray Keating
   and Herb Klein
Manufacturing buyer: David Dickey

 © 1991 by Prentice-Hall, Inc.
A Division of Simon & Schuster
Englewood Cliffs, New Jersey 07632

Printed in the United States of America

10   9   8   7   6   5   4   3   2   1

ISBN 0-13-639824-3

Prentice-Hall International (UK) Limited, *London*
Prentice-Hall of Australia Pty. Limited, *Sydney*
Prentice-Hall Canada Inc., *Toronto*
Prentice-Hall Hispanoamericana, S.A., *Mexico*
Prentice-Hall of India Private Limited, *New Delhi*
Prentice-Hall of Japan, Inc., *Tokyo*
Simon & Schuster Asia Pte. Ltd., *Singapore*
Editora Prentice-Hall do Brasil, Ltda., *Rio de Janeiro*

CONTENTS

8
THE FIVE PENTATONIC MODES   *192*

Anhemitonic Scale Structures in World Musics and in Western
Music *192*

The Pentatonic Modes in Orff-Schulwerk *194*
Theoretical aspects 194
Deciding short- and long-term teaching goals 198
Teaching procedures 200

Arranging Traditional Songs *206*
Sources for appropriate materials 206
Songs in do-pentatonic 207
Songs in la-pentatonic 210
Re- and so-pentatonic 216
The mi-mode 222

Summary *222*

9
RECORDER PLAYING   *224*

The Recorder in Orff-Schulwerk *224*
The instrument 224
The recorder in the classroom 226
Planning the first year 229

The First Steps in Recorder Playing (Call and Chant
Pitches) *229*
The fundamentals 230
Reinforcement 233
1. Exercises involving listening (playing while moving) 234
2. Reading 236
3. Ensemble play (adding recorder parts to a piece) 237

Sequencing Pitch Introduction in Accordance with the Melodic-
Harmonic Development in Pentatonic *239*

Summary *242*

10
WORD AND LANGUAGE IN ORFF-SCHULWERK   *244*

Language and Culture *244*

Small Forms of Oral Lore *247*
The proverb 247
The riddle 251
Poetry 252

PREFACE

Over the past two decades I have taught many workshops and teacher training courses in Orff-Schulwerk. I have been consistently impressed by the dedication and enthusiasm of those attending. Everyone wants to be a better teacher and everyone is striving toward that goal—in this I have not been disappointed. What has continued to distress me, however, is the confusion that persists as to how to become first-rate interpreters of Orff-Schulwerk. Too many are unsure, perhaps understandably so, for Orff-Schulwerk is a complex and many-sided approach. It cannot reveal all of its facets totally and in detail within the limited period of time allotted to us during the training courses. But our schooling as teachers continues in the classroom year after year, as we explore and probe ever further. Because much of the time we must depend upon our own ability to explore and analyze, to contemplate and build, we must be clear about the direction of our search, or else we will rely upon others more than we should and put our faith in rules rather than in our own judgment.

Let me say at the very beginning, therefore, that I firmly believe that, unless we acquire an intimate knowledge of the original five-volume Orff-Keetman work, *Music for Children,* we cannot become informed and effective teachers. Accordingly, the reader is urged to have at hand Volume I of the Orff-Keetman text, to study in conjunction with my discussion and to refer to the many examples from it that I cite.

The essence of Orff-Schulwerk is to awaken and develop musical creativity, which, to a greater or lesser extent, is inherent in everyone. We cannot teach our students how to improvise and create with steadily growing competence unless we as teachers have a clear understanding of how musical concepts evolve from the simple to the complex. Fortunately, the sequence of orderly steps we seek can be found in the original volumes by Orff-Keetman. Unfortunately, these volumes do not spell out the steps in any great detail and it is easy enough to be unsure and, at times, puzzled.

This being the case, I hope to explain in much greater detail the specific steps outlined in the books. In addition, I hope to show that Schulwerk does answer the most important question of all: Why is it that things happen in a particular sequence? Much too often we are satisfied with certain instant successes that are relatively easy to achieve with Orff-Schulwerk materials and teaching techniques. But until we fully comprehend the underlying dynamics of what we do in our classrooms, we will not be able *to make music our own by making music ourselves.* In other words, we will not attain ultimate competence in Orff-Schulwerk. In this regard, our goals for the students must always be our own goals as well. In short, we have to make the same fundamental demand of ourselves as the children make of us, which is to ask questions.

I am aware that interpretations of Orff-Schulwerk differ, and it follows that the answers differ accordingly. This book presents a point of view which comes out of my classroom work and is based on my own perception and interpretation of the approach. Although I have taken pains to verify and research statements dealing with music history, I cannot claim scholarly knowledge in that field.

Finally, it is my hope that music teachers who bring to music education other approaches than that of Orff-Schulwerk will find something of value in this book. In particular, I want to make clear that Orff-Schulwerk is not "just for little children," because, in the end, the improvisation Orff aims for leads to composition, which is the province of adulthood. I have tried, therefore, to be helpful to all those interested in music. If, in some small way, I have succeeded in this, I will have fulfilled a promise I made myself long ago.

ACKNOWLEDGMENTS

During the years this book has been in the making I have learned that writing is painful, very difficult, and lonely. I have also learned that no author can succeed on his or her own without the help and support of many others. It is to these then, and many more whom I have not the space to mention, that I should like to express my deep-felt gratitude.

First and foremost, my thanks go to the Gunild Keetman Assistance Fund and the National Board of Trustees of the American Orff-Schulwerk Association (Arvida Steen, President, 1981) who, through their generous grant, made it possible for me to begin this project.

I am furthermore indebted to the Executive Board of the Middle Atlantic Chapter for their enthusiastic support and encouragement.

To Peter Perhonis, friend and colleague at Key-School, I owe a very special debt. His consistent and deep interest in the progress of the book helped me again and again to overcome lagging spirits and self-doubts. In addition, his careful critiques did much to improve my writing style.

I am indebted to Melba Battin, librarian at Key-School, who always found time to assist me in my search for information.

Louise Bradford-Larkins shared freely and generously with me her invaluable knowledge of children's songs and folksongs. She furthermore provided important copyright information, all of which I gratefully acknowledge.

I have benefitted a great deal from Mary Shamrock's scholarly advice on matters of musicology, in general, and ethnomusicology, in particular.

From among many friends and colleagues I would like to single out Jake Postl, Gin Ebinger, and Rick Layton for their especially generous interest.

I acknowledge with thanks the courteous and patient guidance given to me by the staff of the Archive of Folk Culture and the Copyright Office of the Library of Congress.

To my editors whose expertise cannot be overestimated, I should like to offer my sincere thanks.

I am grateful to the anonymous individuals who initially critiqued the manuscript at the publisher's request. Many of their recommendations proved to be of great value to me.

I also greatly appreciate the assistance given me by the various publishers and authors on matters pertaining to the use of copyrighted material. They are: European American Music, Oxford University Press, B. Schott's Söhne, Louise Bradford, Meredith Stringfield Oates, University of Missouri Press, Harvard University Press, C. F. Peters Corporation, Duke University Press, Kentucky University Press, Harold Courlander, Geordie Music Publishing, Ludlow Music, MMB Music, Hal Leonard Publishing Corporation, Alfred Publishing Co., CPP/Belwin, Orff-Echo of the AOSA, Random House, and Richard Lewis. Individual credit is noted throughout the book.

Brigitte Warner

ORFF-SCHULWERK

1
ORFF,
HIS WORK,
HIS PHILOSOPHY

CARL ORFF AND THE SCHULWERK

At this writing, Orff-Schulwerk: Music for Children is nearly forty years old, not very far from the half-century mark. Although to young people four decades seem to stretch endlessly into the future, for the older generation in looking back they seem to have passed quickly. It comes almost as a shock to the "old guard" of Schulwerk instructors to realize that a new generation of music teachers has grown up for whom Carl Orff is not a contemporary, a living force, the guiding hand behind their work. Who was this man Carl Orff?

In this country most music educators know Orff's Music for Children, and many are familiar with his *Carmina Burana*, an early composition which has become popular through broadcasts and performances, but the majority remain ignorant of his other works. Nevertheless, Carl Orff ranks among the most notable composers of the twentieth century. His Schulwerk, which many take to be his life's work, occupied only a small fraction of his long life (he lived to be 87). However, the development of Schulwerk played an essential part in his evolution as a composer. His years of teaching at the Güntherschule were to determine decisively the direction of his musical expression as a composer. Thus, the music for children and the mature compositions—music for adults—are cut from the same cloth. Though the former uses simpler means of expression, its language and even its themes are similar.

As with other great artists, Carl Orff was fortunate to have grown up in a cultural setting and in a family environment that encouraged his interest in music and the theater. Born in 1895 in Munich, at the age of five he began to study piano under the tutelage of his mother. Family and friends frequently came together in his parents' home to play chamber music. ("Hausmusik" was a widespread custom in Germany among nonprofessional but musically educated people, which I too remember from my own childhood and youth.)

1

The boy's great interest in language and poetry were fostered in school, where classical languages, literature, and essay writing were among his favorite studies. He received his formal musical training at the Akademie der Tonkunst in Munich.

Munich, which before World War I was the capital and residence of the King of Bavaria, was a cultural center where opera, concert music, and drama flourished, all of which the young Orff assimilated at an early age. His special love was for the theater. In 1915, at the age of twenty, he was appointed musical director of the Munich Kammerspiele, which was under the leadership of Otto Falckenberg, one of the greatest stage directors of his time. The years at the Kammerspiele had a profound and lasting influence on Orff's work. He left the theater to serve in the army during the last year of the war (1917–18), and he returned from it a different person to a different world.

Munich teemed with young, enthusiastic, and gifted artists—musicians, dancers, writers, and painters—all seeking to break away from the old ways and traditions, all trying to rebuild on the spiritual and emotional ruins of a terrible war. Although Orff had been an exceptionally creative and prolific composer from early in his life, his search for musical identity led him now in directions that ultimately would result in that special synthesis of word, music, and dance for which he would become famous.

From 1919 on, upon the advice of his mentor and friend Curt Sachs,[1] he immersed himself in the study of Renaissance and early Baroque composers, most notably Claudio Monteverdi, whose operas *L'Orfeo* (1607) and *Ballo dell' Ingrate* (1608) he reconstructed and adapted from old manuscripts. A third arrangement, *Lamento d'Arianna*, Orff based on the only surviving fragment from the opera *Arianna* (1608).[2] Monteverdi's text settings in his recitatives, his closed forms such as the ritornello, the dance song, and the madrigal, his rich harmonies, and his orchestrations became some of the strongest influences on Orff's own musical style. For the next thirty years he returned again and again to this master of early music drama. The third and final reworking of these three dramas, a condensation of all three into one, was performed in 1958 under the title *Lamenti, liberamente tratto da opere di Claudio Monteverdi*.[3]

One of the most significant events of this time occurred in 1923 when he met Dorothee Günther, who envisioned the founding of a school for movement, rhythmic, and dance training. Already he had been deeply impressed and fascinated by Mary Wigman, student of Jaques-Dalcroze and Laban and founder of the modern-dance movement in Germany. He recognized in her dances elemental powers which he was searching for in music. The idea of a training in elemental

---

[1] Curt Sachs, the eminent musicologist and ethnomusicologist, was director of the Berlin Instrumental Collection. Before coming to the United States he also taught at the University of Berlin and the State Academy for Music in Berlin.

[2] The texts of *L'Orfeo* and *Ballo dell' Ingrate* were adapted freely into German by Dorothee Günther, the text of *Lamento d'Arianna* by Orff himself.

[3] The work was recorded in 1974–75 on the BASF label under the title *Lamenti, Trittico teatrale liberamente tratto da opere di Claudio Monteverdi*.

music—a music which is not abstract, but which integrates the elements of speech, movement, and dance—emerged and took shape in his discussions with Dorothee Günther. In 1924 they founded the Güntherschule in Munich. Core studies, taught by several instructors, included gymnastics and dance. As musical director, Orff was responsible for the musical training of the students. Günther, who assumed the directorship of the school, taught classes in theory.

The next six years were a period of exploration and experimentation. Orff began with rhythm as the basic element inherent in music, dance, and speech, combining and unifying them into one language. Improvisation and creation were at the center of his teaching. Because a number of his students had not had previous musical training, Orff emphasized body sounds and gestures for rhythm, and he used the voice as the first and most natural of instruments. He added rattles and other primary "dance" percussion, which were built from exotic models by the students and teachers themselves. He gave great importance to the drum in all its variations of size, shape, and sound. He made the ostinato— whether rhythmic, spoken, or sung—serve as the form-giving element in all improvisations. Since in the beginning no pitched instruments were available, he included piano instruction and group improvisation on the piano in the curriculum.

Orff has acknowledged again and again, in lectures and in writing, that without the assistance and support of many immensely talented and knowledgeable colleagues and friends in the fields of musicology, music education, and dance Schulwerk would not have been born. First and foremost were Gunild Keetman and the dancer Maja Lex, who joined the school as students in 1926 and 1925, respectively. Both of them Orff regarded as gifted equally in music and in dance. Soon they became colleagues and partners in his search for an elemental expression in music and dance. Gunild Keetman's collaboration in particular proved to be of infinite value in the development of the instrumental ensemble and its musical style.

The arrival in 1926 of a xylophone ("Kaffernklavier") crudely fashioned after African models caused great excitement at the Güntherschule. Orff immediately recognized the suitability of simple pitched percussion instruments for elemental music-making and improvisation. During the next years, with the invaluable help of Karl Maendler, a well-known harpsichord builder in Munich, the important barred instruments, which today are simply referred to as "Orff instruments," were designed and built for the school. Gunild Keetman explored their musical possibilities, developed playing techniques, and built up and refined the ensemble.

The same year brought another addition to the dance orchestra, namely the recorder. Again Curt Sachs was the initiator, Gunild Keetman the experimenter, teacher, and designer. (See Chapter 9, "Recorder Playing.") Although in the course of time many more instruments suitable for playing elemental music found their way into the ensemble, the instrumentarium in its basic design was now complete. The curriculum expanded to include instruction on the percussion instruments and the recorder, choreography, conducting, chorus, harmony, and figured-bass playing, all of which were united under the concept of improvisation.

In 1930 Maja Lex and Gunild Keetman founded a dance group and orchestra with students of the Güntherschule, which became widely known in Germany and abroad. The same year saw the first publications, recorder and dance pieces by Gunild Keetman. Soon other publications followed, combining the various works under the main heading *Elementare Musikübung* (Exercises in Elemental Music); the contributors, aside from Keetman, included Orff ("Rhythmic-Melodic Exercises" I and II) and Hans Bergese. Orff was well aware that publishing brought with it the danger that the purpose of the books would be misunderstood. Born out of improvisation, the fluid medium of elemental music does not adapt well to the static medium of print. On the other hand, he realized that only through publication could its educational value be made known.

From 1931 on, lectures, demonstrations, and training courses began to draw the attention of music educators in Germany to the work at the Güntherschule. But plans for a music-educational reform were interrupted in 1933 when Orff's most important supporters in the musical world and in the Ministries of Culture and Education were relieved of their positions. Many fled the country. Although the Güntherschule and its performing group continued to operate, Orff's approach to music pedagogy was declared in conflict with the prevailing ideological and political climate. A number of his published songs were dropped from publication because he had used poems by writers no longer acceptable. Gradually Orff withdrew from teaching at the Güntherschule. In 1944 the school was closed because of political pressure, and sometime later the building and most of its inventory were completely destroyed by bombing. To all appearances, a dream had died.

Orff's pedagogical work at the Güntherschule was fundamental to developing his concept of the unity of the word, music, and movement, but he had other experiences during that time which were also important in his search for a new approach to musical drama. As director of the Munich Bach Society he adapted and staged the *St. Luke Passion* (in all probability not Bach's work) in the style of the traditional Bavarian mystery plays. It was first performed, with great success, under the auspices of the Association for Contemporary Music (Vereinigung für zeitgenössische Musik), which also featured composers like Bartók, Honegger, and Hindemith. Numerous performances took place during 1931 and 1932, and dramatic adaptations of other, similar works followed. A second version of his Monteverdi realizations was also staged through the Association for Contemporary Music.

In 1933 Orff left the Munich Bach Society and from then on devoted himself almost exclusively to composition. Between 1935 and 1942 he created his first three "mature" stage works: *Carmina Burana* and the two Grimms' fairy tales *The Moon (Der Mond)* and *The Peasant's Wise Daughter (Die Kluge)*. Although many other works followed,[4] these three are of direct interest to the Schulwerk teacher because their stylistic relationship to the musical language of Orff-Schulwerk is clearly recognizable.

And here begins the second chapter of Schulwerk. In 1945 another war came to an end. Like most other large cities in Germany, Munich lay in ruins.

[4] See also Chapter 10.

Everyone lacked for the most basic necessities of life. But the need for a spiritual regeneration after this war was even more pressing than after the first. And miraculously, voices that had been silenced for over a decade spoke again, and new, younger ones joined in as well. After years of censorship and indoctrination, of tragedy and great suffering, art, music, literature, and philosophy began a new life.

The rebirth of Schulwerk began with an old, long-forgotten recording of a dance piece Orff and Keetman had created during their Güntherschule years. Walter Panofski, a staff member of the Bavarian Broadcasting Company and an old friend of Orff's, discovered it in a second-hand bookstore. He played the record to the director of the children's radio programs ("Schulfunk"[5]), who sensed immediately that this music would have great appeal to children. At this time working on his *Antigonae*, Orff was contacted and asked whether he could create a series of broadcasts for and with children. At first he was reluctant. His pedagogical work at the Güntherschule had been oriented toward young adults preparing for a profession. But soon his doubts were replaced with enthusiasm, because the task would renew his long-abandoned dream of music-educational reform. He engaged Gunild Keetman to assist in the planning and to work with the children. In September of 1948 the first program, "Children Make Music," went on the air. It was a great success. Youngsters, teachers, and parents demanded more, and it became clear that the broadcasts could not remain an experiment but would have to be presented as an extended series. Between 1950 and 1954, Orff and Keetman wrote down the pedagogical concepts that had grown out of their work with children: a music meant for and created by children. When they had finished, they had written five volumes. Schulwerk, in its re-creation and transformation, had become *Music for Children.*

However, the radio broadcasts lacked the possibility of including the movement aspect, so fundamental to all rhythmic development. In 1949 Gunild Keetman was invited to teach children's courses at the Akademie der Tonkunst Mozarteum in Salzburg, Austria. Only now could movement training be incorporated into Orff-Schulwerk.

The great interest in *Music for Children* among teachers and music educators soon made apparent the need for a comprehensive teacher-training program. Beginning in 1953, therefore, such courses were offered at the Mozarteum. Again, the response among students from Germany, Austria, and abroad was such that within a few years' time the facilities at the Mozarteum were no longer adequate. In 1963 the Orff Institute was opened outside of Salzburg. Still a branch of the Mozarteum, it functions today as an international training center as well as the focal point for the dissemination of Orff-Schulwerk all over the world.

Thus, in retrospect, we see that Orff-Schulwerk emerged in two distinct phases, separated by over two decades during which Orff wrote his first mature compositions. The first phase was a time of apprenticeship in two ways: it laid the groundwork for Orff's own musical style, and it gave him the experience in teaching and in developing the pedagogical concepts of elemental music. The

---

[5] In Germany, "Schulfunk" programs are frequently transmitted directly into the classrooms, which allows teachers and students to develop and expand the lesson after the end of the broadcast.

idea of a comprehensive teaching approach for children developed many years later. In this second phase, as a mature composer, he analyzed and crystallized his musical concepts in the five-volume *Music for Children*. At the core of this work is a kind of musical expression that is able to speak to children without the loss of musical integrity. Therein lies its great significance, its genius.

ORFF-SCHULWERK LITERATURE

First and most important in the Schulwerk literature is *Music for Children*, written by Carl Orff and Gunild Keetman.[6] The first adaptations in English based on the German text were the British edition by Margaret Murray[7] and the Canadian edition by Doreen Hall and Arnold Walter.[8] This literature constitutes the sine qua non of Orff teaching, the foundation upon which all else is based.

Unfortunately, these five volumes have been subjected to much criticism, especially in this country. Skeptics claim that they are not relevant to American culture, or that the music is too difficult. Such judgments tend to be based on misconceptions as to the character and purpose of the texts.

In the first place, Orff and Keetman never intended to write a textbook with detailed lesson plans. Such an approach would negate the Orff-Schulwerk philosophy, which, after all, is based on the inherent creativity not only of the child but of the teacher as well. Instead, they provided us with exercises in speech, rhythm, melody, and harmony, all of which serve as guidelines to a sequential development of the musical concepts. These exercises are meant to be points of departure and motivation for improvisation. The song arrangements and instrumental pieces complement and round out the exercise sections by demonstrating the style and characteristics of elemental music. Some very brief explanations and directions regarding procedures in improvisation are offered in the back of the books.

Most teachers who are products of a traditional music education that does not concern itself with "elemental" music-making find that the five Schulwerk volumes are not immediately accessible, primarily because the elemental style is not familiar enough. The need for more information on the subject has resulted in the publication of many excellent books and articles. The most important among them seem to fall into two categories. On the one hand, there are the teaching manuals, which deal with the practical matter of classroom instruction and development of basic concepts; on the other, there are writings dealing with Orff-Schulwerk from a more philosophical point of view.

It is not surprising that the first thorough and fundamentally important manuals were written by people who helped initiate and develop the first teacher-training courses. These are *Introduction to Music for Children*, by Wilhelm Keller,[9] and

---

[6] *Orff-Schulwerk: Musik für Kinder* (Mainz: B. Schott's Söhne, n.d.).

[7] *Orff-Schulwerk: Music for Children* (London: Schott and Co., n.d.).

[8] *Orff-Schulwerk: Music for Children* (Mainz: B. Schott's Söhne, n.d.).

[9] First edition, 1954; 2nd revised edition, 1963 (Mainz: B. Schott's Söhne). English translation by Susan Kennedy (New York: Schott, 1974).

Elementaria, by Gunild Keetman.[10] The books are invaluable contributions to the understanding of the creative procedures and the development of concepts embodied in the original literature. They lay the groundwork for the craft of Orff-Schulwerk teaching and should be part of the required reading list in every teacher-training program.

Each book has its own focus and objective. In *Elementaria*, subtitled "First Acquaintance with Orff-Schulwerk," Keetman provides fundamental insights on the beginning level by treating each of the basic areas—speech, melody, accompaniment, movement, and improvisation—in carefully developed sequences. Wilhelm Keller limits his discussion mainly to one aspect, that of musical development (including, of course, speech and rhythm), but he offers a perspective of the entire evolutionary process embodied in the original five volumes, along with methodology, pedagogical advice, and suggestions for improvisation. Both works are meant to amplify and complement learning experiences the readers may have already had in classroom teaching. For this reason, they do not address themselves in detail to the matter of sequencing, the order in which new concepts are to be introduced.

The third and most recent publication worthy of mention is the American Orff-Schulwerk edition, *Music for Children*.[11] Its three volumes are doubtless the largest and most detailed Schulwerk teaching manual in existence, broadly designed and reaching across all areas of Orff-Schulwerk. With the objective of using materials suited to the American folk heritage, and of giving American exponents of Orff-Schulwerk the opportunity to share their own ideas and teaching experiences, Hermann Regner has succeeded in the monumental task of putting together a vast collection of materials from American contributors. A few musical examples from the original volumes also are included. The materials are presented in general order of difficulty and are accompanied by articles dealing with the various aspects of Schulwerk instruction. The volumes constitute an important addition to the existing literature, the more so because they speak directly and exclusively to the American audience. Nevertheless, fundamental sequencing and selection of materials accordingly are not, and cannot be, the aim and purpose of these books.

The ability to sequence new musical concepts in a consistent and logical manner begins with understanding the underlying principles of Orff-Schulwerk. To be sure, they have been dealt with from a philosophical point of view in such publications as the three yearbooks of the Orff-Institute,[12] the *Orff Re-Echoes*, and supplementary publications by the American Orff-Schulwerk Association (AOSA).[13] Fascinating as these discussions are, their often esoteric and scholarly nature can make it difficult to see how the philosophical and the practical are

---

[10] German edition: Stuttgart: Ernst Klett Verlag, 1970. English translation by Margaret Murray (London: Schott and Co., Ltd., 1974).

[11] Vol. 1, Pre-school (1982); vol. 2, Primary (1977); vol. 3, Upper Elementary (1980) (n.p.: Schott Music Corp.).

[12] *Orff-Institut Jahrbuch 1962, 1963, 1964–1968* (Mainz: B. Schott's Söhne).

[13] *Orff Re-Echoes*, edited by Isabel McNeill Carley (American Orff-Schulwerk Association, 1977); *Orff Re-Echoes*, Book II, edited by Isabel McNeill Carley (American Orff-Schulwerk Association, 1988).

related. Frequently the two speak at a distance from each other when they are meant to speak in unison as partners.

Let me try, therefore, to restate certain fundamental and philosophical points in such a way that their connection with the practical aspects of Orff-Schulwerk is made clearer. Unless the philosophical aspect can be shown to have a vital relation to the practical, the understanding of these principles will be an understanding *in vacuo*.

THE EDUCATIONAL PHILOSOPHY OF ORFF-SCHULWERK

Although Carl Orff began his educational work with a definite purpose and objective, the specific approach and consequent sequencing evolved and took shape during his and Gunild Keetman's teaching of young adults at the Güntherschule, and later during Keetman's work with children. The title *Schulwerk* is an indication of the educational process taking place, and it gets to the heart of the matter: Schulwerk is schooling (in music) through working, that is, through being active and creative. One might also call it an apprenticeship in music, or one might express the meaning through an equation:

Schooling through working = learning by doing

Children make music in their own way long before they receive musical instruction. Teachers who can learn to understand the child's musical language and to use it in their teaching hold the key to a meaningful and successful educational process.

Research has shown that the music-making of the young child resembles in many ways the music-making of primal cultures. Stylistic similarities between childhood music and that of primal man include the following: The music is rhythm- and movement-oriented. It is not a separate artform, but rather combines the elements of speech and drama, whether recited, chanted, or sung, with those of sound and movement and with rhythm as the most vital force. It is not abstract but functional in its relationship to life's experiences. It is not usually premeditated or composed. It is transmitted orally and therefore liable to change. It is, for the most part, "ensemble music" in the sense that everyone participates.

Such music has been termed "elemental." In its stylistic similarity to primal music, Orff-Schulwerk is elemental. It speaks to the child in a language he understands and is able to respond to instinctively. Elemental music, then, is an ideal vehicle for teaching and an ideal language for learning.

Regarding the learning process of the child, Orff-Schulwerk is in accord with the findings of Pestalozzi, Piaget, and Bruner, to name just a few. Dr. Arnold Walter summarized these findings in a speech given at the 1st National Conference of the AOSA: "Great educators from Froebel to Piaget have always said that teaching was possible only if it addressed a child's powers at the right time and in the right order."[14] In Orff-Schulwerk teaching, the "right order" is teaching a sequence of musical concepts that evolve from simple to complex.

[14] "The Orff-Schulwerk in American Education." Reprinted in *Orff Re-Echoes*, 14.

This sequence may be called evolutionary, as long as we apply the term in a general sense. For instance, the melodic development begins with the recited word; small-range melodies (in the Schulwerk, the chant) appear before larger-range melodies; anhemitonic tunes develop before diatonic tunes (not a universal phenomenon, but nevertheless a frequent one). Movement is the origin of accompaniment as well as of rhythm. It provides the foundation of a steady beat, which keeps an ensemble together. Unpitched accompaniment precedes pitched accompaniment; unchanging drone basses form the first pitched accompaniment and help establish tonality, as well as a fundamental "harmony"; later, harmony without function evidences itself also through parallelism in the voice parts; harmony with function is the last step in a long development. For a long time, melodic development takes precedence over harmonic development.

The following chart illustrates this development of the musical concepts. It also includes other aspects that are an integral part of elemental music and cannot be separated from it.

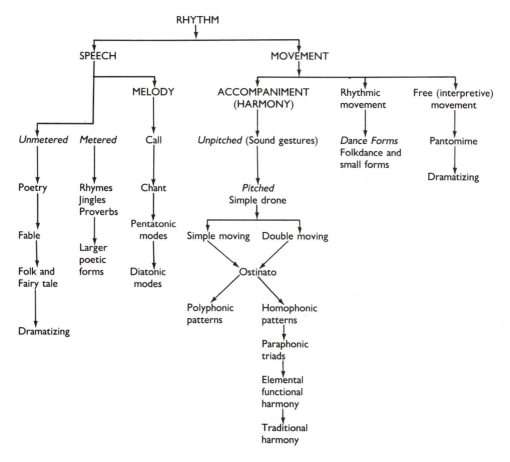

Finally, I would like to emphasize a few other points. First, the musical concepts of rhythm, melody, and harmony as developed in Orff-Schulwerk are those of our Western musical culture. Therefore, Schulwerk leads directly into early music and into the beginnings of traditional harmony. The beauty of the approach is exactly the manner in which we are led through the developmental stages of our own musical culture and thus may gain a much deeper understanding and appreciation for it.

Second, however, I need to stress that the Schulwerk sequence is not a chronological sequence per se, because historical development did not always occur in neat packages of logical, next-step events. Rather, Schulwerk borrows from the historical, ordering significant developments into a consistent and seamless evolution of musical concepts.

My last point has to do with the manner in which Orff-Schulwerk fuses the historical with the elemental. Whereas the historical is embodied in the logically established pedagogical sequence, the elemental represents the language in which the sequence is expressed. This language is nonhistorical, or ahistorical, in that it is always new, actual, and relevant. Thus, the elemental language and the sequence are, in fact, the practical conceptualization of the Orff-Schulwerk philosophy.

Orff-Schulwerk puts us in touch with our musical beginnings, roots most of us lost contact with long ago, but to which the child is still able to respond. The sequence reflects the immediacy of these roots in an unbroken, ever-expanding spiral of understanding. Such understanding, however, comes slowly and only if the sequence is allowed to develop step-by-step through years of consistent and continuous application.

Understanding the organic, step-by-step growth and broadening of the musical concepts is the basis for the improvisation and composition of music. The sequence is demonstrated here through the original Orff-Schulwerk literature, which the reader is urged to have at hand while reading this book. (All references to ''Orff-Schulwerk I'' in this book refer, unless otherwise stated, to the Murray version.) A classroom sequence should also include any music relevant to it, and be adjusted to different age levels and teaching situations. In other words, the sequence is the constant, but the approaches within the sequence are as varied as the teachers themselves. If we understand this, we are ready to begin.

2
BASIC RHYTHMIC CONCEPTS

RHYTHM AND METER: AN ATTEMPT AT DEFINITION

The term *rhythm* has been defined many times, but for the purpose of this discussion it is necessary to do so once more.

The word has its origin in the Greek verb *rheo*—"flowing." In today's general usage, rhythm implies a certain order or organization based on regular occurrences in a space of time. Thus we refer to the change of the seasons, the oceanic flow of ebb and tide, or the phases of the moon as nature's rhythm. Through the systolic and diastolic flow of blood, this same cyclic rhythm is evident on a much reduced time-scale in the human body, which can be seen as the cosmos in miniature. The contracting and expanding movements of the heart are discernible to the ear (through a stethoscope) as a rhythmic pattern, consisting of a shorter and a longer beat. The pulse, on the other hand, is an even beat. It registers the highest point of pressure of the blood flow against the expanding artery walls (systolic). The second, diastolic phase of the rhythmic pattern, which is the release of the blood pressure, is, of course, not felt.

This even, two-beat pulse rhythm is inherent in all regular body movements, be they locomotor—such as walking, swimming, or running—or work-related—such as sowing, kneading, chopping, or scraping. It becomes a musical element when used, consciously or subconsciously, in combination with other "musical" elements, no matter how primitive they may seem. Since the beginning of time man has hummed, whistled, shouted, or chanted while moving along or working.

Today, when people join together to sing in a chorus or to play in an orchestra, a conductor is needed to coordinate the musical ensemble. In the music practices of early and primitive civilizations, it was the motoric pulse rhythm (stemming from motor impulses) that unified the musical activities. The hands, not being occupied with work, could be used for clapping or playing percussion instruments like rattles or drums, while people would sing and dance to the rhythm. Again, such practices are almost timeless, since we still find them today in the clapping accompaniments of children's games and songs and of folksinging.

Pulse rhythm as an accompaniment must stand in a certain relationship to what it accompanies. This other musical element, although it could be a wordless tune or whistle, is more often a text that is spoken, chanted, or sung. The rhythmic structure of the text fits that of the pulse accompaniment in that (1) its individual units stand in an exact metrical (or mathematical) ratio to the pulse (in its simplest forms: the same, twice as fast, or twice as slow), and (2) the stronger accented syllables in the text coincide with the first pulse-beat of the two-cycle pulse-pattern:

Ted-dy-bear, ted-dy-bear, turn   a - round

jump

The example is a jump-rope rhyme in which the jumps in their equal time-length represent the pulse. The first pulse-beat, on which the child jumps over the rope, is the stronger dynamically, whereas the second, weaker pulse-beat is a light rebounding jump while the rope swings overhead. Another regular beat, twice as slow, occurs when the rope hits the ground. This beat is the strong accent and coincides with the strong accents of the words and the jumps:

Text:

Ted-dy-bear, ted-dy-bear, turn   a - round

Jumping:

Swinging rope:

Any further development here ties rhythm to another phenomenon: *meter*. As far as we know, the Greeks were the first to concern themselves in a scholarly way with such matters as meter and rhythm. Their terminology has come down to us, but in the process it has undergone many changes, even to the extent of a complete reversal of the original meaning.

Meter, meaning measurement, has its origin in the Greek system of versification, in which regularly occurring strong and weak syllables (thesis and arsis) combined into specific rhythmic patterns to form "feet" (iamb, trochee, dactyl, etc). In music today, however, meter concerns accent alone. It may be said to be the measurement of equal pulse-beats that form a pattern through regularly occurring accents. The jump-rope rhyme used earlier may serve as an example of duple-meter pattern: ♩ ♩ . The jumping, done in an even, regular pulsation, consists of a stronger and a weaker jump; thus it forms a pattern of two beats, the first of which is stronger than the second. In contrast to this, the regular ticking of a clock or a metronome (being "dead" mechanisms) provides only a pulse in a particular tempo, not its meter, since all the beats are dynamically the same.

To the Greeks, rhythm meant the order of movement. This statement is broad enough to be true even today. But what does this really mean in contemporary usage? Generally speaking, rhythm has to do with the length of beats or notes. These are generally in a measurable ratio, not only to the metrical element, the pulse, but also to one another. The length of the beats is measured in relation to the pulse, by being the same, twice as fast, or twice as slow, for example. Again, the jump-rope rhyme helps us to understand: the jumping and the swinging of the rope give us a duple-meter pattern as well as a tempo. The text gives us the rhythm through the word syllables, which are either the same, twice as fast, or twice as slow as the pulse-beats:

At the same time, these longer and shorter notes of the rhythm are metered through their accentual pattern.

Thus rhythm and meter are interrelated.

RHYTHM AND LANGUAGE IN HISTORY AND IN ORFF-SCHULWERK

Accents and Meter: Rhythmic Patterns as Smallest Units

Often the theory of rhythm is made to seem simple by presenting it as a series of mathematical relationships. This will work with the older student whose mind has developed the ability to think in the abstract, but it does not work well with the young child. Moreover, understanding the theoretical aspects of rhythm in no way guarantees a working grasp that comes naturally and easily. More often than not it becomes a matter of "counting beats" rather than a musical rendering.

In Orff-Schulwerk the basic principles of rhythm and meter are developed through language, because such an approach is the most natural path to follow. Basic elements, such as longer and shorter durational values, accents, and meter, are already present to a degree in language. Since our students, children and adults alike, know how to use language, they already possess the raw material needed for developing rhythmic concepts. They only lack the key to unlock the secrets. This involves freeing rhythm from the bondage of language and allowing it to emerge as a separate entity. The process reflects, in a general way, the historical evolution of rhythm in music-making.

Rhythmic speech occurs out of necessity when a group of people recite or chant together. In the effort to speak alike and stay together, the long and short word-syllables are somewhat exaggerated and begin to form a definite relationship with one another. This relationship is not necessarily measurable in mathematical terms, but it helps to maintain a certain flow (rhythm in the wider sense) in the recitation. The practice of choral speaking may well have had something to do with the development of rhythmic and metered speech. Two reasons support this idea. First, rhythm helped to produce precision in the choral speech; second, in nonliterate cultures the rhythmic and metered flow of a text aided in its memorization. Thus, rhythm bound to the word is at the beginning of all rhythmic development.

In Western culture, rhythm has become a musical element which, independent of the word, can be manipulated in many ways. The development from the word-bound to the word-independent stage is like a gradual freezing of a fluid medium; it has much to do with the development of script as a means of rhythmic notation, for anything transmitted orally is in a flexible, fluid stage without finality, whereas anything notated is unchangeable and final. In a sense one might say that rhythm, freeing itself from the word, has submitted to another bondage, that of the rigidity and finality of notation.

In the various cultures of this world, past as well as present, rhythm has existed in several stages of development in relationship to language and to literacy. We can arrange the relevant stages to support a pedagogical sequence for teaching rhythm and its literacy in our own culture. This sequence consists of three basic developmental stages which are important milestones. One would hope that simplification need not result in misinterpretation. (I must remind the reader that the following is not a scholarly synopsis, but a personal interpretation of historical development.)

Stage One: Word-bound, rhythmically fluid due to oral transmission.

Stage Two: Word-bound, rhythm and meter fixed, due to text transmission through developed script, with rhythm and meter tied to it through a prenotational codification system.

Stage Three: Word-independent, rhythm and meter abstracted into individual symbols and signs.

Stage One.   Cultures without a written language also lack rhythmic or pitch notation. All music and music-related activities and performance practices are handed down orally in these cultures; therefore rhythm, and music in general, is not forced into a set form but stays fluid and changeable.

Children's traditional songs and games belong to this stage. We find many different versions of the same rhyme or game, depending on geographical location and cultural or ethnic group.

Stage Two. From here we take, historically speaking, a big leap forward to Greek culture (disregarding the other cultures on which the Greeks built). Although in Greek music rhythm was still word-bound, there existed a definite, mathematically measurable ratio between longer and shorter word syllables. The smallest time unit, by which all other lengths were measured, was called the *chronos protos* and approximated our eighth-note. The Greeks never developed a rhythmic notation per se, with special symbols for each individual time length and for meter through accent. Indeed, this was not needed since rhythm for them existed through declamation only and not as a separate entity. Therefore they developed a codification system of rhythmic groupings or patterns derived from the syllabication of words. (See also pp. 17–22.)

Today one has to be a scholar of Greek language and literature in order to understand the intricacies of the Greek poetic meters and their terminology. As musicians we do not need to use such a codification, since our rhythmic notation is better suited to express our rhythmic language. But this is the case only because the role of rhythm in music today is different from its role in Greek music. Nevertheless, the Greek codification system represents the transition from the purely oral, rhythmically fluid stage to the notational, rhythmically fixed stage.

In Orff-Schulwerk we also touch upon this transitional stage when we use, through our work with speech, a codification comparable to that of the Greeks, yet with a different purpose in mind. Rhymes, chants, and games, first experienced orally and physically, are now used to extract the basic concepts of rhythm and meter.

Stage Three. Again we leap across many centuries during which the aged, weakening Greek culture even in its decline helped raise and nourish a new, young culture—that of the Christian world. Early Christian culture had no identity of its own. It took hundreds of years for the first sprouts of identity to appear. Musically, one of these was the awakening of a rhythmic concept which eventually led away from the domination of the word.

With the growing awareness of rhythm as an independent musical element, a rhythmic notation ("square notes") expressing definite note values began to be developed. Theoretical works attempted to deal with rhythmic concepts in a methodical fashion (ca. 1200). During the fourteenth century a rhythmic notational system was at last developed sufficiently to express a great many complexities. This gave rise to compositions with highly intricate rhythmic structures. Naturally, this period saw a high development of polyphonic music, for polyphony is based on the independent movement of all parts. In vocal pieces the natural rhythmic and accentual patterns of the text had no bearing on the rhythmic structure. The compositions were *multi*metric rather than *iso*metric as they had been previously. (In multimetric music, phrases and groupings of notes are of irregular lengths, whereas in isometric compositions one meter prevails over a longer period of time.) Musical scores showing simultaneously all instrumental or vocal parts were not yet known. All parts were written out individually, except for such instruments as keyboards and lutes, on which multi-part music could be played.

The decline of polyphony and the growing demands of harmony heralded a new era of thinking. The predominantly horizontal orientation began a shift to a vertical orientation to an ever-increasing degree. Rhythm lost its complexity and again became isometric, having regularly occurring accents and keeping to a specific meter. This rhythmic development was also due to the influence of dance music, which, through its intimate relation to physical movement, is naturally beat- and accent-oriented and therefore isometric. Only about 1600 did the beginning of modern rhythmic notation, showing all parts simultaneously with vertically connecting barlines, become a practical solution. Only now was this possible because now one specific meter synchronized and united all parts in a composition. Rhythm and meter of this type prevailed in Western culture for the next three hundred years.

In relation to Orff-Schulwerk, only a few words need to be said. It is quite obvious that in our teaching we do not recreate the developmental process of rhythm in Western music or the developmental steps of a notation that go with it (Stage Three). We teach the concepts of rhythm and meter, and along with them the notation, in the mold into which they were finally cast. However, the importance of the third stage lies in the fact that it represents the *abstraction of rhythm*, its release from the spoken word, and through this its existence as an individual musical element.

In our teaching the three stages are hardly recognizable, as they flow quickly from one into the other. Yet we must be aware of what we ask of our students in terms of conceptual development and learning. We expect them in a short span of time to assimilate and comprehend concepts that have taken well over a thousand years to evolve. It behooves us to keep this in mind at all times lest we become too impatient.

THE SMALLEST UNITS OF RHYTHMIC PATTERNS

Syllabication of Words

In order to use language for the purpose of developing rhythmic concepts, we must be intimately acquainted with it. We must understand what it can and cannot do, in particular its limitations in relation to rhythm and meter. This in turn will help us to choose the best teaching approach.

If I seem to have spent an inordinate amount of space discussing rhythm in language, I have done so with a purpose. In my teacher-training courses I have found again and again that this aspect of Orff-Schulwerk more than any other causes difficulties for adult students. For this reason and in order to save time, many Schulwerk instructors fall back on the simpler device of using the rhythmic syllables as taught by the Kodály method. This practice ignores the fact that, on the beginning levels especially, rhythm is rendered musical through its connection to the word. Or, to put it differently, metered language becomes unmusical if related to a mechanical recitation of rhythmic syllables. In Orff-Schulwerk, word and rhythm are a unity and must be treated as such.

We pointed out earlier that language becomes musical when it is recited to accompanying pulse-beats, and that it has to adjust itself rhythmically and accentually in order to fit with such accompaniment. We know too that, although there is rhythm in language, language is not always rhythmic. We make it so to meet our needs. Rhythm in language comes about through the interplay of longer and shorter syllables, some of which are more accented than others. In our everyday speech or in prose, the relationship between longer and shorter syllables is not measurable in exact ratios such as 2 : 1 or 3 : 1. We create such an exact relationship when we deal with metered speech. However, such speech is not only a matter of longer and shorter, and of accented and unaccented syllables. It is also a matter of tempo and of emphasizing important words (not the same as accent). Certain problems will arise in notating rhythmic speech, for in the notation available to us it is not possible to express all the aspects mentioned in a completely satisfactory manner, and we will have to compromise.

There are two basic meters, *duple* and *triple*, also referred to as *even* and *uneven*. In the songs of early and tribal cultures as well as of early childhood, duple meter seems to be predominant, but today triple meter is no less important in our music.[1] In even meter the accentual pattern is *strong-weak*, whereas in uneven meter it is *strong-weak-weak*. Any words up to four syllables can be set either in duple or triple meter so long as the strong accents of the words or syllables coincide with the strong accents of the metric pattern. This does not mean, however, that one solution is always as good as another one. Let us look at some examples in a systematic way.

One-Syllable Words. These, by themselves, can give us no clue regarding an accentual pattern; therefore, they cannot determine a meter. There are, however, differences in the way they sound, and this will make a difference in the way they are notated. The few examples given here may help illuminate the importance of clear speech, and of listening to it carefully in order to catch the sound essence most accurately in notation. (Exceptions to rules of pronunciation are not considered here.)

1. Words with long vowel sounds may end with a silent *e*, such as *rose*, or with a soft consonant preceded by a double vowel or diphthong, such as *moon* and *toad*. Whatever the rules of pronunciation are, words with long vowel sounds are best notated through long notes.
2. Hard consonants or more than one consonant at the end of a word tend to shorten the vowel sound: *hut*, *Jack*, *bush*. A shorter note value followed by a rest will best approximate the shortness of the word or syllable.

Two-Syllable Words. Two-syllable words, in their alternation of strong and weak accents, represent the most basic meter, the *duple*, and thus they take on great significance in our teaching of rhythm. In the simplest form the accent occurs on the first syllable, thus starting the word on the *downbeat*: *Ma*ry. Since,

---

[1] For a discussion of *meter*, see also pp. 28–32.

in the tempo of natural speech, the syllable is closer to an eighth-note than a quarter-note, the rhythmic notation of the name is best represented in this way: Mā-ry. However, the first note value introduced to the children is always the quarter-note, because it is the basic pulse (as developed through movement); shorter and longer values develop naturally from it. Therefore, we must notate in quarter-notes, Mā-ry, even though this is not an accurate representation of the speech tempo. To put it differently, the two syllables of a downbeat word are treated— at least initially—as being synonymous with the two pulses of a duple-meter pattern. (See also Chapter 3, page 43.) Later, within the context of a whole phrase and depending on the text, the notation may change, as for instance, in

Mar-y had a lit - tle lamb.

If the accent in a word falls on the second syllable, the first becomes an *upbeat*: Mau-*reen*. The unaccented syllable tends to be shorter than the following downbeat syllable if the latter has a long vowel sound:

Mau - reen
To - day
Be - low

or

The second syllable may have a short sound; in that case it would be notated slightly differently:

Gi - raffe

However, ♪‖: ♩ ⅞ '♪:‖ will work also, even though it does not reflect the short sound as well as the first version.

Three-Syllable Words, Starting on the Downbeat.

1.   Spoken in such a way that all syllables get equal note values, the accentual pattern of strong-weak-weak emerges, thus giving us the other basic meter, *triple*:

or

Hur - ri-cane

2.   Spoken in duple meter, such words will fall into different rhythmic patterns with longer and shorter syllables, resulting in the first divisions of the pulse-beat. The

patterns are either ssl (short-short-long) ♫♩, or lss ♩ ♫, both with the accent on the first syllable. Here are some examples which illustrate that, although all the words shown can be set identically in triple meter, in duple meter they definitely fit only one or the other rhythmic pattern.

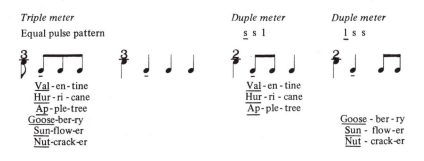

| *Triple meter* | *Duple meter* | *Duple meter* |
| Equal pulse pattern | s s l | l s s |

Some children have trouble hearing in the words the difference between ♫♩ and ♩♫, because they equate "strong" with "long." (See Chapter 3, page 40.) Thus, they would notate "Valentine" ♩♫ instead of ♫♩. If this is the case, it helps to have the children speak the word several times without clapping. Once they pronounce it correctly, the clapping should be added. Finally, the rhythm should be clapped without the speech, and the correct pattern will emerge clearly.

As we look at the two versions of triple meter, it becomes obvious that again it is the eighth-note pulse that is closest to natural speech tempo. In duple time, however, we are perfectly comfortable with the quarter-note pulse, since with three-syllable words the pulse is now subdivided. If we were to choose the eighth-note pulse for these rhythmic patterns, the subdivisions would create sixteenth-notes, too fast for a natural speech tempo. Such are the intricacies and fallacies of notating rhythmic speech!

Children, and newcomers to music in general, cannot be confronted with finer points such as these. It is advisable to stick to the quarter-note count in both duple and triple meter until the students are able to understand (1) the relativity of note values, (2) simple fractions, and (3) the need for changing time signatures. Until then we will have to use somewhat faster pulse-beats than would ordinarily seem appropriate for quarter-notes.

Two-Syllable Words in Triple Meter. The words starting on a downbeat can also be set in triple meter by lengthening the first (strong) syllable: Má-ry. In this way we obtain a different rhythmic pattern. However, the natural speech tempo becomes almost unbearably slow if $\frac{3}{4}$ is used as the time unit. The problem can be circumvented by finding words with long vowel sounds, such as "rosebud" or "moon-light."

Three-Syllable Words, Starting on the Upbeat. Again, several rhythmic patterns can be formed, and it seems that all possibilities work almost equally well:

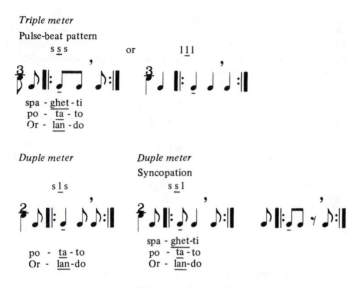

Triple meter
Pulse-beat pattern

spa - ghet - ti
po - ta - to
Or - lan - do

Duple meter

Duple meter
Syncopation

po - ta - to
Or - lan-do

spa - ghet-ti
po - ta - to
Or - lan-do

Four-Syllable Words.   Like the two-syllable words, these four-syllable words
fall most naturally into an equal-note pattern and into duple meter. Many of
them are compounds. Often they contain Greek or Latin roots or are altogether
adopted from another language. A special case in point is the many geographical
names in the United States that have been retained from American Indian tongues.

There are three categories: (1) words with the *accent on the first syllable*,
(2) words with the *accent on the second syllable*, and (3) words with the *accent
on the third syllable*.

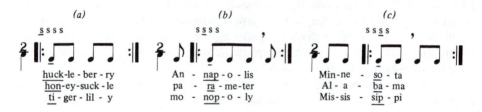

(a)

huck-le - ber - ry
hon-ey-suck - le
ti - ger - lil - y

(b)

An - nap - o - lis
pa - ra - me-ter
mo - nop-o - ly

(c)

Min-ne - so - ta
Al - a - ba - ma
Mis-sis - sip - pi

If spoken slowly and notated in quarter-notes, each individual word unit has its
own duple-meter syllable pattern, starting on the downbeat, whether notated in
simple or quadruple meter. In the examples under (b), the natural accent seems
to shift to the first syllable even though such pronunciation is incorrect.

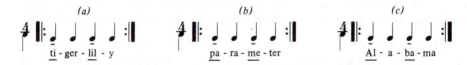

(a)

ti - ger - lil - y

(b)

pa - ra - me - ter

(c)

Al - a - ba - ma

In natural speech, which is considerably faster, the secondary accent is largely
"swallowed," and we notate in eighth-notes using simple duple meter as shown
in the previous example.

Five-Syllable Words. We have already seen in the previous discussion that four-syllable words are "borderline cases" because they can be interpreted in terms of either simple duple or quadruple meter, depending on the speech tempo. It follows that even longer words must also be combinations of simple meter patterns. For the most part they are assimilations of non-English origin. Although they are not usually part of a child's vocabulary and certainly go beyond the beginning stages of rhythmic studies, a quick examination might be of interest to the reader.

In simple pulse-beat rhythm, five-syllable words consist basically of one duple and one triple pattern or vice versa, with a primary and a secondary accent. But as before, fast recitation will eliminate the secondary accent almost completely.

(a) Accent on fourth syllable   *(b)* Accent on third syllable

glo-ri - fi - ca-tion   con-sti - tu-tion-al
pre-med-i - ta-tion   mon-o - syl-a-ble
mis-cal-cu - la-tion   meth-od - ol-o-gy

More interesting rhythmizations are achieved if other than regular pulse-beats are used. In this case, the measures will contain two of the same meter patterns and therefore can be counted either in six or in four:

(a) glo-ri-fi-ca-tion, etc.

(b) con-sti-tu-tion-al, etc.

This classification of words is meant to benefit the teacher, who must be intimately familiar with the possibilities and the intricacies of language and the occasional problems that can occur in developing rhythm through the medium of speech. Only a thorough understanding of these matters will enable the teacher to choose speech examples that exactly fit the intended purpose.

Syllabication in Orff-Schulwerk

The beginning speech exercises in Orff-Schulwerk I (p. 50) deal with the syllabication of words. They demonstrate, in a nutshell, the sequential steps necessary to develop note values, accents, and meters from language.

The choice of words for demonstrating duple-meter in quarter-note pulse is interesting: Pĕar trĕe, and plăne trĕe are actually two words, but their long vowels make the notation in quarter-notes seem much more natural than would be possible with most single words and names. (In the original German edition, the corresponding words, *Birnbaum* and *Nussbaum*, are compounds and also circumvent the problem of speech tempo we spoke of earlier.) Three-syllable words follow immediately and are fitted into the same basic $\frac{2}{4}$ pattern to get the subdivision of the first quarter-note: *ap*ple tree (Apfelbaum) ♫ ♩. The subdivision of the second quarter-note is not shown, but it is a possibility we must not ignore—for example, *bell*flower ♩ ♫.

In the second line of exercises some of the same words are then used in triple meter. The two syllables fall naturally into a long-short pattern in which the strong syllable is also the longer of the two notes: Pĕar trĕe. (This idea of rhythmic variation in word recitation and when to introduce it in the teaching sequence are discussed in Chapter 3, page 55.)

The next exercises are three-syllable words shown in triple meter. Naturally they are in an even-beat pattern of three eighth-notes: Ăpple tree.

After this come words with an upbeat, such as nar*cis*sus. These are not isolated but appear within a group of words.

In Exercise II, names of people are used instead of names of flowers and trees, and different rhythmic possibilities are demonstrated, such as using ♩. ♫ instead of ♫♩ or ♫ ♩. In actual classroom teaching this would come at a much later stage.

The choice of words in some of the examples may seem somewhat unusual (e.g., "fritillary"). Rhythmic development through the use of speech is not Orff's only concern; the examples are also meant to illustrate the expressive quality of language—the hard and the soft sounds, the dark and the light. Rhythmic speech without such shadings becomes lifeless and mechanical. From the very beginning, speech exercises also should include this "musical" aspect of language. (For more comments, see Orff-Schulwerk I, p. 141, "Speech Exercises.")

In none of the speech exercises on this and the following pages are time signatures used. The words are notated according to natural speech tempo, which, as discussed earlier, in duple time with subdivisions appears to call for the quarter-note beat, in triple time the eighth-note beat. The fact that no time signatures are given indicates that Orff was quite aware of the ambiguity of rhythmic speech notation; therefore he notated speech in the way it sounds most natural, that is, with the Greek *chronos protos* or eighth-note in mind. But by omitting time signatures, he left it up to the teacher to make choices as to the basic pulse.

PHRASES AND FORM

From the Greeks, the architects of great buildings, we also learn much about architecture in music as it develops through language. We see how several small units (feet, or podies) are put together to form, according to their numbers, *di-*, *tri-*, *tetra-*, *penta-*, or *hexapodies*, how several of these *polypodies* form a *kola*, and in turn how several kolas make up a *period*.

In Schulwerk the basic principles of form evolve and are understood through the use of language. To be sure, in Orff-Schulwerk the forms are small and uncomplicated, but in miniature they follow the same principles as art music. The rhythmic pattern of a single word is the first building block (to use Gunild Keetman's term). When two building blocks are combined, a half-phrase is formed. Two half-phrases make a full phrase, and two or more phrases are already a short piece (at least in elemental terms), or they can become a section of a larger piece.

Language form	*Musical form*
word	building block
short statement	half-phrase
sentence	full phrase
several sentences/paragraph	short piece
longer story/several paragraphs	piece with several sections

A young child's world is small and he sees himself at the center. The few people surrounding him exist seemingly because of him and serve certain purposes for him. Thus, in my earliest memories I appear like the A-section of a rondo: ME mother ME father ME sister ME brothers. As I grew older, more and more people entered my life and slowly my importance as the center of the universe diminished; I began to realize that the individual is but a part of a larger structure.

If there is a basic law in form and structure, no matter what the structure may be, it is that individual elements of a larger structure must give up a part of their identity for the sake of the whole. The large structure, however, will often display the characteristics of its individual units.

We will encounter this phenomenon as we begin to combine the smallest units, the individual words and their rhythmic building blocks, into sentences, which in music are termed phrases.

Half-Phrases

Let us first look at some examples from Orff-Schulwerk I, page 51, exercise III:

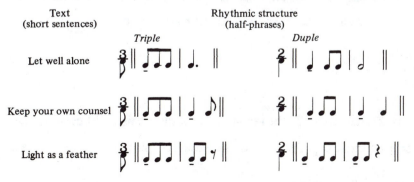

Short statements such as these have two strong accents and are made up of two building blocks, or units. They are only half of what is considered a normal phrase length in music. The examples can be set in both basic meters as long as the strong syllable remains the first beat in the measure. Recitation in duple meter makes the speech somewhat clipped and hard, whereas triple meter results in a smoother and more flowing rendering of the text.

Full Phrases

Full phrases grow from longer sentences, and more often than not they contain four accents or meter patterns. This is true not only of the proverbs shown in Orff-Schulwerk I but also of the majority of children's rhymes and songs, folksongs, and early dance music and dance songs. Apparently the Western European folk idiom has leaned strongly toward a balanced form based on recurrent units of two and four beats. In teaching children, this structure must be basic to discussions of form.

The full phrase in triple meter is a natural outgrowth of the half-phrase. To quote just a few examples from Orff-Schulwerk I, page 51:

#8: Red sky at night, shepherd's delight.

#15: Count not your chickens till they are hatched.

When duple meter is used, we encounter the phenomenon to which I referred earlier, that in a larger structure the identity of the individual unit is weakened. Consider this speech pattern:

#5: Rats desert a sinking ship.

When it is spoken slowly, we hear four accents and a natural phrase length

containing four meter patterns:

However, when spoken and notated in actual speech tempo (as it is in the book), we should call the meter $\frac{4}{\flat}$, in order to retain all four accents:

If the meter is understood as $\frac{2}{\flat}$, the second and fourth accents all but disappear, at least from a rhythmical point of view, because the third note is now a weak beat:

$\frac{2}{4}$ ♪♪♪♪ | ♪♪♩ ‖

This makes clear the fact that, although the first eighth is always stronger within the smallest individual unit of ♪♪, when this unit occurs within a larger structure such as ♩♪♪♪ the third eighth (which would be the first of another couple) loses its accent almost completely.

The matter of emphasis is an important and difficult problem. Metered speech is not only a matter of accents through strong and weak syllables but also a matter of emphasis through meaning, interpretation, and expression. The last proverb cited serves as a good example: "Rats desert a sinking ship." The whole sentence seems to strain toward the last word, "ship." If we imagine a $\frac{2}{4}$ time signature, the word "ship" would fall on a weak beat in the measure:

$\frac{2}{4}$ ‖ ♪♪♪♪ | ♪♪♩ ‖

Notated in $\frac{4}{4}$, the secondary accent on de-*sert* makes the whole statement too square. For a proper interpretation, it is necessary to add dynamic markings:

$\frac{2}{4}$ ‖ ♪♪♪♪ | ♪♪♩ ‖

The example shows that metric accent and meaning emphasis cannot always be achieved through rhythmic notation alone.

Not every speech pattern is so difficult to deal with. Satisfactory results can often be obtained by using an upbeat in order to shift the metrical stress so that it coincides with the "meaning" stress. "Nothing seek, nothing find" (no. 13) is such an example. The notation in the book is:

‖ ♪♪♩ | ♪♪♩ ‖

But one might consider the words "seek" and "find" as the most important ones. The desired accents on these words can easily be achieved by starting on an upbeat:

♪♪ ‖: ♩ ♪♪ | ♩ ♪♪ :‖

Likewise, in speech pattern 18, "All that glitters is not gold," in order to bring out an emphasis on "glitters," an alternative version might be:

$\frac{2}{4}$ ♪♪ ‖: ♪♪♪♪ | ♩ ♪♪ :‖

The choice of suitable texts is essential for working with students on developing a feeling for the phrase length. The teacher must know which are the best and most natural rhythmic settings of the texts before using them with the students or before expecting the students to set them. Only if our illustrations are exemplary models will the children develop a fine sense for recitation. Here are a few simple guidelines that I have found helpful:

1. Determine the accented syllables in the text.
2. Find the words that need to be emphasized to convey the meaning and determine whether they can be synchronized with the rhythmic accents.
3. Choose the meter that seems most appropriate, and then notate the words and syllables according to their time values in rhythmic notation.

Often this is all that is needed. If a text appears to be too problematic it is better to abandon it for a more suitable one.

The following examples are taken from Orff-Schulwerk I, page 52, "Exercises."

Example 1. "*I*dleness is *emp*tiness." There are only two accents, and there is a good solution for triple as well as duple meter:

[rhythmic notation in 3/4 meter]

[rhythmic notation in 2/4 meter]

A version like *[rhythmic notation in 3/8]* or *[rhythmic notation in 3/8]* would accent weak syllables; the second version would furthermore result in an unbalanced three-measure phrase because of the added emphasis on "is." This is not to say that odd-measured phrases are wrong; they are, however, best reserved for later, when a feeling for the natural phrase length has been firmly established. When that stage has been reached, a version like the following will be acceptable:

[rhythmic notation in 3/8]

Example 2. "Where *ig*norance is *bliss*,/'tis *fol*ly to be *wise*."

[rhythmic notation in 3/4 meter with repeat signs]

[rhythmic notation in 2/4 meter with repeat signs]

Differences in longer and shorter vowel sounds can be shown through longer and shorter notes and through rests. Trying to make two phrases, each with four strong beats, will again bring about wrong accents and will distort the text in an unmusical way:

[musical notation]

Distortions of metered speech like the two examples above are not as uncommon as one might hope. They should be avoided under all circumstances when our goal is to find the most natural and obvious rhythm for the text.

Other helpful hints:

In a rhymed text, the rhyming words should fall on the same counts in their corresponding measures:

Example 3. "Touch *wood*, touch *wood*,/'tis *sure* to come *good*." (p. 50)

[musical notation]

[musical notation]

Sometimes a text has an odd number of accents, as in the following example. In such a case it is more difficult to make a choice.

Example 4. "What one relishes, nourishes."

One might hear three accents:

[musical notation]

[musical notation]

However, two accents seem more musical:

[musical notation]

[musical notation]

In either case the result is an uneven phrase length. By placing a rest between the verbs, two half-phrases emerge and the form becomes well balanced because the two important words, "relishes" and "nourishes," correspond in their placement within each half-phrase:

Discussions such as the foregoing tend to sound formidably complicated or hairsplitting, but they are necessary to acquaint the reader with the finer points of metered speech. They show that there is never only one solution. Much depends on interpretation, and this is to some extent personal and subjective.

METRIC VOCABULARY

Lastly, I would like to address the matter of *compound meters*. At first glance this subject may not seem of great importance. Yet within the context of Orff-Schulwerk, with its development of rhythmic concepts *through language*, the matter should raise some questions regarding a consistent terminology for children.

The reader may have noticed that only simple duple and triple meter are used in the examples from Orff-Schulwerk I that I have given (see "Syllabication in Orff-Schulwerk," p. 21). (I have added time signatures which do not appear in the original for clarification.) There are no examples of 4-beat measures in exercises I and II which deal only with individual words and establish the most basic of meter patterns. Even in the proverbs of exercises III the count of four is almost entirely avoided.

The terminology generally used in this country classifies the counts of two, three, and four as simple meters, duple meter consisting of two metric units (counts), triple of three, and quadruple of two duple metric units. Accents (which determine the basic meter) occur once per measure in duple and triple, but twice in quadruple. This second accent is less strong than the first and is therefore called a secondary accent. Compound meters consist of triple units. Duple compounds are those in which two triple units occur in each measure; triple compounds consist of three triple units; quadruple compounds consist of four triple units. Thus, the organization of the simple meters into duple, triple, and quadruple is repeated in the compound meters, and refers exclusively to triple-meter units.

Terminology regarding compound meters is based on conducting patterns. Only the strong beats—that is, the first beat in each meter pattern—are conducted. And, since only the first accented beat in the measure falls on the downstroke, all other strong beats are considered secondary.

In working with language as the basis for development of meter concepts, this terminology, based as it is on conducting patterns, is not relevant to children and may cause some confusion. For this reason I would like to present a different terminology that is more consistent with the rhythmic development from language in Orff-Schulwerk. (I should mention that this approach to metric vocabulary is not my invention, but rather what I was taught as a music student in my theory classes in Germany.) In order to illustrate the difference in approach, let us return to some speech examples from Orff-Schulwerk I:

"*Smooth* as *vel*vet, *rough* as *bad*ger." (Page 51, no. 4. In the book the example is notated in eighth-notes, but notation in quarter-notes combines meter accents and word emphasis more satisfactorily and therefore brings about a more expressive recitation.) The accents stay the same in the speech recitation and are just as strong whether notated in two or in four; that is, there are no secondary accents in the speech:

This being the case, the count of four, consisting of two duple-meter patterns each starting with an equally strong beat (syllable), might be termed a *combined duple meter*.

A speech in simple triple such as no. 17, page 51,

"Chil-dren and   fools must not   play with edged   tools"

can just as easily be notated in six as in three, and this in no way affects the accentual pattern of triple meter and the way the text is recited:

This viewpoint is substantiated by the speech example on page 26, no. 34, "Oliver Cromwell." It is actually notated in $\frac{6}{b}$. The second speech accent is as strong as the first, and the piece could just as well be notated in $\frac{3}{b}$.

These last two examples make clear that the count of six is a combination of two triple patterns and, therefore, can be termed a combined triple meter.

There are several factors that make the standard terminology confusing:

1. The simple meter patterns are named according to the number of pulses they contain: 1 strong + 1 weak pulse = 2 pulses = duple meter; 1 strong + 2 weak pulses = 3 pulses = triple meter. The first inconsistency in terminology occurs with quadruple meter which is also considered a simple meter, despite its being a combination of two duple patterns. In notating rhythms in $\frac{4}{b}$ without speech (which would help to determine meter accents) the children tend to place a strong beat only on the first count of the measure.

2. Disregarding the definition of quadruple meter, we are left with only two simple meters, duple and triple. One would also expect the compound meters to be named on the basis of whether they are combinations of duple or triple units. However, this is not the case. The compound meters are defined solely through the number of strong beats they contain. Thus, a count in six is termed a compound duple although its individual meter patterns are triple patterns. The discrepancy between definition and actual notation is confusing to the children. In writing down their

    own compositions, whether rhythmic or melodic, they notate $\frac{6}{8}$ consistently in group-

    ings of three duple patterns instead of two triple patterns, and they place the accent marks denoting the 2nd strong count on the first note of the 2nd or 3rd pair of eighth-notes:

    (rhythmic notation examples)

    For this reason I have adopted an alternative vocabulary which correlates the primal accentual patterns of speech with the meter patterns in rhythm. In order not to cause confusion with the standard metric vocabulary, I avoid the terms "simple" and "compound." The alternative terminology calls for only two simple meters, the duple and triple which are termed *basic meters* because all combinations are based on these two meter patterns.

Basic duple meters: $\frac{2}{8}$ *(notation)*, $\frac{2}{8}$ *(notation)*

Basic triple meters: $\frac{3}{8}$ *(notation)*, $\frac{3}{8}$ *(notation)*, $\frac{3}{8}$ *(notation)*

Combined meters are those in which a basic meter pattern appears more than once per measure.

Combined duple: $\frac{4}{8}$, $\frac{4}{8}$, $\frac{4}{8}$

Combined triple: $\frac{6}{8}$, $\frac{6}{8}$, $\frac{9}{8}$, $\frac{12}{8}$

Combined meters made up of both duple and triple patterns (in standard terminology, "asymmetric meters") are termed *irregular*.

Irregular combinations: $\frac{5}{8}$: $\frac{3+2}{8}$, $\frac{2+3}{8}$; $\frac{5}{8}$: $\frac{3+2}{8}$, $\frac{2+3}{8}$

$\frac{7}{8}$: $\frac{3+2+2}{8}$, $\frac{2+2+3}{8}$; $\frac{7}{8}$: $\frac{3+2+2}{8}$, $\frac{2+2+3}{8}$

It is not my intention to challenge a widely used terminology, but I do believe that we must be consistent in everything we teach our students. The problem with the two terminologies is that each sees rhythm in a different light. One views it in an abstract, rationalized way, whereas the other allows us to recognize its origins in speech. Perhaps one might say that one terminology is more oriented toward art music, the other toward elemental music.

The reader might like to try a little ''meter game'' that I have my older middle-grade students puzzle over. Its purpose is a review of speech and meter. The text here is a proverb, but could be something else also:

> Early to bed and early to rise,
> Makes a man healthy, wealthy, and wise.

We first set the text in both basic meters, duple and triple. Then we combine the meter patterns. Whereas combinations of the same meter patterns do not produce new meters, combinations of two different meter patterns result in new meters with alternating accents (irregular combinations). The following illustration is simplified in that only one rhythmic version is used in each basic meter, although I have indicated some variations. I usually have the students find one rhythmic variation on their basic version. We also add simple body ostinati to help the rhythmic recitation of the text. The examples are first notated in a quarter-note pulse, but are changed to an eighth-note pulse later on to approximate more closely the speech tempo. Finally, the meter in seven is used. In both combinations, $2 + 2 + 3$ and $3 + 2 + 2$, the second duple pattern loses its accent almost completely because it falls on unaccented word syllables.

One of my classes once suggested a 2 + 3 + 2 pattern, which did not work because it caused too much speech distortion. Nevertheless, it was a valuable experiment; it demonstrated that rhythmic speech, though variable, can be manipulated only up to a certain point, beyond which rhythm must be freed from the yoke of language in order to develop its own potential as an individual musical element.

SUMMARY

Rhythm in its broadest meaning is the order of all things that occur in time. It is a fundamental life force, for without it there would be chaos. Rhythm in music fulfills much the same role. It is the form-giving element in a medium that consists of a chronological order of sounds. In Orff-Schulwerk, as indeed in all elemental music, rhythm is tied to movement and the spoken word because the most elemental human modes of expression are oral and movement expressions.

Rhythm evidences itself in its simplest form through the pulse. Like the heartbeat, which is fundamental to life, the pulse is fundamental to music. Musical training must begin by awakening in the students a physical awareness of the pulse. Thus, movement provides the means by which to develop a conscious perception of pulse.

Speech, on the other hand, in its longer and shorter durations of words and syllables, contains the germ cells of rhythmic subdivision or augmentation of the pulse. The rather vague and imprecise differentiations between long and short in natural speech are brought into exact mathematical relationships in rhythmic speech.

Meter, the measurement of small time units through recurring strong pulses, also finds its beginning in language through the accentuation of individual syllables.

Metered speech, then, is the synchronization of rhythm and meter, because it combines accentual pattern and rhythmization. For this reason, it is the natural foundation from which to develop all basic rhythmic concepts.

For the child as for adults, language is functional in that it serves as a vehicle for communication. We learn to comprehend it and to use it. But beyond the drills and exercises in school that are designed to help us speak clearly and grammatically, we rarely are made aware of its sound qualities, its changes in pitch, its stresses, and its temporal units. Learning to discern these qualities marks the beginning of ear training in music. The understanding of word syllabication is the first step in this direction.

Longer speech patterns introduce the concept of form in music, starting with the half-phrase and continuing to the full phrase. The speech examples in Orff-Schulwerk illustrate clearly that the rhythmization of texts is not as simple as it seems. The teacher must possess an intimate knowledge of language and an understanding of both the possibilities and the limitations of metered speech.

As long as the speech is oral, there is little danger of distorting it, because the speaker instinctively uses correct meter accents, rhythmic flow, and inflections. When it is notated, however, the system begins to exhibit its limitations with respect to the nuances of recitation. The problem is compounded by the fact that our young students' vocabulary is restricted to the most basic concepts of rhythm and meter. Therefore, finer points, such as varying the note value of the pulse-beat to best reflect the speech tempo, cannot be considered for a long time to come. We must use the quarter-note pulse for both basic meters and simply regard it as a flexible temporal unit. Children have no trouble accepting this because they do not yet know that there are other options. Learning rhythmic vocabulary is the same as any other conceptual learning; it begins with the general and only gradually moves into the differentiations that allow for alternatives.

In Orff-Schulwerk, the evolution of rhythm as a musical element, from the word-bound and purely oral stage to its ultimate independence from the word itself, is closely tied to the development of rhythmic notation, as indeed it was historically. However, Schulwerk touches only fleetingly on these stages. The developmental process is almost simultaneous because rhythmic notation is introduced early. Nevertheless, word-bound rhythm is never abandoned altogether in Orff-Schulwerk, even in its most advanced stages, because Schulwerk is elemental music.

3

DEVELOPMENT OF THE BASIC RHYTHMIC CONCEPTS IN ORFF-SCHULWERK

PULSE

Pulse Developed Through Movement

Pulse-beats, though regular, are variable in tempo. The human pulse, for example, differs from person to person, and even within one individual it is changeable. Breathing determines the tempo at which the heart will beat; it varies depending on such factors as physical activity or emotional stress. It is also possible to control the heartbeat consciously through breathing.

One might say that in a similar way music breathes through its pulse. The feeling and understanding of pulse in music, in its regularity and its variability, cannot be learned with a metronome. Rather, it is a process of internalization that begins by experiencing one's own pulse through the physical movements of one's own body.

The younger the child, the more movement-oriented he or she is. I still remember the difficulties I had in the first grade, sitting at my desk for what seemed like interminable hours, and during recess not being allowed to run around to work off stored-up energy. Instead we had to promenade, two by two, around the hall or, weather permitting, around the courtyard. During my first school years my report cards always began with the remark, "Brigitte is a little wiggly tomboy."

Fortunately for the young child of today, this need for physical activity is no longer considered a shortcoming. We recognize it for what it is: a natural developmental stage. Orff-Schulwerk makes use of the child's urge to be active.

The natural locomotor movements with which all children are familiar help to internalize a regular pulse-beat. This is the first and most basic step toward rhythmic development, for unless an established pulse beat can be held steady, further rhythmic development is not possible.

Basic locomotor movements in which the rhythmic patterns are composed of even pulse-beats include walking, jumping, hopping, and running. Emphasis should be placed on the regular and continuous repetition of a movement in all its tempo possibilities, rather than on developing absolute note values for each movement (for example, quarter-notes for the walk, eighth-notes for the run). It is important that breathing exercises precede movement activities.

Often I have been asked whether in a jump the beat falls on the takeoff or on the touchdown. This question takes us back to a similar problem we encountered in speech. There we found that within a larger unit the small units lose some of their identity, but the larger structure reflects the characteristics of its individual parts on a larger scale.

A single jump consists of two movements, a takeoff and a touchdown. (This preparation-release pattern is the same for all percussive sound production.) The takeoff is soundless, but has more dynamic energy than the touchdown; it represents the preparation and is, therefore, an upbeat (arsis). The touchdown, which even in a light jump produces some sound, is the release of the energy and, therefore, the downbeat (thesis). A slow jump can be executed in a duple meter pulse pattern:

♩   ♩

up down

However, normally the takeoff on the upbeat is faster than the touchdown and the following rhythmic pattern can emerge:

♪ ♩

up down

In a series of fast jumps the takeoff merges with the touchdown into one movement:

♫ ♫

jump jump jump jump

Often, every other jump is a rebound and, therefore, weaker, as for instance in rope-jumping:

♫ ♫

jump rebound jump rebound

Other locomotor movements are governed by the same principle, though they may seem a bit different since the feet move alternately in right-left patterns. The hop (touchdown on one foot) can be done in different patterns, such as:

*Stems up denote right foot, stems down, left foot.

The accents occur when the feet change. (Note values are not to be taken literally; they only mean to suggest a slower or faster tempo.) Whereas a basic hop still involves only one foot, walking uses alternate feet. As with the jump and the hop, a single step consists of a lift-off and a touchdown. In a very slow walk, the pattern includes four movements before it repeats:

lift   touch lift   touch

However, in a normal walk at a faster pace, the touchdown of one foot coincides with the lifting of the other as the weight is transferred. The pattern now takes only two beats before it repeats:

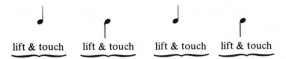

lift & touch   lift & touch   lift & touch   lift & touch

In a normal walk there is no accent on either step, and none should be produced because this would inhibit the easy and even stride that we are trying to develop.

Many other movements, mostly non-locomotor, can be done in pulse rhythm. They consist mostly of two-cycle motions, back and forth or up and down, such as swinging or bending or stretching. The children should be asked to experiment with different body parts using pulse rhythm.

The tempo of the movements will vary among students according to age, body mass, type of movement, and the body part with which it is performed. (For activities, refer to *Elementaria* by Gunild Keetman and the American edition of Orff-Schulwerk.)

Pulse Used as Accompaniment

In music we deal with sounds. Therefore our next step will be to make pulse-beats audible. To some degree this has already happened in the locomotor movements. However, there we preferred light and soft movement to heavy and noisy movement. Now the pulse will be reproduced and made audible in other ways. Just as the feet are natural pulse-producers, the hands are natural sound-producers; through clapping and knee slapping the body serves as instrument.[1] Stamping will be added a bit later; finger snapping is effective only with older children whose fingers are strong enough to produce a sound.

Care must be taken to introduce only one sound at a time, and to start combining two sounds only after individual ones can be executed with ease, correctly and evenly. A simple combination of two sounds involves the hands: In clapping and slapping the sound-producing surface changes, but not the sound-producing tool itself. Starting with the basic pattern of regular alternation, others can be created:

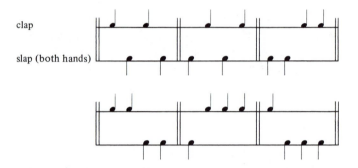

Stamping is not easy because of the problem of balance. Preparatory exercises in shifting the weight from one foot to the other help overcome such difficulties. Unless otherwise indicated, stamping should always be done with alternate feet. The foot should lift off the floor immediately before the stamp-down, so that balance and rhythm are not disturbed.

Children often have difficulty alternating stamps and claps, since the combination is produced by two body parts with different actions. For the clap, the hands and arms move out and in, or, better yet, outward and upward in a circle. The feet move up and down when stamping; moreover, one foot rests while the other moves. The following exercise can help prepare for alternate clapping and stamping: In very slow tempo have the students move their hands apart, using either the out-in or the circular motion, then touch them together again. Then have them stamp whenever the hands move apart. Now change the touching movement into a clap. Finally accelerate the tempo little by little, but make sure that the arms and hands keep up their two-beat motion of opening and closing. (If circular arm movement is used for the clap, the circle should be completed in two beats.)

Orff-Schulwerk I offers only a few examples of pulse-beat accompaniment. They are meant as points of departure for exploration of the many possibilities. In "Rhythms for Ostinato Accompaniments" (Orff-Schulwerk I, p. 60) the progressive combining of different body sounds is demonstrated. Each new combination is first introduced in its simplest form as accented pulse-beat rhythm. The

---

[1] Some teachers in this country prefer the German word for "slapping," which is "patschen."

students should make up similar patterns of their own, which then can be used to accompany rhymes and songs. The very best literature for this purpose is found among the many counting-out and rope-jumping rhymes, the handclap and finger games, and the childhood chants and songs. Very often the pulse-beat is part of these games anyway. Since our purpose at this point is to introduce the basic musical concept of accompaniment, it is not necessary to pay much attention to the rhythmic or melodic structure of the texts and melodies. Rather, we want to make sure that the students understand the broad meaning of the term *accompaniment* and of the pulse-beat as its first step.

As soon as two different body sounds are used for accompaniment, a distinct pattern evolves, and with it another term appears: *ostinato*, meaning a recurring pattern that is used as accompaniment.[2] In this case the pattern is formed through sound alone, as the rhythm consists only of pulse-beats.

BASIC RHYTHMIC BUILDING BLOCKS

The pulse-beat may be considered the simplest form of rhythm. A pulse-beat that alternates between strong and weak may be considered the simplest form of rhythmic pattern. Through subdivision of one or both of these pulse-beats, different rhythmic patterns are obtained which later will become the smallest units, or building blocks, of larger structures.

Patterns with subdivisions are difficult to perform in movement, as they inhibit the natural and free flow of locomotion. Therefore, they should not be attempted with young children or even with older beginners. However, as we have already seen in the previous discussion of syllabication, rhythmic building blocks are developed through speech in a natural way.

Single words or names exemplify the various short rhythmic patterns, and they may serve as "code names" for the patterns before actual rhythmic terminology is used. The different building blocks should not be introduced all at once, and they should follow each other in order of difficulty. For example:

1. Even pulse-beat patterns:
   a. two-syllable words:

   ♩ ♩
   Li - sa

   b. one-syllable words:

   ♩
   Moon

---

[2] Although an ostinato can stand on its own, in Orff-Schulwerk it is usually an accompaniment.

2.   Subdivisions of one of the pulse-beats, from three-syllable words:
     a. subdivision of the first, stronger pulse-beat:

but -ter - fly

     b. subdivision of the second, weaker pulse-beat:

straw - ber - ry

Children, as well as beginners of all age groups, often confuse long sound with accent. It seems that the easiest subdivided pattern is the one in which both coincide, as in 2b. Interestingly enough, the oldest Greek meter seems to have been just this rhythmic pattern, the *dactyl*. Reproduction through clapping or any other percussive movement confirms the same fact: Producing a strong sound needs a larger, more time-consuming movement than producing a weaker sound. For this reason, one might consider introducing the 2b pattern first.

With four building blocks, the children have a rhythmic vocabulary large enough to work and play with for some time. The following pattern need not be introduced immediately:

3.   Doubling the pulse-beat with four-syllable words:

pep -per-shak - er

In all rhythmic patterns, the students should be made aware of the accented syllables representing the strong beat. This helps to lay the foundation for meter and phrase feeling.

Still other rhythmic patterns, such as , and ♪♩ ♪, do not make good building blocks, as they are difficult to reproduce when taken out of context. However, they are likely to crop up, and are entirely acceptable in speech recitation or rhythmic improvisation in the absence of notation. Their conceptualization is possible only later, after the children have understood the basic meter patterns of strong and weak beats.

On Notation

So far I have mentioned nothing regarding musical notation, although it has been used in the examples. The question of when and how to teach it cannot be answered in terms that would apply to all possible situations. Musical literacy, although part of the whole process of musical development, is not the main objective in Orff-Schulwerk. Taking a realistic look at music education today, we know very well that, in spite of the lofty objectives prescribed in many curricula, the final goal cannot be the same in every situation. If little time is available for musical instruction—and this is often the case—priority should be given to the practical aspect of making music rather than the theoretical aspect. After all, Western culture made music for thousands of years without feeling the need to write it down, and most of the world's music is still made without notation.

In the light of history, the need for a precise notational system developed as music in Western culture became an art form, premeditated and composed. The evolution of rhythmic notation went hand in hand with the development of rhythmic conceptualization and theory. It underwent many changes until, by the end of the sixteenth century, it had essentially taken on its modern form.

If music education, particularly Orff-Schulwerk, is to achieve its goals—namely an understanding and enjoyment of our musical heritage through creating, singing, and playing—then musical literacy is indeed a necessity. Orff-Schulwerk demonstrates this clearly, as during the developmental process its elemental style incorporates more and more characteristics of traditional music:

1. Pitched bar instruments which require playing from memory (since the eyes are occupied finding the bars to play) are joined by traditional instruments, such as recorders, other wind instruments, and strings, all of which eventually necessitate the reading of music.

2. The simple orchestrations and short forms of the beginning stages become larger and can no longer be committed easily to memory.

3. As the concepts become more complex, improvisation takes on aspects of composition.

The ability to read and write music finally becomes essential. Thus, the evolutionary process in Orff-Schulwerk is similar to that of Western music.

As to the actual teaching of notation, the instructor may choose his own approach. There are only two basic guidelines to observe: to teach the children when they are ready, and to teach only as much as they can handle at a given time. Musical notation is the abstraction of a sound language. Before an abstraction into sound symbols is attempted, the language must be spoken and internalized first, even if only to a limited degree. Rhythmic notation should be taught first. Pitch notation can wait for quite a while until it is really needed. If taught too early, it will inhibit the development of pitch recognition, since the child will rely on visual rather than aural perception.[3]

How to introduce rhythmic notation and terminology depends a great deal on the age of the students. With older ones it is really not necessary to go through a series of preliminary symbols and terms. With younger age groups we have to be more patient and inventive. Each teacher will want to use his or her special approach. I will describe one possible path to notation.

---

[3] For the introduction of pitch notation, see Chapter 5, page 122–123.

I usually introduce symbols once the children have internalized the pulse-beat and its subdivision into the two basic building blocks, ♩ ♫ and ♫ ♩. From the start, I show the notes as they really appear, rather than in stick notation, because the concept of their function is evidenced through both the heads and the stems. (Too often, in the effort to make learning easy, we embark on unnecessary "detours.") However, I use a different device, imagination, to enhance the learning process. If the notes are written with stems downward, they look like "stick-people." The children regard these beats as living creatures and become very interested in them. The eighth-notes are twins who hold on to each other, whereas the quarter-notes are the grown-up beats. The measures—$\frac{2}{4}$, later $\frac{4}{4}$ and $\frac{3}{4}$—are houses with numbered rooms (the counts). The twins, being much smaller, naturally share one room together; the grown beats, on the other hand, need their own rooms. The story of the beats gets longer and more involved as more rhythmic concepts are added. In the end, a hurricane blows the roofs off the houses and the transformation into measures has taken place. The story varies from year to year as I tire of repetition.

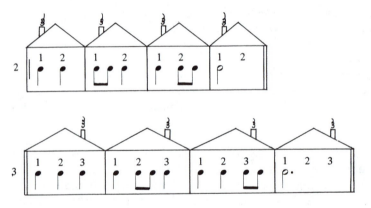

DEVELOPMENT OF THE HORIZONTAL AND VERTICAL SOUND ASPECT

Time is the force that governs life. Everything we do happens in a sequence measured in terms of time, and it is expressed through words such as "before," "after," "while" "then," and "now." Language, in itself a sequence of words expressed in time, has another dimension: it can be notated. In Western culture the successive time element is shown by a horizontal line.

Like language, music is a succession of sounds. Depending on the source of the sound, the horizontal line depicts a rhythm or a melody. Unlike language, music is also notated in a vertical way, for sounds can be heard simultaneously. The vertical line creates harmony, in the Greek sense of the word, meaning "sounding together."

Everything we teach in music has to do with its horizontal and vertical aspects. Already in our beginning work with speech we see the two concepts separated. The spoken text represents the horizontal line and therefore carries the seed of melody; the accompaniment adds the vertical dimension and therefore carries the seed of harmony (simultaneous pitches).

Horizontal Development (Form)

The Smallest Units: Names and Words. Words with the same or different rhythmic patterns can be strung together, recited, and clapped over an accompaniment of pulse-beats:

Red - bird,   red - bird,   chick - a - dee,   chick - a - dee,   barn swal-low   barn swal-low

Such word sequences do not yet imply a specific musical form, as they can go on ad infinitum. But each word in itself is recognized as a rhythmic pattern. When notation is used, the symbols show the specific, single units which, in time, will become parts of a larger unit.

Half-phrases. In learning how to speak, the child generally progresses from single words ("naming things") through combinations of words to short statements, and finally to complete, fully developed sentences.

Learning to speak the language of music is a similar process. A rhythmic building block represents the single word, the half-phrase a short statement, and the whole phrase a full sentence. In order to be able to improvise, the students must first acquire a feeling for, and an understanding of, these short rhythmic structures, since they are the beginning of all form in music.

Work with speech again will help to develop a sense for musical structure. The rhythmic counterpart to short statements in language are the half-phrases, made up of two building blocks (two simple meter patterns with two strong beats). Using everyday speech for examples, imperative sentences work well:

Eat   like a   la - dy

Please,   clean your   room.

Children often have difficulty in making up short sentences to fit the half-phrase, although they may understand the basic concept. It is easier for them to work from given texts. In any event, we should soon proceed to less prosaic language and find texts that are instructive as well as artistically rewarding. As can be seen already in the first speech examples in Orff-Schulwerk I, Orff is concerned not only with the rhythm of speech but with language as an art form—with the sounds of words, with the poetic or dramatic qualities of a text, and with the thoughts behind the words. Such qualities we find in the vernacular poetry of folk idioms, proverbs, weather sayings, riddles, even magic spells and curses. They represent the beliefs and the wisdom of our forefathers, and thus have much human and educational value.[4]

The speech examples in Orff-Schulwerk I (p. 51) include some short proverbs:

Nothing seek, nothing find	♩♫ ♩ ♪ ♩♫ ♩ ♪ (♩ ♫ ♩ ♩ ’ ♫ ♩ ♩)
Look before you leap	♩ ♫ ♫ ♩ ♩
Watch your step[5]	♩ ♩ ♩ ♩ ♩ ♩

There are also similes:

Light as a feather	♩ ♩ ♫ ♩ ♩ ♩ (♩ ♫♫ ♩ ♫ ♩)
Flat as a pancake	♩ ♩ ♫ ♩ ♩ ♩ (♩ ♫♫ ♩ ♩ ♪)
Mad as a hatter	♩ ♩ ♫ ♩ ♫ ♩ (♩ ♫♫ ♩ ♫ ♩)

(In the book, the next-to-the-last example starts on an upbeat with the word "As." I deleted it, because in all likelihood the children will not yet be familiar with the upbeat.)

Most speech patterns can be performed in both duple and triple meter, as illustrated. However, in beginning rhythmic training only duple meter will be used.

Speech patterns such as these should not just be recited in order to make a point and then discarded; rather, they should be used in different ways to reinforce the new concept. For instance, they may serve as a starting point, or as a central idea, for experimentation and improvisation in movement and dramatic play. They can be used to build melodies, and often they lend themselves to canonic treatment:

Round   as   a   pan - cake,   round   as   a   pan - cake,   round   as   a   . . .

Round   as   a   pan - cake,   round   as   a   pan - cake,

---

[4] See also Chapter 10.

[5] The note values in the last measures of lines 2 and 3 have been changed to better express the vowel sounds.

Canon creates a new vertical sound picture. Instead of one horizontal line being accompanied, there are now two equally important lines. Although identical, they follow one another at some time distance.

The successive time element of two identical ideas can be shown visually through color patterns, pictures, and so on. One of my second-graders once drew a double canon with colored-in squares. Without color, it can be represented by a graphic pattern:

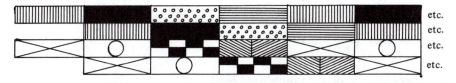

Combining Several Half-Phrases. The combination of several half-phrases into a longer form is best illustrated with nursery and childhood rhymes. These rhymes are metered speech and usually consist of two to four lines but sometimes are longer. The individual lines are half-phrases, and this clear separation helps the children to recognize them as such.
Short two-liners:

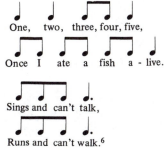

Typical four-liners:

---

[6] Texts from Emrich, *Folklore on the American Land.*

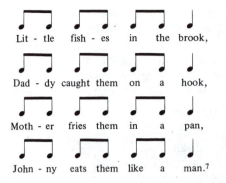

Lit - tle   fish - es   in   the   brook,

Dad - dy caught them   on   a   hook,

Moth - er   fries them   in   a   pan,

John - ny   eats them   like   a   man.[7]

Not all rhymes consist of even-numbered lines:

Ears   like   a   mule,   or:

Tail   like   a   cot - ton   ball,

Runs   like   a   fool.[8]

One,   two,   tie   my   shoe,

Three,   four,   shut   the   door,

Five,   six,   pick   up   sticks,

Sev - en, eight,   lay   them straight,

Nine,   ten, a   big   fat   hen.[9]

Often, however, a clear separation into half-phrases cannot be made. For example, the four-liner,

---

[7] Text from Opie, *The Oxford Book of Nursery Rhymes*.
[8] Text from Emrich, *Folklore on the American Land*.
[9] Text from Opie, *The Oxford Book of Nursery Rhymes*.

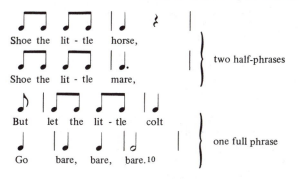

Shoe the lit - tle horse,

Shoe the lit - tle mare,   } two half-phrases

But let the lit - tle colt

Go bare, bare, bare.[10]   } one full phrase

consists of two half-phrases and a full phrase, a form often found in English nursery rhymes. However, although the two half-phrases begin on the downbeat, the full phrase starts with an upbeat. This is confusing to the children if rhythmic notation is used, because in the text the upbeat is the first word in a new line, whereas in the rhythmic notation it belongs to the previous measure, even though it marks the beginning of the next rhythmic phrase. In my experience it is best to select rhymes where this problem does not occur. Later, when the upbeat is studied, texts containing such problems can be chosen for illustration.

In notating a speech pattern, I have the class first find and underline the accented words or syllables. In doing so, we have already determined the beginning and end of the building blocks (houses, measures, or whatever term is used), as every accented syllable is the starting point of a new unit. When working with young children whose writing skills are not yet well developed, I make a set of flash cards for each child. The sets contain several cards of all the building blocks the children are familiar with. These can be laid out in proper order instead of notating the speech patterns.

Full Phrase Length. In order to demonstrate the full phrase in metered speech, we shall turn to weather sayings. They seem to work especially well because most often they are conditional sentences with two clauses. Musically speaking, these proverbs consist of antecedent and consequent half-phrases.

① No weath-er is ill if the wind is still.

② The sharp - er the blast, the soon - er it's past.

③ Rain-bow at noon, more rain soon.

The same proverbs in duple meter:

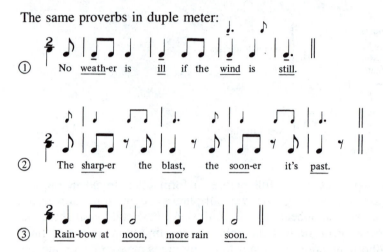

① No weath-er is ill if the wind is still.

② The sharp-er the blast, the soon-er it's past.

③ Rain-bow at noon, more rain soon.

Sometimes an upbeat beginning will help to emphasize important words better than would a downbeat:

(a) When the dew is on the grass, rain will nev - er come to pass.

(b) When the dew is on the grass, rain will nev - er come to pass.

Example b is rather monotonous when recited, an ever-present danger in using metered speech. By starting the rhyme on an upbeat, the important words— *dew*, *grass*, *never*, *pass*—will fall on the downbeat. In this way, word accent and speech emphasis are combined, and the recitation will sound more natural.

Finally, I would like to remind the reader that the time signatures of even meter $\left(\frac{4}{p}, \frac{2}{p}\right)$ are not identical in meaning, as they imply a difference in the number of stresses within the measure. Thus, they will bring about a different speech recitation:

A storm of hail brings frost on its tail.

A storm of hail brings frost on its tail.

The one-phrase proverb, although self-contained, is rather short to qualify as a musical form in itself. Like the half-phrase, it needs to be lengthened through repetition (echo, canon, etc.) in order to become a structure that satisfies our sense of musical architecture. However, it is the single phrase which is the basis for all further development of elemental music forms, and therein lies its significance. Extensive work with one-phrase speech patterns such as proverbs will help the children to understand this basic form-unit.

Two or More Phrases. Texts consisting of two full phrases give a sense of wholeness and completeness which the smaller structures lack. A form results which, though still small, can justify its existence as it stands.

There is an abundance of material—proverbs and weather sayings, street games and jingles, jokes and riddles, and cures and spells—that can be used in dramatizations, for making songs and canons, for building rondos, and other such experiments with form. Research on such literature need not come only from books. The children should be asked to share their own store of traditions and those of their parents. There is danger that such verbal lore may disappear, and for this reason it is all the more important to save from oblivion that which still lives in the varied ethnic and regional cultures. Some may be hesitant to use such material, considering it archaic and out of touch with the modern world. These fragments of folk traditions *are* still relevant today, however, as they teach us about our own roots and identities, those of other peoples, and the world around us. Therefore the choice of meaningful texts is of the utmost importance (see also Chapter 10).

Vertical Development: Accompaniment

After having followed horizontal development to the point where form is definitely established, we will now examine the vertical dimension. As we have seen earlier, the pulse-beats are the simplest and most natural way to accompany rhyme, chant, or song. The next developmental step makes use of subdivisions of the pulse, the building blocks, in repeating patterns called ostinati.

Ostinati have been used as a compositional technique throughout the ages and throughout the world. However, whereas all extant historical examples in Western tradition deal with melodic or harmonic ostinato forms, in Orff-Schulwerk we start at a more elemental level, using speech, rhythm, and even movement.

For the sake of clarity it is again helpful to use terminology carefully and consistently, differentiating between the various ostinato types, such as speech ostinato, rhythmic ostinato, and movement ostinato. As a general rule, a pattern should be heard at least four times in order to qualify as an ostinato. The simplest form of *speech ostinato* consists of a single word, but it may be longer.

(a) Red - bird,   blue - bird,   chick - a - dee,   barn swal - low,

speech ostinato
bird - watch-ing, bird - watch-ing, bird - watch-ing, bird - watch-ing,

(b) Car - di - nal,   blue - jay,   wood - peck - er,   duck,

speech ostinato
Let's   feed the   birds,   let's   feed the   birds,

spar - row,   tit - mouse,   chick - a - dee,   wren.

speech ostinato
let's   feed the   birds,   let's   feed the   birds.

(An example of a speech ostinato can be found in Orff-Schulwerk I, p. 26, "Oliver Cromwell.")

A *rhythmic ostinato* is, as the term implies, purely rhythmic, with no words attached to it. Separating rhythm from the spoken word is a rather important step in the learning process, for it makes rhythm an independent musical element. The pulse-beat is the first "wordless" accompaniment. However, it is in a strict sense not yet a rhythmic ostinato, as all the beats are of equal length. Although there is pattern in its alternation of strong and weak, without supporting words it is not readily recognizable. We might regard it as a "pre-form" of rhythmic ostinato.

A rhythmic ostinato is formed through the repetition of rhythmic motifs. An almost infinite number of patterns is possible, and for this reason they provide a good basis for improvisation. Again, the buildup from simple to more complex forms takes considerable time.

In the beginning stages, rhythmic ostinati must stay simple, for it is not a simple matter for the child to play a rhythmic pattern while reciting a text or singing a song. Although skill development is only one aspect of musical training, we must allow plenty of time for it, as all music-making depends on coordination. The examples in Orff-Schulwerk I cover a development of many years.

We now have four building blocks that can be used simultaneously to create a variety of accompaniments. I explain to the children that this "stacking" of ostinati is like building a multistoried house. Two-story houses may look like this:

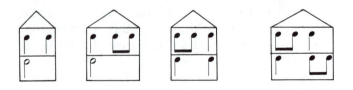

and three-story houses like this:

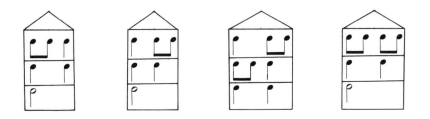

How far such a building process can be carried at one time depends on the age and skill development of the students. Adding a new story to the houses should be undertaken only after the "foundation" has "settled." The activities should take the form of exploration and improvisation rather than being teacher-directed. After the idea has been demonstrated on the blackboard by the teacher, the children can go to work on their own in small groups, constructing their two- and three-story houses. For this purpose they can use their flash-card collections, which we call rhythmic construction kits.

These activities lead to the discovery of several new concepts. Until now the building blocks have been used only within the framework of word-recitation, an order of succession that has been shown through horizontal notation. Now the simultaneous occurrence of sounds or patterns can be visualized through the vertical picture. Our two- and three-story houses are nothing less than the basic principles of scoring. (With older beginners the term *score* can be introduced immediately, as can the term *measure* instead of "house.")

The building of multistoried houses leads to yet another concept, that of *rhythmic complementation* or *contrast*. An accompaniment is not the same as the part it accompanies, nor are the ostinati themselves all alike; all parts are different and contrast with one another. The principle of complementation is basic to music and should be introduced early, even if only in simple terms.

Complementation or contrast occurs also in other ways. In sound textures, for example, we have talked thus far only about body percussion; now it is time to take a look around the music room and discover some of its secrets! Under the teacher's guidance the children should experiment with various unpitched percussion instruments. They will soon find out which instruments produce clear sounds even when played quickly, and which instruments are better suited for long, sustained sounds. Learning to differentiate between tone colors and to understand how they can be mixed to achieve an interesting texture are basic lessons in instrumentation. As a class project, students may create a large chart that supplies information about the instruments, either in pictures or in writing. The information should include the name of each instrument, the duration of its sound, its possible dynamic levels, and its most appropriate uses. Naturally some instruments will fit into almost every category.

Unpitched Percussion Instruments

Instruments	Sound		Dynamic levels	Uses: Good for playing		
	sustained	short	loud to soft	fast & many notes	slower & fewer notes	special & seldom
Membranes						
Hand drum		x	←→	x	x	
Tambourine		x	←→	x	x	
Bass drum		x	←→	(x)	x	x
Timpani		x	←→	x	x	x
etc.						
Metal						
Big cymbals	x		←→			x
Finger cymbals	x		⊢→		x	x
Hanging cymbal	x		←→			x
Triangle	x		→		x	x
etc.						
Wood						
Claves		x	⊢→	x	x	x
Woodblock		x	←→	x	x	x
Temple blocks		x	⊢→	x	x	x
etc.						
Rattles & Shakers						
Maracas		x	→	x		
Sand rattle			→	x		
Jingles			→	x		

"Rhythms for Ostinato Accompaniment" (Orff-Schulwerk I, p. 60) illustrates the development of the whole range of body percussion from one sound up to four sounds, using the clap, slap, stamp, and finger-snap. Naturally it will take years before the students are able to perform the more difficult patterns. However, such ostinato exercises are essential for the development of coordination and must be practiced from the very start and at ever-increasing levels of difficulty. Ostinato patterns should be created through improvisation rather than taught through drill. For instance, the instructor might give the rhythmic framework through clapping only and have the children "orchestrate" with different body sounds. In this way a rhythmic pattern can go a long way. For example: Teacher claps a basic pattern | ♪♪ ♪♪ | ♩ ♩ |

Improvisation with two sounds:

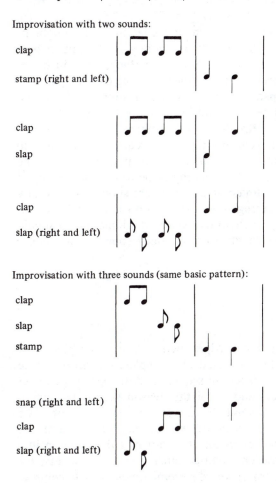

clap

stamp (right and left)

clap

slap

clap

slap (right and left)

Improvisation with three sounds (same basic pattern):

clap

slap

stamp

snap (right and left)

clap

slap (right and left)

"Exercises for Knee Slapping" (Orff-Schulwerk I, p. 76) again provides materials for many years. These and similar examples made up to suit specific levels of skill development are an excellent preparation for instrumental play with alternating sticks. They may serve as a rhythmic framework to develop bordun forms. They can be used with advanced students as reading exercises and for developing skill and coordination. And finally, they may be adapted for playing on hand drums, bongos, or timpani (consult notes in Orff-Schulwerk I, p. 142).

Rhythmic Speech Pieces with Ostinato Accompaniment

There are several larger pieces in Orff-Schulwerk I that exemplify the horizontal and vertical aspect through the use of metered speech or song, with nonpitched ostinato accompaniment.

Speech ostinato is added to metered recitation in "The Campbells Are Coming" (p. 25) and in "Oliver Cromwell" (p. 26). Depending on the age and areas of interest of the students, other texts should be set in similar ways. Body ostinati accompany two songs, "My Little Pony" (p. 72) and "Old Angus" (p. 73). Since singing grows out of metered speech, a preparatory step might be choral recitation of the texts. The rhythmic ostinato setting is difficult in both songs, but it can be simplified if necessary. "My Little Pony," for instance, might be accompanied all the way through with just the beginning ostinato patterns; or, if a change is desired, a new pattern might consist of simple pulse-beats. Under the teacher's guidance, other texts should be developed by the students.

A third group of pieces are the "Rhythms over Ostinato Accompaniment" (p. 62). Here words have been eliminated and rhythm appears as an element in its own right. The examples illustrate the use of complementation between the parts, resulting in "rhythmic polyphony," a stepping-stone to true polyphony.[11] Exercises in building rhythms with ostinato accompaniment should be carefully sequenced, beginning with simple arrangements such as example #1 (p. 62) and developing slowly to more complex rhythms. Again, rhythmic pieces should grow out of improvisation and not be taught from arranged compositions alone.

OTHER RHYTHMIC CONCEPTS

Triple Meter

The reader might well wonder where triple meter fits into the picture of rhythmic development. It has already been used in examples, but no reference has been made to its placement in the teaching sequence. Although triple meter is the second of the two basic meters and is for this reason very important, it should not be introduced before the students have a strong foundation of basic rhythmic concepts and are conversant with the full phrase length in duple meter.

There is no single recommended procedure for initiating the children into triple meter. I prefer using longer speech patterns rather than single words, for in the larger unit the accentual pattern is heard several times, which helps to establish its "otherness" more clearly. A simple text can be recited in even note values and, regardless of the speech tempo, should be notated in $\frac{3}{4}$ time:

Chil - dren   and   fools must not   play with edged tools.

---

[11] The term is used in Keller, *Introduction to Orff-Schulwerk.*

The accentual pattern of strong-weak-weak can be easily heard and thereby clearly established. The dotted half-note at the end will in all likelihood be a new note value to learn. Since the children are already experienced in the use of building blocks in duple time, new ones can now be made up to fit the triple meter. One might start by systematically subdividing each of the quarter-notes:

1.‖ ♫ ♩ ♩ ‖   2.‖ ♩ ♫ ♩ ‖   3.‖ ♩ ♩ ♫ ‖

Or two quarter-notes might be combined into one half-note:

1.‖ ♩ ♩ ‖   2.‖ ♩ ♩ ‖

Later, other patterns can be created with four eighth-notes. All examples should first be practiced through clapping, and then turned into body ostinati. This is a good time to start using three different sounds, since three-beat patterns fall quite naturally into three different body levels of sound production:

In working with speech, single two- and three-syllable words or names used formerly in duple meter can now be reintroduced in triple meter for comparison:

Mar -y or Mar - y,   Jon - a-than or Jon- a - than,   sun - flow - er or sun - flow - er

With this exercise, a new concept appears—the *rhythmic variation*. As we have seen, there is more than one way to set a word or text. Improvisations and exercises using this idea should follow.

Within the context of rhythmic variation, one might also introduce the dotted quarter-note, which seems to fit naturally into triple meter, especially when used with speech. The dotted half-note has already introduced the function of the dot, and the same principle can now be applied to the dotted quarter. Still, my experience has been that young children do not always understand the mathematical aspect of the dot. Ties can be used instead, at least to prepare the introduction to dotted quarters:

♩ ♫ ♩

Many words and names formerly spoken in an even pulse-beat, or in duple-meter patterns of ♫ ♩, can now be varied to fit the new rhythmic pattern:

Jonathan:

The natural locomotor movement in triple meter is the *waltz-step* or *waltz-run*. The strong beat should be shown through an extended step rather than a loud and heavy one. Children often have difficulties with the waltz, since the accent falls on alternate feet.

The Upbeat

Before the upbeat can be introduced, the teacher must make absolutely sure that the class understands and can hear, in speech as well as in rhythm, the strong and weak syllables and corresponding beats. The children should be comfortable with the improvisation of rhythmic phrases in both simple duple and triple meter. Without such background and practical experience, they will not understand the meaning of this new rhythmic idea or be able to use it correctly.

The upbeat is introduced most easily with the help of longer speech patterns (i.e., not individual words), because they show clearly how the beginning and end complement each other to form a whole measure (and thus complete the phrase):

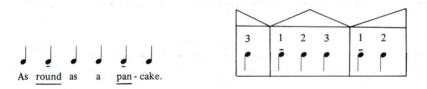

(A flashback to the old name-game is often useful and fun; children may compare their names to find out which ones start with an upbeat.)

Once the students have comprehended the idea because they can *hear* the pickup, rhymes and songs consisting of several phrases should be used:

> Two *bodies* have *I*,
> Though *both* joined in *one*,
> The *stil*ler I *stand*,
> The *faster* I *run*.[12]

---

[12] Opie, *The Oxford Book of Nursery Rhymes*.

These longer texts demonstrate that, as a rule, if the first phrase starts with an upbeat all the others do also. (This, by the way, applies also to melodic phrases.)

The two preceding examples are both in triple meter and notated in a quarter-note pulse. It has been my experience that the use of this meter and of the quarter-note pulse makes it easiest for the students to understand the duration of the upbeat: The long note preceding the upbeat is always twice the length of the pickup note; in $\frac{3}{4}$ time we thus only deal with half-notes and quarter-notes, with which the children are familiar. In this manner, even a second-grader will be able to understand how the phrase ending on the downbeat forms a complete measure with the upbeat beginning of the following phrase.

Matters are a bit more difficult in duple meter with the quarter-note as the pulse. Here, the note marking the phrase ending is three times as long as the succeeding upbeat. This occurs most often in rhymes consisting of two half-phrases and one full phrase (the following example is from Orff-Schulwerk I, p. 16; see also above):

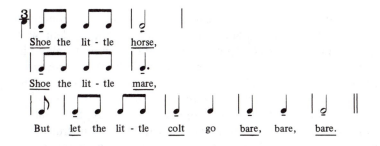

In the next example (from Orff-Schulwerk I, p. 52), all phrases start on a pickup. Although the text is actually more natural in triple meter, it can be put into duple meter also:

The cock does crow

To let you know

And thou be wise

'Tis time to rise.

In these last two examples the note before the upbeat must either be a dotted quarter-note or a quarter followed by an eighth-rest, symbols that young students are probably not yet familiar with.

When the time has come to introduce dotted quarter-notes, single eighth-notes, and eighth-rests, names or individual words can be used again to demonstrate the differences in the length of sounds and how to notate them as precisely as possible:

Clau - dine   Ma - rie   Y - vonne   Je - rome

but: Y - vette   Co - lette   Gi - raffe   etc.

(As can be seen, many words or names starting on the upbeat and with the accent on the last syllable are of French origin.)

With advanced students the finer points in the use of the pickup should be discussed, as for instance how it can influence word emphasis and expression in metered speech.

IMPROVISATION

There was a time when a person's musical education was considered incomplete unless he or she was able to improvise and compose music. The student was instructed in the art of composition and improvisation while learning to play his or her chosen instrument. Thus, one's instrumental skills and ability to improvise balanced each other and developed hand in hand. J. S. Bach's *Klavierbüchlein für Wilhelm Friedemann* and Leopold Mozart's *Notenbuch für Wolfgang* are living monuments to the nature of musical instruction in another age. Today, the creative aspect has no part in traditional elementary music education or in instrumental instruction. Unfortunately, what has been omitted in early music training can never be made up completely in later years.

The Orff-Schulwerk philosophy once more recognizes the importance of involving the student actively in the process of creating. For this reason, improvisation is an integral part of its musical instruction. Learning is meaningful only if it brings satisfaction to the learner, and satisfaction arises from the ability to use acquired knowledge for the purpose of creating.

Mind-Challenging Games

Activities in improvisation need to be well planned by the teacher. They are most meaningful and successful if used with a specific objective in mind, limited to one concept at a time.

Creativity starts the moment the children are asked to find different names or words fitting the rhythmic building blocks they have learned to recognize. Often, especially with young students, such improvisations take the form of games. They teach fast reaction and clear thinking; their value cannot be overestimated. Children as well as adults have always delighted in playing mind-challenging games. In a classroom such games are an enticing way to reinforce newly learned concepts. The following are a few examples of creative activities, each with a specific objective.

Word Game

Objective: To Make Correct Use of the Building Blocks.

Text: Little Tommy Tittlemouse
       Lived in a little house,
       He caught fishes
       In other men's ditches.

The children stand in a circle, reciting or singing the rhyme accompanied by body percussion. When they have finished, one child in the middle—Tommy Tittlemouse—starts "fishing." He moves around the circle, touching each child as he sings or says:

> One fish,
> Two fish,
> Red fish,[13]
>
> . . .

The fourth child he touches must say a new fish name which fits the rhythm of a building block chosen before the game started. Such building blocks might be:

goldfish ♩♩

silverfish ♫ ♩

sea-nettle ♩ ♫

If the child finds a fish fitting the rhythmic pattern, he will be the new Tommy Tittlemouse. Naturally, most students cannot think of a new fish fast enough; to make matters easier, the different fish for the various rhythmic patterns can be "caught" beforehand and listed on the blackboard, so that it becomes only a matter of choosing the right one. In yet another variation, Tommy Tittlemouse decides which building block is to be used, and he announces it by clapping the pattern four times as an introduction to his song.

Objective: Timbre and Memory. All children sit in a circle. The teacher selects one building block to be used throughout the game. The first child plays the pattern twice with a body sound of his or her own choice and all repeat it twice. The next child repeats again, but then plays the pattern in a new way, also twice. All repeat the first and the second sound pattern. The third student then plays both patterns and adds a new one. This goes on until everyone has added a new sound, or until their memory fails. (Most often the children remember better than the teacher.)

---

[13] Dr. Seuss, *One Fish, Two Fish, Red Fish, Blue Fish* (New York: Random House, 1960).

Objective: Rhythmic Contrast.   The game involves as many students as there are building blocks familiar to them. One child claps a pattern four times, then a second student joins, clapping a contrasting pattern. This continues until all the building blocks have been used, when the game begins again with other children.

Objective: Instrumentation.   In a more advanced version of the previous improvisation, each rhythmic pattern must be reproduced with a different body sound. Finally, the same can be done with small unpitched percussion. The instruments are scattered in the middle of the circle; each child quickly must select an instrument that provides a sound contrasting to those already in use.

The last two activities become more difficult as more building blocks are used. Young beginners perhaps can handle only two different patterns; however, if they manage well, they should be urged to add a third pattern. Older students will progress more quickly.

These improvised patterns can also be used to accompany rhymes and songs.

Developing a Feeling for Phrase Length

Children learn to speak by imitating their elders. *Echo-play*, or *imitation*, is at the beginning of all musical improvisation; it is done rhythmically as well as melodically, and it continues through all stages of musical development.

The teacher will start the echo activities with small units, such as the half-phrase consisting of two building blocks. Soon the children can take turns in making up similar short phrases to be imitated by the whole class. Since the phrases are short, it is advisable to use only one body sound per phrase to insure smooth and fluent playing.

Echo-play of half-phrases develops into a rudimentary form of *question-answer* when the children are asked to make up a different pattern in answer to the one the teacher has played. This exercise may be first illustrated through speech, but I have found that children often have trouble finding answers in the right phrase length quickly:

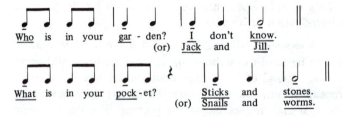

To maintain interest in question-answer games, ways must be found to vary the same basic idea. For instance, the answer may be done with a different body sound than the question. Or, if the question and answer are played by two individual children, the whole class might be asked to repeat both phrases. This exercise leads directly into echoing of a full phrase.

Improvisation of full phrases continues in the same way. Attention should now be given to the endings. In speaking, the conclusion of a statement is heard through the dropping of the voice to a lower pitch. A question, I have observed, apparently can end on either a lower or higher pitch. In a rhythmic statement a clearer sense of finality is achieved by ending it on the strong beat than by ending it on a weak beat. (The Greek differentiation between male and female endings in a line of verse is rather amusing in this regard—I am sure no explanation is necessary as to which ending was which!) The students should learn to distinguish between the two different endings and to use them with discrimination. For this purpose, the question-answer improvisation might be set up in such a way that the antecedent phrase concludes on a weak beat and the consequent phrase on a strong beat (i.e., the last strong beat in the phrase):

Just as in actual conversation the answer relates to the question, a relationship exists between antecedent and consequent phrases regarding their rhythmic content. As long as the rhythmic vocabulary is limited, not all of the following possibilities are feasible:

1. *a, a¹ structures*, in which the answer represents a variation of the question:
   a. The answer repeats the beginning of the question, but concludes differently:

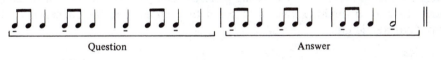

   b. A rhythmic element of the question is varied in the answer:

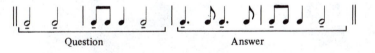

   c. The end of the question is repeated in the beginning of the answer:

2. *a, b structures*: The answer is simply a contrast to the question:

These possibilities should be demonstrated, discussed with the students, and then practiced in both duple and triple meter. Among the given structures, the varied answer (a, a¹) and the contrasting answer (a, b) are the simplest solutions and should be introduced first. Numbers 1b and 1c presuppose more experience in listening skills and a greater rhythmic vocabulary.

Once the students are comfortable with the question-answer play and have no more problems feeling the phrase length, it is time to have them improvise two phrases. This is not difficult if they think of the two phrases as a question and an answer.

The Rhythmic Rondo

The rondo provides an ideal framework for improvisation. At the same time it introduces the children to their first larger musical form.

The structure of the elemental rondo resembles the rondeau of the seventeenth-century French clavecinists, but in every other respect it is much more flexible. The recurring A-section is performed by the whole class (= tutti), while the intervening sections are improvised by solo players or small groups. If each student wants a turn as a soloist, a rondo may well take the better part of a class period!

A rondo can be designed in different ways. There are speech rondos, rhythmic rondos, instrumental rondos (which can also be danced), and song rondos (in which different songs form the interspersed sections). The idea of the rondo—alternation between same and different—can even be shown in movement by posing as "sculptures," or by drawing pictures. Once I asked a class of second-graders to draw a rondo (I wanted to see if they understood the concept). Here is my favorite picture:

In a rhythmic rondo, the improvisations between the A-sections can be set up in a number of ways:

1. Question-answer between two solo players: The length of the improvisation should correspond to the length of the A-section. If A is eight measures long and repeated, the two solo players should go twice through the process of inventing a question and an answer. Even better, they should try to play the same question or answer the second time around.
2. Four students per section improvise one phrase each.
3. One child improvises a question, to which the whole class responds with an answer. It does not matter that everyone plays something different, as long as all feel the phrase length and end together.
4. An echo can be built into the improvisations by having each solo phrase repeated as a tutti phrase.

Adding ostinato accompaniment not only enhances the improvisations but also helps to keep the tempo steady. As the students become more experienced and competent, the individual improvisations should be lengthened to two phrases each.

Improvising Canons

Rhythmic echo-play leads to another form of imitation, the *canon*. It differs from the echo in that the imitation begins before the original phrase is finished.

Rudimentary canonic structures may have developed in the antiphonal singing of tribal cultures when the chorus started the response before the leader had finished. This is only a reasonable assumption, however, and other practices may have contributed to this type of simultaneous imitation.

In Orff-Schulwerk, elemental canons are developed through improvisation in the same way and are therefore a direct outgrowth of echo-play. They can be introduced as soon as the children have an active working vocabulary of half-phrases. At first, the teacher will have to be the leader, but soon the students can assume this role also. It is important that the leader's instrument be louder and of a different sound texture than that of the imitating group. For instance, the leader may clap while the class slaps, or use a drum against the group's clapping. Preparatory steps leading to such open-ended canon improvisations should be sequenced similarly to the following "recipe":

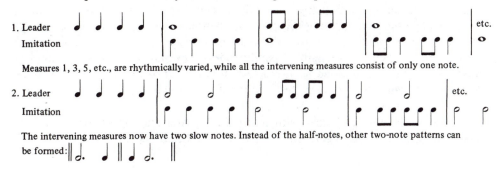

3. Leader

Imitation

etc.

The alternating measures have three notes. Other three-note possiblities:

It is important that the improvised rhythmic patterns in the even-numbered measures always be different from the recurring simple "beat-patterns" in order to prevent overlapping.

These three steps cannot be developed all at once, because the listening skills of the children need time to grow. The response of the class will tell the teacher when to move to the next step. The exercises should also be tried in triple meter and while moving.

A true canon without recurring measures should be attempted only when the students can handle the preparatory steps. Now the leader's task is more difficult, as he or she has to constantly create new rhythmic patterns which will be in clear contrast to the preceding one. Only in this way will it be possible for the children to hear the new pattern while echoing the one before.

Models for Improvisation in Orff-Schulwerk I

In looking at the "Rhythmic and Melodic Exercises," we must again remember that they exemplify a musical development of many years, and that they are not a lesson plan certain portions of which can be completed in a given class period. Imitation and question-answer activities, for instance, are used at every developmental stage, though always with new and increasingly difficult rhythmic concepts. Thus, two lines of examples in the book may contain rhythmic materials worth two years of instruction. It goes without saying that the pace of teaching and learning depends on the age of the students, on class size, and on the number of classes scheduled per week.

"Rhythms for Imitation," starting on page 53, are examples of echo-play. No instruments are "prescribed," and only the rhythmic development is shown. Naturally, echo exercises should start with the simplest body percussion, the clap and the slap. From there, one will proceed to a combination of sounds, such as clapping and slapping together, or stamping and clapping. Different dynamic levels should be considered; small percussion instruments may replace body sounds. There are so many possibilities for echo-play, even with the simplest rhythmic materials, that one need not fear running out of ideas. Rather, it is the sequential organization of ideas that is difficult but absolutely necessary to successful improvisation.

Exercises nos. 1–3 deal with half-phrases, first starting on the downbeat and ending on a strong beat. Somewhat later, upbeats appear, as well as weak endings and more complicated rhythms. It is perhaps possible, though unlikely, that older students can handle all these rhythmic concepts while still improvising with half-phrases only. In my experience, children progress to working with the full phrase long before they have accumulated a rhythmic vocabulary as extensive as the one contained in these examples. Exercises nos. 5–7 are examples of echo-play in the full phrase length.

Section II on pages 54–55 demonstrates imitation in triple meter along the same lines of development. Notice that triple meter is notated here in quarter-note pulse rather than in $\frac{3}{8}$ as is the case in the rhythmic speech examples (see also discussion of speech tempo, Chapter 2, pp. 17 and 22). On page 64 we find question-answer games under the heading "Rhythms to Be Completed." Each example illustrates alternative answers to the question. An antecedent phrase starting on the upbeat is followed by a consequent phrase beginning in the same manner. The students should be made aware of this basic principle of upbeats (see p. 56). Exercises nos. 6–8 include some asymmetrical phrases, a much later development.

The "Exercises" on page 66 are rather advanced in their use of rhythmic vocabulary; however, they deal with the finer points of question-answer improvisations and in that regard are of great value to us. Each of the antecedent phrases contains a specific rhythmic idea—dotted eighth-notes, two or four sixteenth-notes in succession, dotted quarter-notes, or triplets—which is then used in the consequent phrase. From this we perceive that a question can be used to deal with one specific rhythmic idea (perhaps a newly introduced concept), which then can be taken up in the answer.

There are three models of complete *rhythmic rondos* (pp. 67, 68, 71), as well as a number of A-sections for which the intervening sections are to be improvised. Again, the rhythmic vocabulary and the skill development needed for these specific pieces go well beyond the beginning levels. But to put them aside because they are difficult may mean cheating ourselves and our students of something valuable. Difficult playing techniques and complexity of design can always be scaled down. More important are the basic concepts on which these models focus. And once the basic concept is recognized, it can be applied to all developmental stages. The ability to identify such basic concepts in the models is one of the most important skills the teacher has to learn in dealing with the Orff-Schulwerk books.

The examples of A-sections contain something that was not used in the other rhythmic rondos. Instead of a rhythm with ostinato accompaniment, the A-sections here are composed of two or more equally independent rhythmic parts. In other words, we now deal with several horizontal lines, each complementing the others. Here, then, we find the origins of polyphony, for without rhythmic independence in all voices there cannot be polyphony.

We now face the task of communicating to our young children the difference between horizontal and vertical orientation. Since polyphony and homophony are basic musical concepts, I believe that their beginnings, as we find them in rhythmic structures, must be taught early. Speech represents a horizontal orientation, since it happens successively in time. In this respect it becomes the forerunner of rhythm and melody. For this reason, we will illustrate to our students the horizontal concept as it appears in the example on page 67, by using speech. This A-section consists of two rhythmic parts, played by two groups. If we add text to the rhythms the piece becomes a conversation between two people.[14] (I leave it to the reader to find titles.)

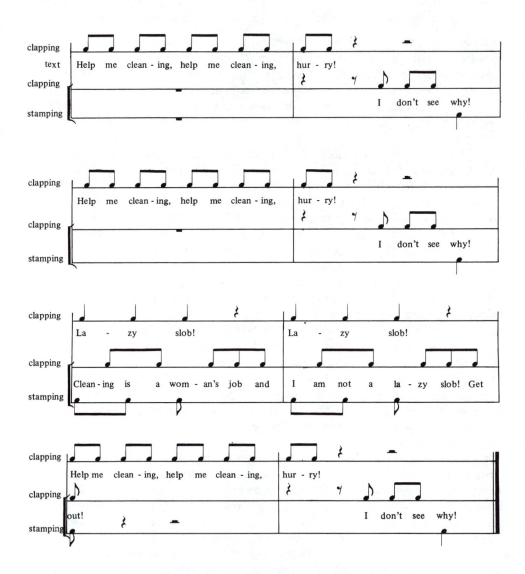

____

[14] The dynamic markings of the example have been omitted here.

A conversation usually centers around a topic. The people involved express their thoughts and also respond to the remarks made by others. Sometimes everyone talks at the same time (but with the result that nobody understands anybody else). Thus, a conversation contains the horizontal as well as the vertical aspect. Adding speech to multipart rhythms as in the example above will help to demonstrate these concepts to the class; it is also an aid in learning rhythms more quickly and without having to resort to counting. Care must be taken, however, that the conversation makes sense both horizontally and vertically and that the speech accents fit the meter accents in order to avoid distortion of language. Tutti phrases with the same rhythms are easier to understand if all parts have the same text.

Improvisations of *rhythmic canons* developed through continuous imitation are demonstrated on pages 74 and 75 of Orff-Schulwerk I. As pointed out earlier, it is difficult to follow in canon when identical rhythmic patterns are played in successive measures, such as in nos. 4 and 9 on page 74, and no. 2 on page 75 (see pp. 63–64).

A number of examples use two body sounds, which opens up a whole new field of possibilities. Canonic improvisations with more than one sound need to be built up in careful steps. The following is an example of how one might start out with even beats and regular changes, using two, later three, different body sounds.

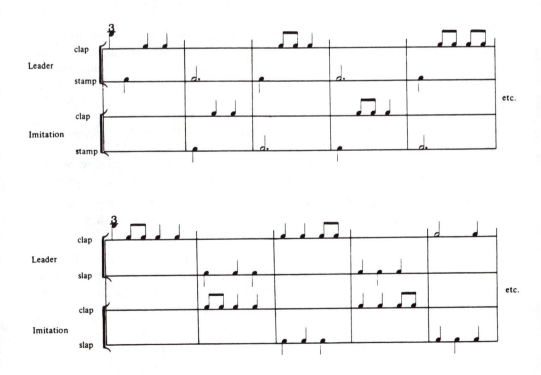

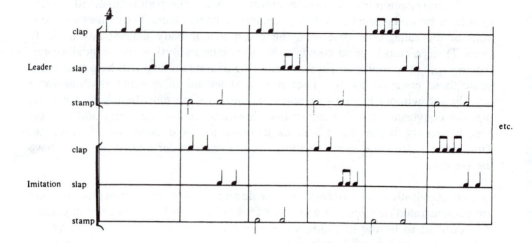

SUMMARY

It has always seemed to me that the beginning stages of musical development are the most important as well as the most difficult to teach because they form the foundation. This foundation must be well built in order to support the musical growth of our students.

So far, only the rhythmic concepts have been dealt with, and each of them was developed somewhat further than the mere laying of a foundation would warrant. My intention has been to show an uninterrupted growth—from an unidentifiable seed, so to speak, into a recognizable plant. The simultaneous growth of other musical aspects is another matter which, one would hope, will come into focus once they have all been dealt with. Perhaps Orff and Keetman had this in mind when they decided to place the essential parts of rhythmic development in Volume I, rather than dividing it up among all the volumes.

To clarify the course of rhythmic development, I will recapitulate briefly what appear to be the main concepts. A chart may further clarify the development.

Pulse. As the origin of all rhythm, pulse is experienced, internalized, and made conscious through movement. It becomes audible through simple body sounds or small percussion and is used to accompany rhymes and songs.

Subdivision of the Pulse and Meter. Rhythmic patterns (building blocks) are developed through speech. Duple meter, with its accentual pattern of strong-weak, evolves as the first meter. Triple time, the second of the basic meter patterns, is introduced only after duple meter is securely established. Quadruple meter, a combination of simple duple patterns, can be used after the two basic meters have been internalized.

Form. The succession of sounds (words, rhythms, or both) develops the form concept: from single word to the half- and full phrase, and finally to multi-phrase structures.

Accompaniment. The vertical aspect of music involves more than one part sounding simultaneously. Through ostinato accompaniment, the concept of contrast is introduced. Ostinato exercises help to develop coordination, rhythmic assurance, and instrumental playing skills.

Rhythm. Removing language from a rhythmic pattern brings about the emergence of rhythm as an independent musical element. Rhythmic notation represents the abstraction of the rhythmic language.

Improvisation. Musical competency evidences itself in the ability to speak the musical language. It is achieved in part through improvisation, which must be practiced on every developmental step with already familiar materials, incorporating the new concepts as they are introduced.

PULSE-MOVEMENT
(Two-cycle movements, locomotor and non-locomotor)

HORIZONTAL DEVELOPMENT
(Form)

Rhythmic Speech ——————————————————— Rhythm Alone

Single word   Building block
↓   ↓

Short statement   Half-phrase
(proverbs, etc.)
↓   ↓

Full sentence   Full phrase
(one-line riddles, proverbs, etc.)
↓   ↓

Several sentences   Multiple phrases
(rhymes with several lines)
                                                            ↓

Forms with sections—rondo, AB, ABA, etc.

VERTICAL DEVELOPMENT
(Accompaniment)

Pulse
(body sounds and small percussion)
↓
Ostinato
(speech, rhythmic)

This recapitulation is an attempt to show rhythmic development in a general way. Obviously details would only obscure the essential points. Such details include the refinement and extension of rhythmic vocabulary—the whole range of note values and their corresponding rests, syncopation, combined meters, the relativity of note values, and so on. Their introduction can be treated in much the same way a foreign-language teacher will gradually enlarge the vocabulary and grammar skills of the students in order to refine their expressive faculties. Let us never forget, however, that understanding of the basic concepts and the ability to use them correctly must come before any refinement can be attempted. This objective is achieved by limiting the vocabulary and by keeping to the essential for a long time.

4

BEGINNING MELODY AND ACCOMPANIMENT

GENERAL CONSIDERATIONS

This chapter will deal with the beginning of melody and pitched accompaniment. Looking at the two concepts objectively, we see them as separate musical elements, not equal in importance; for, whereas melody can exist by itself, accompaniment cannot. In the musical practices of children, however, the two are of equal importance and one is never in evidence without the other. What sense does it make to a child to recite a jump-rope rhyme if he or she does not skip the rope? Why bother singing a silly little song without simultaneously practicing a challenging clap pattern with a partner? The whole purpose of childhood music is to play a game, and both the word and the action are needed for this purpose. Because both are of equal importance, it is difficult to determine during the act of performance which of the two—word or action—is the accompaniment. Yet, since the voice produces the words and the physical action reflects the pulse, the first leads ultimately to melody, the latter to accompaniment.

The words of a game are often chanted or sung. Thus the children themselves have provided us with a melodic beginning which, in Orff-Schulwerk, we use as the foundation for further melodic development. Children's melodies are simple, so simple in fact that they need not be taught. Although each child creates these tunes, they all sound alike. It is as if the same tune were born over and over again. Let me illustrate my point in a more tangible way.

As a child I spent many vacations with relatives who lived in the Franconian Alps. One of my fondest memories is the evening walks with my uncle and my cousin which often took us to a hillside overlooking a small valley beyond which the forest started. We would sit on the hilltop and watch the deer grazing in the evening dusk. Frequently, however, no deer appeared and we children, growing impatient, would call out loudly for them to come. I remember the fascination with which we listened to our voices coming back to us from the dark woods. In time we developed a whole repertoire of questions and calls which we would send again and again into the forest like a ritualistic inducement to the deer. What we would most often get in return was not the appearance of the deer but the faint and mysterious singsong answer of the echo.

I did not know then, but realized much later, that our calling game was done entirely on the falling minor third and the three-note chant, the age-old song that children have always sung and does not need to be taught.

Call and Chant

In the previous chapter we have seen how language, through its longer and shorter syllables and its inflections, combines all elements of rhythm and meter. The accented and unaccented syllables indicate a slight change of pitch in the speaking voice, and in that way they become the germ cells of melody. We can actually follow this evolution of the word-originated melody: the louder a word is spoken, the greater difference in pitch between the accented and unaccented syllables. For example, say "Mary." Now repeat the name with more emphasis and in a raised voice as if calling her from another room. Finally, call to her loudly as if she were up the street: "Maaa-ry!"

In a call, especially when the word or name is drawn out, the interval formed by the two pitches approaches a minor third. If the same call is repeated softly like an echo, the voice quite naturally takes on a singing quality and the falling minor third is heard clearly.

Just as spoken word sequences do not qualify as a grammatical form, name-calling on the falling minor third cannot yet be called a tune, as it lacks formal structure. Such a structure is provided if a metered text takes the place of individual words. In the following example the two pitches of the melody are determined solely through the word accents.

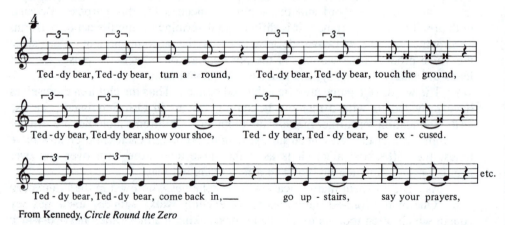

Ted-dy bear, Ted-dy bear, turn a - round, Ted-dy bear, Ted-dy bear, touch the ground,

Ted-dy bear, Ted-dy bear, show your shoe, Ted-dy bear, Ted-dy bear, be ex - cused.

Ted-dy bear, Ted-dy bear, come back in,___ go up - stairs, say your prayers,

From Kennedy, *Circle Round the Zero*

However, when the single word is replaced by a short sentence, more often than not the melodic content expands also. It reaches above the higher of the two pitches and so extends the total melodic range to the interval of a fourth, and the common three-note chant emerges. The nucleus of these chant-songs, however, is still the falling minor third, while the new pitch, La, acts as an upper auxiliary note. The most prevalent formulas used by children are shown below; again, they follow the natural word accents and are therefore easy to sing.

Chant formulas

Starlight, Star Bright

Star - light,   star   bright,   first   star   I   see to - night, I

wish I   may, I   wish I might   have the wish I   wish to - night.

Arre, mi burrito

New Mexico

Gid-dy - up my   bur - ro, we're go - ing to Be - lén,

Fies - ta is to - mor - row, and one hot day a - gain.

From Bradford, *Sing It Yourself*

In the chapter on syllabication we observed that words or names starting on an unaccented syllable present rhythmically the upbeat. Singing such names results in these patterns:

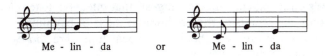

Me - lin - da   or   Me - lin - da

The upbeat formula starting on the tonic is one way to introduce the new pitch, Do or C, and metered rhymes with upbeat phrases will resemble the following example:

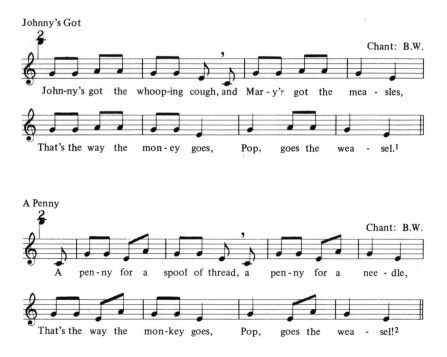

Similar songs can be found in Orff-Schulwerk I, "Bye Baby Bunting" (p. 8) and "Ring Around a Rosie" (p. 9). Although the tonic note is not used in the upbeat phrases, it can be substituted for the E.

I have heard the song "Ring Around a Rosie" also sung with the ending on the tonic:

Here, then, we find the tonic note used in yet a different way, namely as *finalis* (or *final*, last note). In this particular song this makes sense in several ways: The last text word is "down," and the singers fall down; rhythmically, the text ends on a strong beat; and melodically, the feeling of finality is reflected in the drop to the lowest pitch in the tune.

Observation of children's chanting and singing suggests that intensive listening to language unlocks not only the secrets of rhythm but also those of beginning melody. The most natural, and therefore best, beginning vocal tunes are those that have not yet lost their affinity to the spoken word.

---

[1] Text from Fowke, *Sally Go Round the Sun.*
[2] Ibid.

Pitched Accompaniment

Pitched accompaniment presents a somewhat different problem since, unlike melody, it is not inherent in childhood music. Rather, it exists in an embryonic state only as rhythmic action, and it must be developed accordingly.

The first step toward conceptualizing accompaniment is to make audible a pulse movement. In Chapter Three we have seen how the body with its different sound-producing possibilities serves as the most basic instrument, and how the use of small percussion is the first adventure into the world of "real" instruments.

The transition from unpitched to pitched accompaniment is made when the pulse-beat rhythms are transferred onto the barred instruments and played in the form of drones.

In general usage, the word *drone* (French: *bourdon*; German: *Bordun*) implies inactivity. A drone is the nonworking male bee, or a lazy person. Applied to sound, the term again denotes inactivity or monotony; in standard musical terminology, drone, bourdon, or Bordun indicates a low note of long duration, and it has become synonymous with pedal or organ point.

The simultaneous sounding of a melody and sustained notes occurred early in man's history and in many parts of the world. In Western music culture, instruments such as the hurdy-gurdy (tenth–fourteenth centuries), the vielle (thirteenth–fifteenth centuries), the bagpipe, and the dulcimer attest to the fact that the droning of melodies has been a widespread practice in folk music throughout the centuries.

From the evolutionary point of view, the use of drone accompaniment signifies an awareness of tonality and the beginning of a harmonic development. This applies not only to historical music, but also to Orff-Schulwerk.

The drone usually consists of two notes a fifth apart. The lower of the two pitches provides the tonal basis; thus the melody above is not free to roam at will but is bound to a tonal center. The fifth of the drone strengthens the feeling of tonality. *The drone contains the seed of all harmonic development.*

Although a drone can be played in many different ways (see Chapter Six), beginning accompaniment should be limited to a simple pulse rhythm, both hands playing at the same time. All basic melodies, from the falling minor third to the three-note chant and even the full pentatonic, can be accompanied in this way if need be. Only after the children have gained complete rhythmic assurance and some measure of instrumental skill is it time to move on to different and more difficult drone patterns. Some children will reach this point faster than others, but this is never a problem since each student in the ensemble can be given a part he can handle.

For the most part children have less trouble in the physical act of playing a simple drone pattern than in playing it in time with the rest of the ensemble. In my experience it takes a class of first-graders several months before they can handle two rhythmically different drone patterns simultaneously in an ensemble. As teachers we easily become impatient and want to move on to more challenging tasks. We must never lose sight of the fact that what is easy for us is new and difficult for the child. We expect the student, as a member of an ensemble, to do several things simultaneously:

1. Sing the song
2. Play the two drone notes on the barred instrument
3. Coordinate his pattern not only with his own singing but with the whole ensemble.

All this requires careful listening to others and perfect control over the physical movement of the droning. The drone accompaniment should be kept as simple as possible, so that their concentration will not be fragmented by attempting to fulfill several difficult tasks at once. Rather, it should be directed toward the most important tasks, those of listening and adjusting their pattern to the ensemble.

THE PRACTICAL ASPECTS OF TEACHING THE BEGINNING CONCEPTS OF MELODY AND ACCOMPANIMENT

Melody

metered speech: accents
↓
pitch: high-low concept
↓
two definite pitches (call)
↓
chant

Pitch Awareness.   With young children the concept of high and low in reference to pitch cannot always be taken for granted. To some, high is synonymous with loud, and low with soft. Curt Sachs tells us that such confusion of dynamic intensity with pitch exists in a number of tribal cultures, and he suggests that it may reflect the greater or lesser force needed in the vocal production of a higher or a lower pitch.[3]

Since such ambiguity might exist in the vocabulary of our young students, conceptualization of pitch and understanding of its terminology must come at the beginning of all melodic improvisation. A lesson built around "listening" will lead to the exploration of beginning pitch concepts. This involves three steps, each of which flows smoothly into the next one:

---

[3] Curt Sachs, *The Wellsprings of Music* (New York: Da Capo, n.d.), p. 55.

1. Recognizing *different* pitches
2. Identifying the difference as *higher* and *lower*
3. Identifying the higher and lower as two *specific pitches* (the falling minor third)

The following example may serve as a suggestion regarding activities for each step. (Note: In exercises 1a, 1b, and 2a, sing or play all the notes in the same time value so that the students relate the being "different" to pitch and not to time. The children should listen with closed eyes, as this will greatly increase concentration.)

1. Recognizing different sounds
    a. *Sameness*: After singing or playing a note over and over again, the teacher asks the children how many different sounds or tones they have heard. The answer will be (we hope!) "Only one."
    b. *Difference*: The teacher alternates between two sounds, playing them in different ways:
    • Many high notes and one low note
    • One high note and many low notes
    • Some high, some low, and again some high notes
    • Some low, one high, some low notes
    • Mix high and low notes frequently
    The answers to the same question should in every case be, "Two different tones." The listening can be made more challenging by changing the two pitches for every pattern.
2. Identifying the difference as higher and lower pitch
    a. The teacher alternates between two pitches, similar to 1b. This time his question for the children will be, "*How many times* did you hear each of the two tones?" Since now the children need to specify in their answers *which* note they are talking about, adjectives for differentiation will become necessary. In all likelihood some of the children will already use the terms "higher" and "lower." The concept can now be illustrated for all to see by holding a barred instrument upright while playing the low and high notes.
    b. Use body levels to show high and low sound. In this exercise the children have to start out with a body level that will allow them to go higher or lower.
    • The teacher plays a tone and the children react (from the second sound on) with an appropriate change in body level. More than two pitches are used in this exercise since it continues over a period of time. The children should be asked to react appropriately to smaller or larger leaps (if they can already hear them). Slow glissandi may suggest a flowing and gradual change of level.
    • The teacher shows different levels with his or her hand, to which the children respond vocally. Although they are not expected to sing specific pitches yet, smaller and wider distances between two notes should be explored vocally.
3. Identifying the lower and higher pitches as two specific pitches, the falling minor third.

The most instructive approach is to have the children discover the interval by themselves. To this end we play "echo," a reenactment of my own childhood memories. The children are asked to turn themselves into trees, representing a forest. From the other end of the room I begin calling names, and the children whose names I have called sing back the echo in a soft voice, matching pitch and tempo as accurately as possible. Soon the children take turns in calling forth the echo, which may extend into little phrases.

Older students do not like to play such "childish" games. However, the echo idea still serves best to illustrate the emergence of the falling minor third from the accented syllable; it can simply be demonstrated and explained without play-acting.

Metered rhymes soon lead into the first songs, and the concept of tune or melody is introduced. Practically all the tunes can be "invented" by the children themselves, quickly and spontaneously. It is important, however, that rhythmic recitation precede the singing, since the speech accents dictate the order of the two pitches. As adults we may fear that the children quickly will tire of hearing the same tune over and over again. I have found that young children are very word-oriented; as long as the text changes, it is a new song for them, even though the tune stays the same.

A word of caution on the selection of texts is in order here. Texts that are basically a series of calls or short, imperative statements ("Tinker, Tailor," "Teddybear") are more likely to be sung spontaneously on the minor third (without any other pitches) than are texts with longer sentences or teasing phrases, for example.

The process of pitch conceptualization is not yet complete. So far, only the *relationship* of two pitches to each other—an interval—has been discussed. No fixed pitches were necessary, as the instruments needed at this stage were just the voices. With the introduction of the sound-bar instruments, fixed pitches have to be established. Our sequence of pitch development continues, therefore, with two more steps, marking the beginning of instrumental play. The two steps are:

4. Transferring the falling minor-third tunes onto the barred instruments, and
5. Using pitched accompaniment.

These steps further serve the purpose of introducing the two basic mallet techniques, alternate and simultaneous sticking. When playing a tune the hands alternate, whereas when playing a drone the hands play the two pitches simultaneously. (Other ways to play a drone will be explored later.)

Whether to first introduce the playing of melody (step 4) or of accompaniment (step 5) is a matter of choice. In any event, both steps will occur almost simultaneously. Before making a choice, the teacher should weigh the following points.

First, transferring the two-tone call to the instruments is a smooth and logical continuation of the previous activities in pitch exploration. It can be handled in a creative way, having the children themselves discover the pitches on the instruments. Playing the falling minor third necessitates alternate sticking, which is often difficult for children; however, the coordination between the two hands will greatly improve with this technique. Recreating the call tunes on the barred instruments will also teach careful listening, since the two pitches do not always alternate in a regular pattern.

Second, introducing the drone is a smooth and logical continuation of the rhythmic and motor-skill activities used in body-percussion accompaniment. It is, however, *not* a natural outgrowth of pitch exploration, but rather a new concept, that of simultaneously sounding pitches for accompaniment. In other words, it is the beginning of harmony. In its simplest form the drone is played with both hands simultaneously, thus developing directly from the familiar slapping. For most children this is easier than alternate sticking. (The development of fundamental playing skills and coordination will be discussed on page 91 of this chapter.)

To sum up, it does not make much difference whether instrumental playing starts with two- and three-tone melodies or with drone accompaniment. Each approach has its own merit. Beginning with the playing of melodies may be a bit more difficult in terms of coordination, but it improves pitch perception; beginning with the playing of drones necessitates the introduction of a new concept, but requires less coordination.

Preparation for Steps 4 and 5: Getting to Know the Instruments.   The children ought to have a general idea of the instruments they are about to play. For this reason I first acquaint them with the complete instrument—that is, with all the bars on the soundboxes. While exploring the higher and lower pitches and their placement, the children find out that the letter names make a seven-note pattern which appears twice (less one note in the highest octave), and that the size of the tone bars is in direct relationship to their pitches.[4]

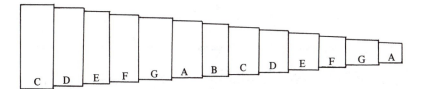

I have found it helpful to differentiate between the two octaves right from the beginning by adding the adjectives "low" (or "first") and "high" (or "second") to the letter names of the respective octaves.

The pitches of the various instruments are then compared, but without attaching to them absolute pitch terms (C1, C2, etc.). The different sound quality of the metal and wooden bars sometimes makes pitch identification difficult. For example, not all children will be able to hear that an alto glockenspiel and a soprano xylophone have the same pitch. (The reader who is not familiar with the barred instruments and their pitch ranges is referred to the introduction to Orff-Schulwerk I, which offers a short description of the instrumentarium.)

The names of the instruments, especially when the terms "alto," "soprano," and "bass" are added, frequently pose a memorization problem. A large chart, to which the children can easily refer, may be displayed in a prominent place in the music room. I construct such a chart in three sections, which can be combined by hanging them above each other. Chart 1 is for the beginners. By looking at

---

[4] Some instruments on the market use different ranges.

the instruments within one family from the bottom of the chart up, the meaning of bass, alto, and soprano—low, middle, and high sound—will become clear. The instruments can be lined up as the chart shows, and then their pitches can be played and compared. For the students who have learned to read pitch notation, the second chart, which demonstrates the actual sound, is added. Advanced students will learn about transposing instruments by comparing the third chart displaying the staff notation with the chart of actual sound production. (B-Bass, A-Alto, S-Soprano, X-Xylophone, M-Metallophone, Gl.-Glockenspiel.)

CHART 1: *Our Barred Instruments*

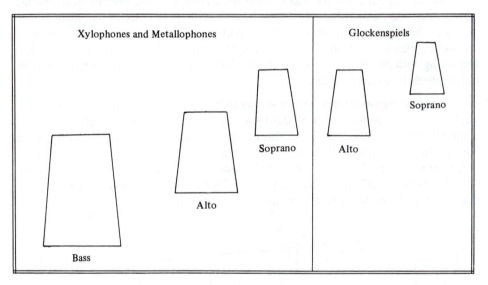

CHART 2: *Ranges in Actual Pitches*

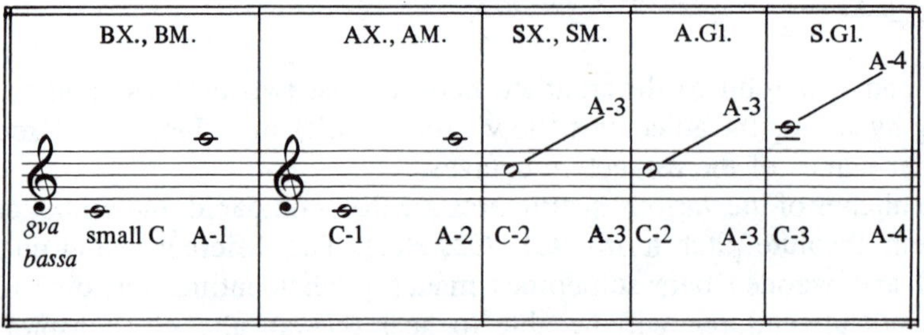

CHART 3: *Notation of the Barred Instruments*

(This part of the chart to be added only when needed.)

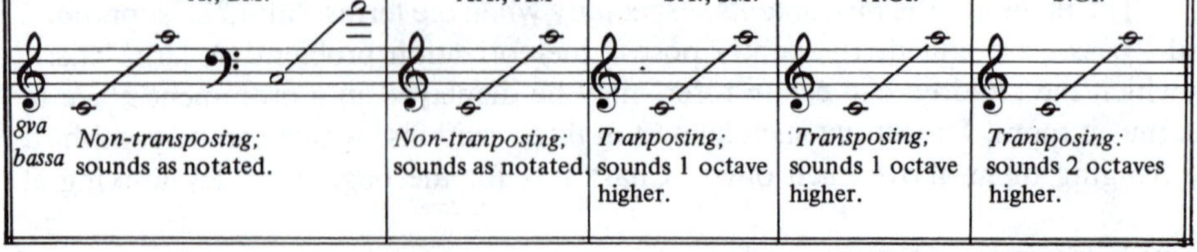

Finally, a few comments on good playing skills are in order.[5] The instruments should be adjusted to the correct height so that the students need not sit or stand hunched over. Frequently the children stand or sit much too close to the instruments, which interferes with the natural movement of their lower arms and wrists. In order to illustrate posture and proper distance from the instruments I again resort to a childhood experience. My mother's rules on good table manners included that we sit straight as if wearing a little, light crown, and far enough from the table that a rabbit could sit on our lap. The same can be applied to "instrumental manners." The mallets should be held as one holds a toothbrush, and the arms should move freely and not be pressed against the body. To illustrate good tone production, I ask the children to think of pulling or drawing the sound out of the bar rather than striking down. We experiment also with finding the best spot on the bars to produce a good tone; it is, of course, in the middle, which allows the bar to vibrate.

Emergence of Two Specific Pitches. After singing a call or a call song on the falling minor third (which the teacher has pitched on G–E), the class will quickly discover the matching tones on the instruments. For easy orientation, the F-bars between G and E should now be removed in the lower and higher octaves. Among the variously pitched instruments there are a number of different G–E pitches, which often confuses the children. For this reason I establish the singing pitch (G1, E1) in the first octave of the alto xylophones and alto metallophones as a reference point to which all the other G and E pitches are then compared.

The falling minor third is now explored through the already familiar word and name calls and their rhythmic building blocks:

It is important that singing always precede playing, and that all students be able to reproduce a given pattern with ease before they explore a new one. This is the time when playing habits are established. If a teacher, for the sake of convenience, allows a student to play entirely with one hand, it will be difficult later on to convert him or her to alternate sticking.

We start with the basic call pattern, derived from two-syllable names:

A sequence of words may end with a one-syllable word on the pitch G:

---

[5] See also, Keetman, *Elementaria*, and Keller, *Introduction to Orff-Schulwerk.*

Chev - y,   Vol - vo,   Dat - sun,   Ford

The next two call patterns contain eighth-notes, as they evolve from three-syllable words. The sticking is now a bit more difficult, since it requires repetition of a note, depending on the pattern:

croc - o - dile

Using only one of the two call formulas at a time, the children learn to play it while singing the word sequences:

Croc - o - dile,   pan - da bear,   el - e - phant,   moun-tain goat.

Next, the call formula is combined with the basic pattern in a longer sequence, for example:

Dol - phin,   croc - o - dile,   sea - horse, whale,   el - e - phant, moun-tain goat,   pan - ther, moose.

or in a half-phrase:

Bil - ly,   come to me.

Now the children are ready to play the songs they ''invented'' earlier when they were only singing. We have noted that the texts resulting in the falling-minor-third pattern are most often made up of calls (e.g., ''Tinker, Tailor'') or imperative half-phrases (e.g., ''Teddybear''). It is also interesting to observe that in these texts the call formula (*a*) seems more prevalent than the one with the eighth-note on the second beat (*b*):

(c)

This latter pattern, as well as pattern (*c*), may be developed in a similar fashion. Frequently, though, the children themselves initiate new formulas, either purposely or accidentally. In any case, the teacher must be flexible enough to adjust his or her own planning to pick up and develop ideas from the class.

If these beginnings seem somewhat tedious, we must remember that instrumental practice need not be a drill but can and should be used as a creative experience.

At this stage melodic improvisation on the instruments is of necessity limited. It will manifest itself mainly in using the call formulas with different texts. However, exploring the orchestration and performance possibilities leads to a variety of ideas. In one way or another, they all make use of antiphonal practices, be they echoes, repetitions of longer sections, or question-answer phrases. Antiphony can take place in different ways. It may be:

1. based on *numbers* of players or groups, regardless of instruments used:
   solo—tutti
   tutti—solo
   solo—solo
   tutti—tutti

2. based on *instrument families*:
   all xylophones—all glockenspiels
   all xylophones—all metallophones
   all metallophones—all glockenspiels
   and all other possible combinations

3. based on the *different pitch levels* within one instrument family:
   soprano glockenspiels—alto glockenspiels
   soprano xylophones—alto xylophones
   alto xylophones—bass xylophones
   soprano xylophones—bass xylophones
   and the same combinations of metallophones

4. based on the *same pitch level*:
   alto glockenspiel—soprano xylophone
   alto glockenspiel—soprano metallophone
   soprano xylophone—soprano metallophone
   alto xylophone—alto metallophone
   bass xylophone—bass metallophone

Instrumental echo- and question-answer play is used mainly for the purpose of pitch conceptualization and ear training. The notes of the falling minor third are vocally conceived and cannot be organized into strictly instrumental tunes without sounding artificial and contrived. Interestingly enough, Orff-Schulwerk I offers no instrumental pieces with only two, or even three, notes, but starts immediately with pentatonic melodies.

The Chant.

As we have seen earlier, certain texts lead naturally to the call formula while others lead just as naturally into the three-note chant.

On close inspection it seems that all chant formulas are variations of the call, in that either one or both eighth-notes on the second beat are replaced by the pitch A (or La). Yet, unlike the call, more than two beats altogether are necessary for the A to occur, because it does not stay suspended but falls back to the G. A half-phrase is the smallest structure into which the chant formula can be fitted. Children's teasing chants are classic examples of one such half-phrase (see also p. 73). Longer texts that fall naturally into the chant melodies are usually a series of statements in half-phrase or full-phrase format. Often they tell a story or describe a game. Traditional chant examples can be found in Orff-Schulwerk I, nos. 4–7; text examples to be set to chant tunes are on page 10, but many more are available in source books of traditional children's poetry.

No more suggestions are necessary in regard to the introduction of the third note. Very often the chant appears unplanned in the children's singing as a result of the text structure. In such cases one need only pick it up and expand on it. In any event the introduction of the third note is not a dramatic step. Its importance lies in the fact that it allows for development of form concepts. Understanding of form is fundamental to all improvising and creating of music.

At this point we have at our disposal a number of melodic fragments, or formulas:

1. The basic call, two counts in length, in four rhythmic patterns:

2. The chant half-phrase with four beats, the second of which contains the new pitch A. Depending on the rhythmic pattern—that is, the structure of the text—the following variations are possible:

---

[6] Depending on the text, the chant formulas may have slightly different rhythmic structures. For example, if a text ends on a strong beat, the pitch will be G.

In making up melodies to texts, the use of only one formula—either the call or one of the chants—results in successive *a*-phrases; the use of both formulas for the different phrases of the text results in *a,b* forms.

The following illustrations are what I consider good forms because they originate with the voice and are therefore natural song tunes. The letter names refer to half-phrases.

1. Songs which are, through the textual content, a series of *a*-phrases. Either the call or the chant formula will make a simple, natural tune:

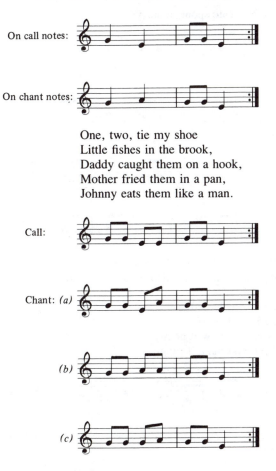

One, two, tie my shoe
Little fishes in the brook,
Daddy caught them on a hook,
Mother fried them in a pan,
Johnny eats them like a man.

2. Texts which work as *a,a,a* form in call or chant, but which also lend themselves
    to *a,b* form:

One, two, three, four, five,
once I caught a fish alive.

An *a,a* form young children might create spontaneously:

a, b forms (call and chant):

(The reversal of *a*- and *b*-phrases does not result in a convincing tune.)

3. Texts which seem to be basically chant but which also work in *a,b* forms, including
    the call phrase:

Jeremiah, blow the fire,
Puff, puff, puff.
First you blow it gently,
Then you blow it rough.

[7] The song appears in this version in Vol. 1 of the Canadian edition of *Orff-Schulwerk: Music for
Children*, by Doreen Hall and Arnold Walter.

4. Texts possible in *a,a* form, but also in *a,a,b,a*:

> Little Tommy Tucker
> Sings for his supper.
> What shall it be?
> White bread and butter.

5. Finally, there are longer songs in which the *a*- and *b*-phrases can be used in a variety of ways. The following text, for example, seems to fall naturally into two sections. The first one consists of two questions and answers which are preceded by a statement. All the phrases might be sung on the call, the statement in tutti and the question-answer phrases antiphonally. In the second section one of the chant formulas might be used, again sung by everyone:

Instrumental Tunes. Although the three notes offer only a limited melodic vocabulary, it is possible to arrange them in other ways than chant formulas. However, the attachment to the chant is very strong, as the pitches are essentially word-originated. Furthermore, texts help to retain the proper phrase lengths without the need of counting. For this reason I have serious reservations about the benefit to the children in having them create purely instrumental tunes.

There are certain differences between word-oriented and instrument-oriented melodies which children at this beginning stage cannot yet perceive. An untrained voice does not naturally change pitches on quick notes, but rather repeats the same pitch. The only exceptions are the following chant patterns:

On an instrument, fast changes are easier to accomplish. In contrast to the plainer, syllabic style of vocal tunes, instrumental melodies are more ornamental and embellished. If the class is receptive (which is usually not yet the case) the teacher might begin to point out such differences in instrumental echo and question-answer exercises: Not only can fast notes be used in pitch changes, as shown in (a) below, but the sequence of notes as well as the rhythmic structure need not be a typical chant pattern, as in (b):

But there is little else that can be done at this developmental stage beyond making such rudimentary observations. On the whole, improvisations will consist mainly of creating tunes on given texts. In these activities the teacher should make sure that the children are able to sing their tunes before they transfer them to the instruments. If this is not done, a conscious pitch awareness will not develop. The texts for melodic improvisation often lend themselves to dramatic play or movement activities, as for example, "Wee Willie Winkie" (Orff-Schulwerk I, p. 7). (More will be said about instrumental improvisation in Chapter Seven.)

Drone Accompaniment (Step 5)

Playing simple drones is most easily developed from slap patterns, since the same arm and wrist movements are used in both.

All melodies, from the word sequence to the chant and longer songs, may be accompanied by drones. Although these can be played on different pitches (higher and lower octaves), a ground bass should always be present underneath the tune, even when higher instruments and pitches also are used, because it provides a solid foundation.

The basic, beginning patterns are:

They may be played in the lower octave of the instrument only, or their position may alternate between low and high:

etc.

Both basic patterns can be combined to provide a rhythmic complement and to obtain a fuller sound.

AX.

BX.
BM.

I familiarize the students quite early with the drone's *inversion*:

in which the drone stands on its head, so to speak. Alternation between root position and inversion should be practiced.

The two drone pitches can also be played alternately, much like the pitches of a melody. In this case the pattern is referred to as a "broken drone." In its simplest forms it may look like this:

inverted:

Naming the Two Drone Notes. From the beginning I refer to the lowest note as the *root* and the upper one as the *drone fifth*. When the drone is inverted the names still apply.

With these possibilities a simple drone can be used for a long time before more complicated patterns are introduced. For a comprehensive discussion of accompaniment forms, the reader is referred to Chapter 5.

Developing Instrumental Skills and Coordination

Young children getting their first experience on the barred instruments often have problems coordinating their hands. The production of a percussive sound involves an up-down, or vertical, motion which is identical for both hands. Yet, if we listen to and observe the youngsters playing a simple drone such as the one shown below, we can discern a difference in the way the hands work.

Whereas one hand is on the beat and the target bar, the other one is a split-second late, often missing the tone bar halfway or altogether. In a broken drone, also, we frequently notice one hand playing more forcefully and louder than the other. Of course, all of this has to do with being born right- or left-handed. Our first task, therefore, prior to any instrumental improvisation, must be to improve the playing ability of the nondominant hand so that coordination between the two hands will be easier to achieve.

Exploration: Discovering the Dominant Hand. After some preliminary playing of a simple drone pattern, during which I observe the children's sound production, I engage them in a conversation about their hands. (One such simple drone is shown below.)

We determine our writing hand and discuss other skills we perform with one hand only, such as throwing a ball or brushing our teeth. The children discover quickly that they prefer the use of one hand over the other. Next, we hold our hands in front of us and look at them closely. They are mirror images of each other, exactly alike, but with reversed sides. Why then can't they both be equally skillful? Most children will already be familiar with the meaning of right- and left-handedness, but the important point to impress on them is that, in order to play our instruments well, both hands must function equally well. We cannot treat one hand as we would an unloved, disadvantaged stepbrother; we must give it the opportunity to become just as clever as our dominant hand. Most children begin to feel sorry for their "step-hand" and are ready for some practice activities.

Mallet Practice, Echo, and Improvisation.   Whereas good coordination is char-acterized by economy of movement, the opposite is true of poor coordination. In playing the barred instruments, economy of movement must be developed to a much finer point than, for instance, in knee-slapping. Playing the barred instru-ments requires more delicacy in the use of the striking force, and more accuracy in finding the much smaller target. Restraint is more difficult than force. Economy of movement is achieved by keeping the mallets close to the bars so that the downward stroke (coming from the wrist) is quick and efficient.

1. Playing with Both Hands Simultaneously.   The advantage here is that the dominant hand becomes the ''leader,'' and the other hand copies its movement simultaneously. We begin by resting the two mallets next to each other on two sound bars—let's say C and D. The children compare the two hands to make sure that the mallets are held in exactly the same way. Then we strike ever so softly, lifting the mallets no more than about an inch above the bars. By having the beaters so close together, the motions can be perfectly coordinated. In this manner we play a number of even pulse-beats. We then move the right hand one pitch up to E and repeat the process. The same is done with the mallets a fourth and a fifth apart. (For this exercise the F-bar need not be removed.) After that, each child may play the whole sequence alone while the class listens carefully to determine whether or not both pitches sound at the same time and with the same dynamic force (which is *pianissimo* at this point!). It is quite wonderful to watch how the children become completely absorbed in this activity and for once are utterly quiet! Naturally, the concentration will not last forever, and the teacher must change to another activity before interest has waned.

The same process should be repeated frequently, gradually increasing the distance of the mallets from the sound bars, but only as much as is needed and is possible for perfect mallet control and sound production. In order not to be too repetitive, little variations can be built into these practice sessions. For example, the pitches can be repeated less often or not at all before the right or left hand moves to other sound bars. In time, the children may create short sequences of pitch changes with one hand (not to exceed four beats) while keeping the other stationary. (In this activity, the F- and B-bars should be removed.) However, the teacher should set limitations as to how far apart the two hands may play, because the greater the distance, the more difficult it is to control the coordination:

Echo-play may also be used to help the children recognize a few intervals by their sound and soon to identify them by name. To this end, we again limit the range to a fifth and remove the F-bar. This leaves only four intervals: unison, second, third, and fifth. (The unison as an interval should be played with both mallets, one of them being placed slightly higher up on the sound bar than the other.) In order to help the pupils start out correctly, I tell them the two pitches on which I will begin. (Later on, I forego this initial assistance.) Before allowing them to repeat my tone sequence, I ask them to tell me which hand was moving. After a replay, I finally have them imitate me. Thus, a sequence of echoes might be set up in the following way:

Starting with unison

On C, right hand moving   etc.

left hand moving   etc.

Also, on G, D, E

Starting with a third

E-G, left hand moving   etc.

right hand moving   etc.

C-E, right hand moving   etc.

left hand moving   etc.

Also possible, A-C

Starting with a fifth (here, the interval of a sixth can hardly be avoided)

C-G, right hand moving   etc.

left hand moving   etc.

2. Alternate Sticking. The inferior hand is weaker simply because we use it less frequently. When alternate sticking is used on the barred instruments, this weakness results in a dynamically uneven sound production. We again must devise little exercises to minimize the problem. However, we must be patient and, above all, consistent in our efforts—a ''one-time shot'' won't do any good.

As before, I have the children themselves discover the problem by letting them play individually either a sequence of pitches with alternate sticking or a sequence with one hand which is then repeated with the other:

After each child has determined his nondominant hand, practice begins with playing repeated pitches, always starting with the dominant hand in order that the other can practice copying the dynamics as precisely as possible. For example:

On any one pitch:	*Dominant hand*	*Inferior hand*
	4 times	4 times
	2 times	4 times
	1 time	2 times
	2 times	2 times
	1 time	1 time

The idea here is to give the inferior hand more practice than the superior one.

Then two neighboring pitches are used (stems up denote right hand, stems down left):

We then move on to pitches a third and a fifth apart.

Although the children play all together, occasional solo turns are necessary to check on the sound production of each individual student. Also, the teacher should make sure that the children have the opportunity to play on different instruments, because each family and each size within the family of barred instruments requires a different touch.

Finally, I have the class repeat pitch sequences (not melodic phrases) with their ''step-hand,'' moving from stepwise motion to leaps:

So that the students don't become bored, they need only do these and similar exercises for a few minutes at a time, as a regular preparation before other instrumental activities.

Ambidexterity can be promoted through many activities outside of the music room. For instance, bouncing or throwing a ball, using a spoon or fork, brushing one's teeth, or opening a door can be practiced with the inferior hand. I urge the children to select two such movements each week to be executed with their "step-hand" exclusively.

Mirroring arm and hand motions away from the barred instruments is another activity the children love to do. In these exercises the horizontal aspect of mirror movement is explored. We begin by drawing large numbers in the air in one single, sweeping arm motion. Both arms move simultaneously, the left arm in an exact mirror image of the right arm. We accompany the drawing of each number with mouth or voice sounds to describe the dynamics of the movements. Next, the students write these oversized numbers on the blackboard where they can see the results. (Those children waiting for their turn at the blackboard can practice on walls and floor, without chalk!) Finally, with a colored pencil in each hand, we draw on large sheets of paper:

At another time I might ask the children to write with their right hands the first letter of their own names while simultaneously writing the mirror image of the letter with their left hands. Then we proceed to the second letter of their name. The right hand places the letter to the right of the first one, the left hand to the left. We continue until each student has completed his or her name. It might look like this:

But there is more to these exercises than mere entertainment. They allow each hand to develop horizontally oriented skills simultaneously and naturally. Our Western notational system caters exclusively to the right-handed person. We write, as is natural for right-handed people, from left to right. Letter formation, especially script, is designed to allow for smooth execution with the right hand. Does it not follow that the left-handed person would write most naturally from right to left, with the letters formed in mirror image? Of course, I am not suggesting that this become a standard for left-handers. However, it seems to me that today's practice of allowing left-handed children to write with their dominant hand often results in awkward and labored handwriting, at least in the first years. Perhaps it would be no less frustrating in the long run to simply develop the right hand as the writing tool from the beginning, and in general to encourage and develop ambidexterity through a variety of games and exercises.

Removal of Tone Bars, Transposition

We know that the sound bars on the instruments are removable so that any bar not needed can be taken out for easier playing. Thus, if only simple drone accompaniment in the C tonality is required, every bar but the C and G can be removed. If a call pattern is played, only the two tone bars forming the minor third need be retained. However, I have found that it is hardly necessary to remove all nonessential bars. School-age children readily recognize the three-plus-two pattern of pentatonic without F and B.

The five remaining tone bars are like the rooms of a home: although the child is familiar with all of them, certain ones have more significance to him than others (his own room, the kitchen, and the recreation room, for instance), and these are where he spends most of his time.

The advantage of using the pentatonic setup from the beginning is twofold. First, the children can *see* that the three notes C, E, and G are part of a larger unit. By singling them out we can establish them as the most important pitches in the five-note pattern. Second, from the start the students can experience the relationship between tune and accompaniment because, again, they can see it:

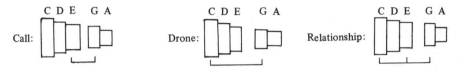

(The latter point holds also if D and A are eliminated.) As teachers we are aware of the harmonic implications: The three tones are all part of the tonic triad, consisting of a major third with a minor third on top of it. Even after the second and sixth scale notes are included later on, the tonic triad will remain the structural backbone of all melodies based on a major modality.

The removable sound bars have another purpose besides that of eliminating tones not in use. By making F or G the starting point of the three-plus-two pattern, a transposition of the major pentatonic scale can be obtained:

Thus the two-note call or the chant can be sung in F or G.[8]

The advisability of confronting beginning students with the concept of transposition is a matter that needs to be weighed carefully. There is no doubt that the children are able to recreate the three-plus-two pattern on F and G without any problem. It is doubtful, however, that they comprehend the underlying principles of pitch relativity and of transposition. A quick-thinking student might want to relocate the pattern on D or E, but he will not understand that this pattern produces a different sound from that built on C, F, or G:

---

[8] For a detailed discussion of the transposition of pentatonic modes, see Chapter 8.

On D   On E

When this happens in class, how does the teacher explain? At this stage of development the child does not know about whole and half-steps or about major and minor intervals. He or she perceives the pattern only through the eye, which is deceptive since the basic design of the instruments is diatonic: Whole or half-steps are not a function of the perceived distance between the bars since each bar is equidistant from the next. This means that the interval of a third *looks* the same whether it is major or minor. A child, having just learned about high and low pitch in general and about the call-melody which we set on the specific pitches G and E will not yet be able to discriminate with certainty between a major and a minor third.

The teacher's answer to the quick-thinking student who builds the three-plus-two pattern on D or E would have to be, "Sorry. It doesn't sound right, but I can't tell you why yet because you wouldn't understand. It only sounds right on C, F, or G."

All the songs and instrumental pieces in Orff-Schulwerk I are set in the major pentatonic mode based on C, and nowhere in the "Notes and Instructions" is mention made of possible transpositions to other keys. This has occasionally given rise to criticism. Are we really to suppose that Orff and Keetman simply forgot about the possibility of transposition? Hardly so. They probably felt it important that the child become conversant and comfortable in one key first before moving on to another. The idea of transposition, a device of Western art music, became possible in a thoroughgoing way only after the invention of well-tempered tuning (completed ca. 1700, after a long period of experimental development). Instruments with fixed pitches, from early Western culture as well as in other cultures, were tuned with five to seven notes to the octave. Never was the octave divided into twelve equidistant semitones. This means that, although different modes could be used, transposition of the specific modes was not possible. The Schulwerk instruments are modeled after this elemental idea of a fixed diatonic scale. (Transposition on the pentatonic level is not ignored in Orff-Schulwerk, as Gunild Keetman deals with it in her three xylophone books.[9]

The discussion of transposition leads to a related problem that every Orff-Schulwerk teacher must face and think about. Today it is a widespread practice to combine elements of Orff-Schulwerk with elements of the Kodály system. Kodály's relative solmization syllables of movable Do have little relevance to Orff-Schulwerk, since all the instruments, barred percussion as well as recorders, are based on absolute pitches and fixed letter names. The Kodály method, in contrast, deals (at least in theory) with the voice only, which indeed is an instrument without a fixed pitch. What makes eminent sense in one approach does not necessarily make sense in another. Therefore, the question is: Will a combination of the

[9] *Spielbuch für Xylophon I, II, III*, (Mainz: B. Schott's Söhne).

two approaches, whose basic premises and ultimate objectives are simply not the same, bring about better results than if each were taught as its originator envisioned? Or, rather, will such a combination complicate matters unnecessarily and ultimately weaken each system's respective strengths?

Hand signs can be a helpful stepping stone toward the conceptualization of pitch notation, even if their meaning is tied to fixed letter names rather than to solfège syllables. First, they can be "read" and thus facilitate faster learning of melodies to be played. Second, they also aid conscious pitch discrimination when the children are asked to translate what they have heard into hand signs before they play.

The First Song Arrangements in Orff-Schulwerk I

The reader is likely to be confused and puzzled when looking at the first song arrangements in Orff-Schulwerk I. Nowhere will he or she find drones in simple, accentuated pulse-beat patterns. Even the very beginning tunes on the falling minor third and those using the chant notes have accompaniments that not only are conceptually complex but also exceed by far the instrumental skills of beginning students. Indeed, a consistent criticism of volume I has been that it is so difficult as to be unusable.

This criticism is correct if one reads and uses the book as most books are usually read—by starting at the beginning and working one's way page by page to the end. But Orff-Schulwerk is not an ordinary book. The volume is divided into three sections, the central focus of which is Part II, "Rhythmic-Melodic Exercises." Orff and Keetman had their reasons for placing these exercises between Part I, "Nursery Rhymes and Songs," and Part III, "Instrumental Pieces." Part II is, first of all, a thought and direction indicator, not just for Volume I but for the following volumes also. In the "Rhythmic-Melodic Exercises," the basic ideas are presented. It is here that the concepts of rhythm, melody, and harmony are introduced and developed. Here is the classroom where the learning takes place—*the heart of the Schulwerk*. If this is part of the "shop" (as Werner Thomas calls it) where the apprentice learns the craft of music-making under the guidance of the teacher, Parts I and III constitute the exhibition halls of the masters' work. Here the concepts of Part II reappear, not in their basic form but transformed and shaped into models of the elemental music style. These models do not illustrate the growth process itself in detail, but the results of such processes. They are not meant to be used and taught as they appear on the page, nor are the students expected to create examples of equal complexity and sophistication.

The growth process is briefly outlined in Section II and clarified further in the "Instructions and Notes" at the back of the book. The teacher must fill in what is not spelled out in detail. In this respect Orff expects from the teacher as much creativity as the teacher expects from the student.

This excursion into the basic layout of Orff-Schulwerk I was necessary to explain the virtual absence of simple arrangements. In particular, the use of a simple pulse-beat drone accompanying two- and three-note tunes need not be illustrated, since it is concisely explained in the "Notes and Instructions" on page 142: "The simple drone can be used for every melody in this volume."

A detailed discussion of the contents of Volume I may be found in Chapter 7.

SUMMARY

There never has been, nor is there today, a "songless" culture in this world. Singing has always been humanity's second language, and no one had to go to school to learn it—everyone learned to sing simply by singing along. I remember from my childhood and many years of teaching that the child who could not sing on pitch was rare. Today, though, I find that every class has students who cannot hit pitches precisely, although their pitch perception in instrumental echo-play is not necessarily worse than that of the other children. This may have something to do with the fact that today, as a society, we sing less, that children have few opportunities to learn to sing. The entertainment media have usurped singing as a social or communal activity. Of course, children do sing along with whatever they hear on the radio or television, but more often than not these models do not encourage natural voice production. What is missing is that special early childhood experience of sitting on Mom's or Dad's lap and speaking or sing-songing nursery rhymes along with them. As we have seen, these elemental forms contain the beginnings of melody. Because of their small melodic range, they are never outside a child's voice range, and for this reason the child is able to sing on pitch. Most of our young students entering school have not been exposed to nursery-rhyme chanting, whether at home or in preschool. As a result, more of those who are not "natural singers" end up singing off pitch.

The simplest form of singing, alternation between two pitches, has its beginnings in the accentual strong-weak pattern of the spoken word. This accentual pattern turns into the falling minor third when sung. A third pitch, La, appears as the upper auxiliary to So when, instead of single words, short sentences are chanted. Since the new pitch always occurs on the weak beat of the phrase, the falling minor third still forms the structural basis of the chant. Children's own chants usually consist of a half-phrase, two duple-meter patterns, so that La, which must descend to So, falls on the weak beat of the first meter pattern in the half-phrase.

Combinations of the call and the chant are the beginning of form in melody. The smallest true structure is the phrase consisting of four meter patterns. The call pitches must occur twice to balance the double length of the chant. The form is *a,b*, each letter name referring to a half-phrase only:

The phrase can, of course, be an *a,a* form, utilizing only one instead of both formulas. Longer texts result in the two basic form structures, *a,a,a,b* and *a,b,a,b* (half-phrases).

The introduction of the basic rhythmic building blocks, as well as of the half-phrase later on, should be immediately combined with singing so that the rhythmic and the melodic aspects are presented in an almost simultaneous process. As a matter of fact, one can just as easily start with singing and extract the rhythm and meter pattern of the text from the chant. This is possible because rhythmic speech and chant are closely related.

Unlike the two melodic formulas, which are intuitive, pitched accompaniment does not originate with the child himself. But it is an easy step to transfer the percussive pulse-beat clapping or slapping that accompanies the song to the barred instruments, because they too are percussive in nature. The bordun or drone is an elemental accompaniment that occurred early in Western music as well as in other cultures. The importance of the drone lies in the fact that it establishes tonality and marks the beginning of harmony.

Although the barred instruments are relatively easy to play, some practice is necessary in order for the children to learn the fundamental skills. From the beginning, both techniques of sticking are in evidence, alternate sticking for the melody and simultaneous sticking for the drone. After these have been mastered, the bordun may be varied by either breaking it or inverting it, or by a combination of both.

Ensemble play, however, is difficult for beginners, and it should not be attempted before they have reached a degree of rhythmic security and an awareness of being part of a group. Listening to one another is the first step toward developing sensitivity in general. In this way, ensemble playing can help to serve a larger purpose, namely that of establishing a fundamental mode of communication.

5
COMPLETING
THE PENTATONIC

BASIC CONSIDERATIONS

If I have devoted what may seem an unreasonable amount of space to the discussion of the call and the chant, it was done with two considerations in mind:

1. The chant forms the nucleus of a specific pentatonic mode which is based on a tonic pitch we might call Do. In other words, once the chant is established it cannot develop in any other way but toward the pentatonic Do-mode. The absence of the pitches that produce the two half-steps (the 4th and 7th scale degrees), as being of no immediate importance, is already built into the chant; the 4th is skipped over, and the 7th lies outside the chant range.
2. The chant comes from the child himself. Hence, the development of the Do-pentatonic is set by the child.

Although these arguments may seem reasonable enough, we will find that the road leading to this "predestined" melodic development is not easy to follow, that there are snags in which we might get entangled, and that the road signs are sometimes deceptive. As always, we must know the terrain before we can decide how to cross it.

The term *pentatonic* can be defined in more than one way. Within the context of Orff-Schulwerk it refers to anhemitonic, or half-tone-less, scales and their modes in which the octave is divided into five steps, three of them major seconds, the other two minor thirds. In Orff-Schulwerk I only the Do-mode based on C is used. Thus, its scale pattern is 1–2–3—5–6—8, or, presented in terms of fixed pitches, C–D–E—G–A—C.

After the call and the chant have been established, the next most important pitch is the tonic. Its function is determined by its placement at the lower end of the scale. A note without tension, it both precedes and follows the buildup to tones of higher pitch and intensity, representing the point of release and rest. Thus, its basic functions are those of beginning and concluding a melody.

The upbeat formula of the call and chant has been discussed already in Chapter 4. Of course, the upbeat is not the only way the tonic may serve as the starting point of a tune, but it is the most natural way since it grows out of word and text recitation.

As the final of a melody, the tonic is often reached from the call or chant in a stepwise, falling melodic line. The second scale degree naturally becomes a passing note:

Among the five pitches of the Do-mode, the supertonic is the only note we need to "handle with care." It does not fit within the context of beginning accompaniment which, in conjunction with melody, consists either entirely of the tonic triad or of alternating tonic and submediant triad sounds (see also Chapter 6):

The supertonic note is part of the dominant triad, and our ears expect it to be treated as such when it occupies a prominent place within a melody, as for instance:

1. On strong beats in the measure:

Do-mode on F

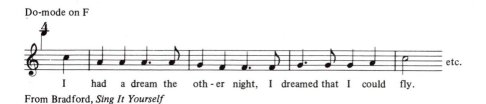

I had a dream the oth - er night, I dreamed that I could fly.

From Bradford, *Sing It Yourself*

2. On phrase endings:

Do-mode on G

Sail - ing   east,   sail - ing   west,   sail - ing   o'er the   o - cean.

From Landeck, *Songs to Grow on*

3. On strong beats before the final:

Do-mode on C

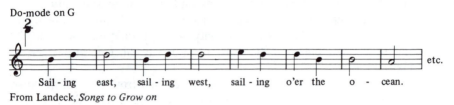

The   old   hen she   cack - led,   she   cack - led in   the   loft.

From Crawford Seeger, *Animal Folksongs*

In all these examples the supertonic needs to be harmonized with the dominant. Here then, we have come to a deceptive road sign, because the mere absence of the 4th and 7th scale degrees does not automatically make a melody pentatonic. The decisive factor is the manner in which the five pitches are distributed. Tunes with strongly accented and exposed supertonic notes are simply an incomplete diatonic major and belong to a category sometimes referred to as "gapped" diatonic tunes. The literature of children's songs and folksongs abounds with such melodies. I cannot emphasize strongly enough that these pseudo-pentatonic songs which call for harmonization rather than drone and ostinato accompaniment should not be used until concepts of harmonization have been introduced to the students. The teacher should choose songs in which the 2nd scale degreee appears as a passing tone only. Such songs are not easy to find, as Carl Orff apparently realized.

In selecting materials for Volume I, Orff turned to a collection of German children's songs and games, the first of its kind, published in 1897 by Franz Magnus Böhme.[1] In his introduction Böhme makes some observations on the nature of the child's singing which, as far as the chant is concerned, clearly have guided Orff. Böhme says: "The child's song, unless influenced by school or kindergarten, knows basically only one melody. It originates in the major mode, has two $\frac{2}{4}$ measures, and is constantly repeated.

There follow examples of three basic groups of formulas which, he states, make up the range of patterns used by children. The first group consists of the three-note chant. In the second group, the tune is composed of the broken tonic triad centered on the tonic note while touching the upper 3rd as well as the lower 5th scale degree:

---

[1] *Deutsches Kinderlied und Kinderspiel* (Leipzig, 1897; reprint, Nendeln, Liechtenstein: Kraus Reprint, 1967).

Do-mode on G

The third group consists entirely of melodies in diatonic major, incorporating the semitones. No mention is made of pentatonic, which I found puzzling. But an analysis of the songs produces some interesting and surprising results. Among approximately 370 tunes (not including the chants), there are only 42 without half-steps. Among these, 17 have a strong supertonic and are, therefore, gapped diatonic major. Nine melodies make use of the tonic-triad formula, which does not qualify them as pentatonic either, although they work with drone accompaniment. The remaining songs are based on the chant, with lower or upper tonic added. The 2nd scale degree does not appear at all!

A study of a somewhat later song collection, Johann Lewalter's, *Deutsches Kinderlied und Kinderspiel*,[2] was even more disappointing. Excluding the chant, I could not discover a single pentatonic tune among the over 900 examples.

In view of this state of affairs, Orff had no choice but to create pentatonic tunes. Only a very few songs in his first volume are traditional. The same applies to the English version by Margaret Murray, who for the most part adapted English texts to the Orff tunes. (In the Hall-Walter English version a number of traditional songs are utilized—more of this later on.) We might well question where Orff got the idea of using the pentatonic mode. Although it is impossible to be certain, I feel sure that he did not have in mind the reconstruction of a missing link in some Darwinian conception of musical evolution. Rather, as a musician and composer he must have recognized that pentatonic offers to the creative but unsophisticated minds of the young an immediate and direct manner of music-making because it is not subject to the demands of our traditional harmonic system. Orff used the major-oriented Do-pentatonic because it evolves naturally from the chant and leads just as naturally into diatonic major, the mode of the German children's song.

As to the historical aspect, we know that pentatonic modes have existed and are still extant in many cultures. The fact that German children's music, outside of the chant, shows no trace of the pentatonic does not disprove its existence in bygone ages. Until fairly recently, folk music has been an oral tradition. Although some of it was used by composers and in this manner found its way into the literate music world, nobody bothered preserving it for its own sake. Collecting our folk heritage, including children's lore and music, began in earnest only during the last century. By then, however, the songs were heavily influenced by art music. This is true especially of Central Europe, where there was close contact between the nonliterate and the literate populace. We simply have no way of knowing anything about children's singing in a much earlier era.

Not surprisingly, the Do-pentatonic mode in the traditional children's song

[2] (Kassel: Carl Victor, 1911).

literature of the North American continent shows certain similarities with its Middle European counterpart. Although there seems an abundance of available songs, under close scrutiny the majority turn out to belong to the pseudo-pentatonic variety, gapped major diatonic with a strong cadential feeling. Few melodies are shaped as would serve our purpose best, namely call- and chant-centered, with the supertonic note as passing tone. Perhaps it is for this reason that the English adaptation of Volume I retains Orff's own tunes.

However, one need not be confined to these examples. There is nothing wrong with creating new song tunes. Orff did so, after all, and we are advised in the book to use the many short rhymes listed for exactly that purpose. Those who prefer traditional song literature and are having difficulty finding enough suitable material might try eliminating cadential effects by making small changes in a given tune. Care must be taken, though, to leave intact the basic melodic structure. I believe such an approach is justifiable because we are dealing with music of oral traditions which is not meant to be cast into a final mold anyway. The following example will illustrate my point:

Do-mode on C (original in D)

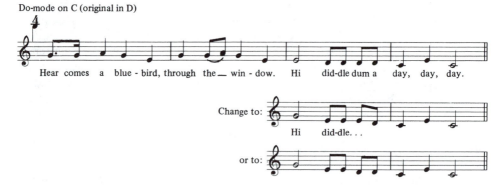

From Bradford, *Sing It Yourself*

In traditional North American children's songs, a melodic motif similar to the chant-centered tune is found, but with the pitches in a different order. They oscillate between So and La; Mi is reached in a direct leap from La, instead of descending from So. The strong and weak word syllables do not coincide with higher and lower pitches, which seems to make this a different formula. Although I do not know how widely it is used in this country, apparently its roots are not in the Middle European chant. Since it occurs in the song games of black children, I believe it to be a mixture of the African and European cultures:

Do-mode on C

From Kennedy, *Circle Round the Zero*

This motivic alteration of the three chant pitches appears not only in combination with the descending pitches Re and Do but also by itself. I have not included this formula in the chapter on chant development because it does not evolve naturally from speech rhythm and speech pitches.

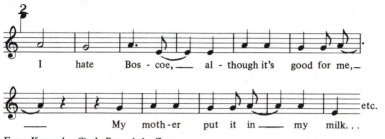

I hate Bos - coe, ___ al - though it's good for me, ___

___ My moth - er put it in ___ my milk. . .

From Kennedy, *Circle Round the Zero*

The next example introduces a new type of tune:

alternatives:

Do-mode on C

Old Aunt Di - nah, ho - pee, ho - pee, Old Aunt Di - nah, ho - pee ho.

From Bradford, *Sing It Yourself*

The suggested changes in measures 2 and 4 eliminate the strong supertonic. A tune like this represents a step forward in melodic development because it is not based on call or chant nuclei. The lower scale degrees are now used more prominently and in varying configurations. The reader may ask, "For heaven's sake, what's the big deal? After all, there are many ways to arrange the five pitches to form a melody!" This is true, of course. We must remember, though, that the moment we abandon the call- and chant-centered tune we leave behind the truly child-originated song, which, after all, consists only of a number of formulas with limited variants. The more advanced pentatonic tune, be it a folksong or a newly created song, is conceived *for* the child rather than *by* the child; it is *child-oriented* rather than *child-originated*. The young child would not think of starting a song on the tonic unless this has been part of his or her experience. But another more compelling reason has to do with the rhythmic structure of the text. In the simple, child-originated song, accented syllables generally coincide with higher pitches in the tune (with the exception of the "Afro-American formula"). This is no longer the case in the songs that have just been introduced. Consequently, we are entering a new stage in melodic development, even though it does not seem all that dramatic a change.

SONG TUNES WITH LARGER RANGES

The expansion of the melodic range to a full octave allows for a great variety of song tunes, whether traditional or newly created. Traditional materials will now be easier to come by, although the problem with the accented 2nd scale degree still exists. It can be solved in the same manner as before:

Do-mode on C

Krink-um, Krank-um is   my song, An' 'ts'all   I   sing   it   all   a - long,

alternative:

From my   el - bow to   my thumb, I   sing   it   back an' hug 'em some.

From Bradford, *Sing It Yourself*

Songs containing the "Afro-American formula" seem to incorporate the upper tonic note into another specific pattern: C2 (Do2) substitutes for A (La) before the descent to E (Mi):

Do-mode on C

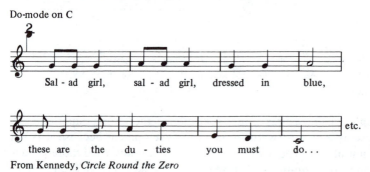

Sal - ad   girl,   sal - ad   girl,   dressed   in   blue,

these are   the   du - ties   you   must   do. . .

From Kennedy, *Circle Round the Zero*

The result is a leap of a sixth downward, very different from most other traditional tunes, which reach or leave C2 in smaller intervals of thirds or fourths. Tunes such as this one will help the children to recognize and internalize the sound of a sixth.

A number of children's songs consist entirely, or nearly so, of the broken tonic triad, like many songs of the European tradition (see also pp. 104–5). Although such tunes are not strictly pentatonic, they lend themselves well to drone accompaniment:

Do-mode on C

Pass one win - dow,   Ti - de - o,   Pass two win - dows,   Ti - de - o,

From Bradford, *Sing It Yourself*

Pass three win-dows, Ti - de - o,   Jin-gle at the win-dow, Ti - de - o.
Ti - de - o,   Ti - de - o,   Jin-gle at the win-dow, Ti - de - o.

Do-mode on C
(Original in F)

Had me a cat, and the cat pleased me, Fed my
cat in yon-der tree, The cat went fid-dle-i - dee.

From Sharp, *English Folksongs of the Southern Appalachians*

So far, we have discussed tunes with a range of an octave or less. They were in the *authentic* form of the Do-mode, because they did not reach below the tonic (or final). Song tunes such as these are in a comfortable singing range, and for this reason they need not be transposed.

I am aware of the differing points of view among music teachers regarding the training of the child's voice. Some believe strongly in developing and utilizing from the start the higher registers, the beauty and clarity of which are exemplified in the many excellent children's choirs around the world. This approach makes necessary the transposition of authentic tunes to higher pitches, such as F or G (in order to be usable with Orff instruments). Others maintain just as strongly that vocal training should begin in the lower register, closer to the speaking voice, because children with pitch problems will thereby have more success in learning how to match pitches.

The preference for one viewpoint over another depends on the ultimate goal. The vocal teacher interested in developing a first-rate children's choir, mainly for performance purposes, will choose differently from the teacher with somewhat broader objectives. The Orff specialist must keep in mind that Orff-Schulwerk is not a vocal approach for which Orff-type arrangements are occasionally used. The approach does not specialize in one single aspect of music such as singing; rather, its objective is to convey an understanding of music and skills in creating it. Therefore, the Orff-Schulwerk teacher needs to adhere to a teaching sequence that considers all musical aspects equally important; developing the upper voice range is only one among several aspects to be considered.

Perhaps a more important concern ought to be avoiding uncomfortably *low* singing ranges. Innumerable songs—even though their melodic circumference may not exceed a sixth—reach below the final:

One may, of course, position such tunes an octave higher, as indeed is done in Orff-Schulwerk I. However, once these melodies encompass an octave (G1–G2) most children's voices, unless specifically trained, will have difficulty in reaching the highest pitch. I have found it very helpful to coordinate the introduction of transposition with the introduction of songs which, because of their range (either too low or too high), need to be transposed. In this way, the children comprehend the reason for the procedure. The simplest transpositions of the Do-pentatonic (the scale pattern built on C), are to F and G, since neither will require sharps or flats.

Plagal melodies are defined by their ranges. They extend from the 5th scale degree above the final to the 5th degree below it. The definition and classification of melodies according to their authentic or plagal ambitus originated with the church modes of the Middle Ages and was the concern of theorists for several centuries. This terminology refers to a categorization of the diatonic modes which reached its final form during the sixteenth century. In applying a similar classification to our pentatonic tunes, we must keep in mind that we are dealing with a folk idiom that does not conform thoroughly to the rules and terms established by early theorists. Categorizations are generally applicable only to a limited degree anyway, as they do not make allowances for all existing tunes (unless we add a category of "unclassifiables").

Keeping these limitations in mind, three types of tunes emerge, all extending below the final:

1. Songs Starting on the Upbeat, 5–1.   In the beginning of this chapter a short reference was made to the upbeat in the call and chant formulas. The text, beginning on a weak syllable, was represented by the 1st and 3rd scale degrees, and the following accented syllable or word by the 5th scale degree. All these pitches are part of the tonic triad:

In comparison to this, the more sophisticated song frequently expresses the same rhythmic structure of the text with the pitch formula 5–1, a subtle but nevertheless interesting difference (Do-mode on F):

Do-mode on F

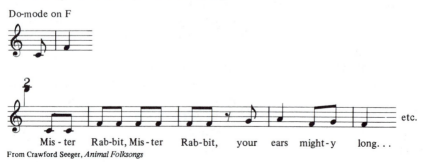

Mis - ter   Rab-bit, Mis - ter   Rab-bit,   your   ears   might - y   long. . .

From Crawford Seeger, *Animal Folksongs*

Since the lower 5th degree has no significant part in shaping the melody but is rather only a consequence of the text beginning, songs with the upbeat formula 5–1 need not be considered plagal.

2. Songs Including the Lower 6th Scale Degree (6–1). The 6th scale degree as the lowest pitch can be found often as a note preceding the final, at phrase endings as well as at the conclusion of a song:

Do-mode on F

Hush lit-tle ba - by,— don't you — cry, You'll be an an - gel — by 'n' by.

From Bradford, *Sing It Yourself*

Such ending formulas, persistently avoiding the half-step by leaping over it, seem like archaic precursors of the cadence ending on the scale degrees 7–1 (see also Chapter 8, pp. 193–94):

Do-mode on F

In other songs we find the lower submediant note as part of a melodic phrase reminiscent of the chant. However, here the chant pitches appear in the plagal range of the melody, as 6–1–2 (La–Do–Re) instead of 3–5–6 (Mi–So–La), which seems to strengthen the submediant harmony:

Do-mode on G

Who built the ark? No - ah, No - ah, Who built the ark? No-ah and the Lord.

From Bradford, *Sing It Yourself*

In some tunes the lower 6th is used more frequently. As a group, they constitute a transition between the authentic and true plagal ranges. Important to us is the fact that they need transposition, just like the first group of tunes.

3. Plagal Songs. In plagal melodies the 5th and 6th scale degrees are utilized more extensively below the tonic than in the examples above. As a matter of fact, the pitch progression 5–6–1, or 1–6–5, occurs with such frequency that one might consider it another formula:

Do-mode on F

Cot-ton needs a pick-in' so bad,— Cot-ton needs a pick-in' so bad,—

From Bradford, *Sing It Yourself*

Cot-ton needs a pick-in'   so   bad,— Goin' to   pick all   o - ver this   field.

Expansion of the melodic range will be helpful in clarifying and understanding concepts of form and in acquiring good musical judgment for improvisation. Although the forms discussed in Chapter Three are still the basic models, the individual phrases of a song will be more distinct from each other because they may lie in different ranges of the octave. Although the divisions are flexible and overlap, two areas can be defined within the octave:

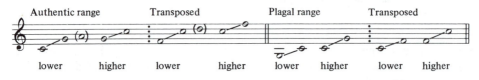

Authentic range		Transposed		Plagal range		Transposed	
lower	higher	lower	higher	lower	higher	lower	higher

The authentic tune of ''Krinkum'' (p. 108) is a perfect example of a clear phrase division. The three *a*-phrases are in the upper tetrachord, while the *b*-phrase consists only of the three lowest scale degrees (form: *a,a,a,b*).

Not all traditional songs display such a clear division of phrases. In order for the children to be able to create good song tunes it is advisable, at least initially, to give them models with clearly defined phrases.

Sequencing Tonal Expansion.   Attending to matters of form and style is only one part of the whole picture of tonal range expansion. To set up a sequence that takes care simultaneously of a number of difficulties in a progressive order is a real challenge. I would like to offer some points upon which the teacher should reflect before making song selections.

The first point concerns intervallic relationships within a melody. The greater the number of different pitches there are in a song, the greater is the variety of intervals that can appear. As a general rule, smaller intervals are easier to sing than larger ones. However, one cannot make a strict rule of this and introduce new intervals with regard to their size alone, proceeding from the third to the fourth to the fifth and so on. Much depends on the harmonic (triadic) configuration of which these intervals are a part. For instance, the fifth Do–So (ascending or descending) is easier to sing than the fourth La–Mi (here not meant as part of the chant formulas) and Re–So, because the first interval belongs to the tonic triad whereas the latter two do not. This is especially true when, as will be mostly the case, the song is accompanied by a bordun that firmly establishes the tonality.

The following is an illustration of all intervallic progressions and their triadic affiliations which can occur in Do-pentatonic (seconds and sevenths are not considered, as they are not parts of a triad structure).

Do-pentatonic scale on C:

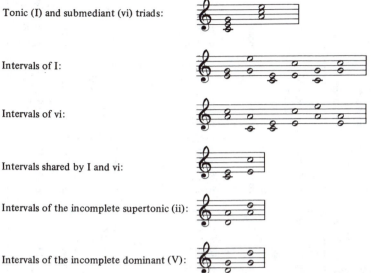

Tonic (I) and submediant (vi) triads:

Intervals of I:

Intervals of vi:

Intervals shared by I and vi:

Intervals of the incomplete supertonic (ii):

Intervals of the incomplete dominant (V):

Obviously, there is no single way in which to introduce these intervals in a progressive order for singing. The difficulty seems to shift back and forth between the physical aspect of acquiring vocal skills and range and the auditory aspect of acquiring and internalizing pitch relationships. In the end both belong together as neither can exist without the other.

So far we have examined tonal expansion as a purely horizontal development. My second point concerns the vertical sound picture. The reader should recall the discussion earlier in this chapter regarding the placement of the 2nd scale degree in a given tune. Although melodies with a strong supertonic pose no problem in singing, they require adaptation in the accompaniment, or in other words, a fairly well developed vertical pitch discrimination and advanced knowledge of harmonic concepts. For this reason they are part of harmonic rather than melodic development, and their introduction ought to be coordinated accordingly.

The question arises as to what constitutes a strong 2nd scale degree. Two combined factors render a supertonic strong enough to sound cadential and therefore to require adaptation in the accompaniment: (1) the supertonic appears on a strong beat; and (2) it lasts through the entire count. For example:

DEVELOPMENTAL STEPS IN MELODIC EXPANSION

Song examples are taken from the following texts:
Orff-Schulwerk: *Music for Children*, Vol. I, Murray edition;
Orff-Schulwerk: *Music for Children*, Vol. I, Hall-Walter edition;
Sing It Yourself, by Louise Larkins Bradford;
Circle Round the Zero, by Maureen Kennedy.

The examples are illustrations of certain types of tunes in the original Orff-Schulwerk I, and their counterparts in traditional literature. For traditional song examples only two sources are listed. They do not, by any means, exhaust the available literature. *Note:* Some examples from Bradford and Kennedy have different tonal centers, and need to be transposed to correspond with this chart.

Developmental Steps	Sequencing	New Pitches	Song Examples			
			O.S.I. Murray	O.S.I. Hall	Bradford	Kennedy
Step I *Untransposed Do-pentatonic* *Call- and chant-centered tunes* Tunes beginning on the downbeat start on E or C. Tunes beginning on the upbeat start on G.	1. Range of fifth and sixth. a. tonic as final reached in a descending motif; supertonic is passing tone. b. lowest three pitches in various configurations. 2. Range of one octave.	[music notation]	1. a. p. 113, #32 b. none 2. p. 18, #21 p. 18, #22, p. 19, #23	1. a. p. 14, #13 p. 15, #14 p. 16, #15 p. 62, #50, b. none 2. p. 20, #19 p. 22, #21 p. 94, #2 p. 21, #20 (strong 2nd)	1. a. p. 28, #55 (strong 2nd) b. none 2. none	1. a. p. 14, *The Clock, Gypsy* b. none 2. p. 14, *Old Man Mosie* p. 16, *Salad Girl Banana*
Step II *Untransposed Do-pentatonic* Breaking away from call- and chant-centered tunes. Melodic structures more varied, although a certain flavor lingers on. Songs begin on all pitches except the supertonic.	1. [music notation] 2. [music notation] 3. [music notation] Proceed similarly as above.	no new pitches	1. p. 11, #12 p. 45, #41 2. none 3. p. 19, #23	1. p. 13, #12 2. p. 18, #17 3. p. 19, #18	1. p. 13, ##27, 28 p. 30, #59 2. none 3. p. 58, #115 p. 61, #121	1. none 2. none 3. p. 46, *One, Two, Three*

Step III

5th and 6th scale degrees below the tonic prepare for the emergence of plagal tunes. Transposition is introduced. For singing, only Do on F is used.

	Pitches				
1. Tunes with upbeat 5–1. Final F. Ranges: (a) (b) (c)	[staff notation]	1. a. none / b. none	1. a. none / b. none	1. a. none / b. p. 71, #143	1. a. none / b. none
2. The 6th degree below the tonic as a formula in traditional songs. Final F. Ranges: (a) (b) (c) (In order to reinforce the concept of transposition, Do on G may be used also, as long as the tunes do not exceed the 5th scale degree (D2).)	no new pitches	2. a. none / b. none / c. none	2. a. none / b. none / c. none	2. a. p. 20, #42; p. 21, #44 / b. none / c. p. 63, #126; p. 64, #128	2. a. none / b. none / c. none
3. True plagal tunes. Final F. Ranges: (a) (b) (c) Authentic tunes transposed to F may also be used, as long as their range does not exceed a sixth (D2).	no new pitches	3. a. none / b. none / c. none	3. a. none / b. none / c. none	3. a. p. 48, #96; p. 48, #97; p. 40, #81 / b. p. 73, #149 / c. p. 86, #168; p. 87, #169	3. a. p. 41, *Hambone*; p. 34, *Down, Down, Baby* / b. none / c. none

Alternatives to Step III or to be interspersed with Step III

Step IIIA

Teachers interested in developing the higher voice register earlier may use untransposed, plagal tunes.

The range of a tenth allows for authentic tunes.

	Pitches				
1. Range of a sixth. Final C2.	[staff notation]	1. p. 16, #16; p. 44, #41	1. p. 30, #28	1. none	1. none
2. Range of an octave. Final C2.	no new pitches	2. p. 16, #17; p. 17, #20; p. 22, #28	2. p. 17, #16; p. 23, #22	2. none	2. none
3. Range of a tenth. Final C1.	no new pitches	3. p. 32, #37; p. 47, #41	3. p. 36, #33	3. none	3. none

Step IIIB

Introduction of the La-mode (minor modality) in transposition to D.

A detailed discussion of this mode follows in Chapter 8.

	Pitches				
1. Range of a fifth. Final D1.	[staff notation]	1. none	1. none	1. p. 21, #43; p. 19, #40	1. p. 52, *Ama, Lama*
2. Addition of lower 7th degree.	no new pitches	2. none	2. none	2. p. 49, #99	2. none
3. Range of an octave.	[staff notation]	3. none	3. none	3. p. 65, #131	3. none

If, on the other hand, only one of the two factors applies, as happens so frequently in the syncopated patterns of traditional American songs, there is no need for harmonic change:

DEVELOPMENTAL STEPS IN TONAL EXPANSION

In the following chart are listed the developmental steps in tonal expansion. Although the examples given refer to song tunes, instrumental melodies can be treated similarly. The teacher need not adhere strictly to the sequence shown. Some steps will consist merely of adding a note or two for the purpose of range expansion; in such cases it does not matter greatly whether the new pitch is added at the lower or the upper end of the scale. Other steps need to be treated more prudently, as they necessitate introduction of a new musical concept. Generally speaking, melodic expansion and other purely horizontal concerns should take precedence over harmonic (vertical) concerns. In practical terms this means that tunes in which the melodic structure allows for bordun and ostinato accompaniment throughout should be used before those requiring harmonic changes. Children have less trouble with the transposition of a pentatonic scale pattern than with coordinating sounds vertically—that is, adapting an accompaniment pattern to a tune. This topic will be discussed in a later chapter.

For completeness' sake, the sequence below includes the La-pentatonic as an alternative step, although we have not yet discussed this mode (see Chapter 8). I like to introduce the La-pentatonic after the children are well versed in authentic Do-mode tunes within an octave's range. After this stage, transposition in one way or another is the next step. Those who prefer to continue with the Do-mode will now move into the plagal ranges. An alternative is to introduce the La-mode, which also needs transposition in order to be within a comfortable singing range. I prefer this latter approach because it introduces a new and interesting dimension.

The song examples on the chart clarify and underline certain points discussed in this chapter:

1. The available song literature, both Orff-Schulwerk and traditional, does not cover all the developmental steps. This is especially true of the beginning stage, when we deal with call- and chant-centered tunes. Thus much opportunity is available for the teacher and the students to improvise and create. The reader is referred to Orff and Keetman's *Paralipomena*,[3] the first section of which contains several more song tunes appropriate to Step I. (The texts, however, are all in German.) In Steps II and III cross-referencing will cover most possibilities in melodic development.

---

[3] (Mainz: B. Schott's Söhne).

2. In comparing the Orff-Schulwerk songs with the traditional songs, some interesting observations can be made in regard to the melodic structure. Orff's tunes, whether authentic or plagal, show a clearly elemental harmonic design. For the most part they are anchored firmly to the tonic-triad sound. At the same time, though, a constant swing to the submediant harmony is implied in the way the 3rd and 6th scale notes are positioned. The melodic and formal structure of the tunes is designed so as to make ostinato accompaniment possible.

Many traditional tunes seem to have a different tonal structure because they were not necessarily conceived with the idea of pitched accompaniment in mind. Other factors, such as a comfortable singing range, may have been more important. Perhaps for this reason there is an abundance of traditional songs in plagal or near-plagal ranges. In these songs, the plagal portion almost always conforms to the specific melodic motifs illustrated earlier. Such motifs are not a part of Orff's tunes. Sometimes the minor modality is not just implied but strongly expressed by means of the broken submediant triad (for example, Bradford #42, verse).

Accompaniment to such tunes presupposes a greater awareness of harmonic change than accompaniment to those oriented toward the tonic triad, because one single drone pattern cannot always be used without interruption throughout a song. The examples in Step III were chosen to minimize such problems, and the teacher should try to do the same when making selections. Arranging more problematic song tunes will be discussed in Chapter 8.

The chart should provide several years' worth of materials concerning tonal expansion and the development of melodic concepts connected with it. Pitches beyond E2 may very well be introduced only during the diatonic stage. On the other hand, range extension can continue to take place within the pentatonic realm as well. In the suggestions below, the numbers do not imply sequence, but merely alternatives.

Addition of E2.

1. Untransposed Do-mode; see Step IIIA.
2. Transposition of Do-mode to G; follow Step III/1,2,3.
3. La-mode untransposed; range of a fifth and sixth (subtonic added).
4. La-mode transposed to E; range of an octave and a ninth (subtonic added).

Addition of F2.

1. Authentic Do-mode, transposed to F; range of an octave.
2. Plagal Do-mode on F; range of an octave and an eleventh.

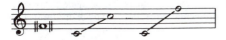

INSTRUMENTAL MELODIES

So far, the discussion has concentrated on theoretical matters because my objective has been to present the range expansion and the structure of melody in synchronization with the vertical aspect, the tonic-triad–oriented drone accompaniment. Moreover, the sequence of pitch introduction was based exclusively on vocal tunes and took into account the gradual increase of the child's voice range.

Matters are somewhat different when we deal with instrumental tunes, because on the barred instruments there are almost two full octaves available right from the start. This does not mean, of course, that once the five pitches of the Do-pentatonic have been established, the melodies are free to roam across the entire range of the instrument. It does, however, allow for more freedom and a more accelerated pace of sequencing melodic expansion.

Orff-Schulwerk I does not provide any obvious clues to the order of pitch introduction. There are no examples of melodic echo-play such as the "Rhythmic Imitation" exercises in Part II that would at least hint at a sequential development of melodic range. And although Part III, "Instrumental Pieces" (p. 94), contains a number of examples with small melodic ranges, they are placed in the advanced section because they are illustrations of polyphonic ostinato accompaniment, which accounts for their simplicity.[4] The only examples indicating the range appropriate for beginning instrumental melodies are the first two pieces in Part III (p. 94). In no. 1 the tune moves between C and G in the *A*-section, including the pitch A in the *B*-section; no. 2 advances to the octave C1–C2.[5]

Using the hexachord C–A as a point of departure for echo and question-answer activities, there are several options to expand the tonal range. One option makes use of the authentic positions first and then moves on to the plagal ones. The ranges of the tunes will therefore appear in the following order:

1. Sixth C1–A1, final C1, authentic.

2. Octave C1–C2, final C1 or C2, authentic.

---

[4] Nos. 5, 20, 26, 27, and 29 (pp. 104–10).

[5] Both examples contain supertonic pitches on the strong beats of the measures, colliding openly with the drone fifth. This may raise the question whether it is really important to avoid the accented Re. Obviously, in their early attempts at instrumental improvisation children cannot be expected to manipulate pitches according to specific melodic or harmonic considerations. These matters, however, will take on importance as the children acquire better instrumental skills, develop pitch discrimination, and become more experienced at improvisation.

3. Sixth G1–E2, final C2, plagal.

4. Octave G1–G2, final C2, plagal.

Option two gives first priority to the smaller range:

1. Sixth C1–A1, final C1, authentic.

2. Sixth G1–E2, final C2, plagal.

3. Octave C1–C2, final C1 or C2, authentic.

4. Octave G1–G2, final C2, plagal.

It does not matter which option to choose first, although the second one may be slightly more advantageous for ear training because it places the three-plus-two scale pattern immediately into the reversed two-plus-three position.

The range of an octave, in both authentic and plagal positions, offers so many different possibilities for creating tunes that it is unnecessary for a long time to go beyond that range. As a matter of fact, most instrumental melodies in the book are within this range also.

Echo-Play Instrumental echo-play is of fundamental importance not only to develop conscious pitch discrimination but also to provide examples of good melody building. Although echo-play should be practiced regularly and frequently, it need not take more than a few minutes of class time. I use it often (but not exclusively) as a warm-up so as to set the tone with concentrated listening.

After having played the phrase to be echoed, the teacher must carefully observe the response by the class. If only a few children echoed correctly, the phrase obviously was too difficult. In that case it is better to abandon it and begin with a simpler version, rather than playing it over several more times.

Repeating the same phrase too often is not an echo, but teaching by rote. Here are some more suggestions:

Begin an echo activity by having the class play the whole range of pitches that will be used.

Tell the students on which note the first phrase will start, and begin each new echo on the pitch that ended the previous phrase.

Have the children listen with eyes closed; this helps them to concentrate better and to use their ears.

To begin with, play only in simple quarter-note rhythm and move stepwise where possible.

Introduce eighth-notes into the phrases on repeated pitches.

Thus, a little sequence of echo phrases might consist of altering the original phrase in some small way:

As the children improve their listening and playing skills, the echo phrases should become more challenging.

Improvisation   Part Two of Orff-Schulwerk I contains three pages of "Melodies to Be Completed," examples of question-answer play. Their purpose is not merely to illustrate tonal expansion, because this aspect is only one of many to be considered in a sequential development of melodic improvisation. Since the exercises cover a development over many years, tonal expansion is basically attended to within the first three examples. The others imply that improvisations should focus always on specific musical ideas or playing skills: dotted quarter-notes, upbeats, eighth-notes, specific meters, and so on. Examples 8, 9, 10, and 11b offer an interesting alternative, in that questions are to be created for already existing answers. Concerning musical structure, all the illustrations except two (6 and 11a) adhere to an *a,b* form. This form may be somewhat easier to create, especially once the melodic range of an octave is available, because there is more freedom in choosing an answer. An *a, a¹* structure requires instant comprehension of the question in order to make the response similar. It is closer to echo and therefore grows directly out of imitation exercises. However, as long as only small ranges of a fifth and a sixth are used, it works better than an *a,b* form, since it is perhaps the more elemental form structure.

Before starting a question-answer activity I always explain the specific focus of the improvisation. First, we play the range of pitches to be used and determine the "home tone" (the tonic). If the children have difficulty in keeping to the imposed tonal limitation the bars not needed may be removed. I discuss with them how in an *a,a¹* form the answer is similar to the question. The most obvious change in the answer is to go home, which the question never does (at least at the beginning). Other changes, such as using two eighth-notes in place of one quarter-note (see also echo example above) or filling in skips, may be incorporated later. Here are some examples of questions in the authentic range of a sixth that lead to an *a¹*-answer:

Questions in the plagal range of a sixth that lead to an *a¹*-answer:

Questions that allow for filling in skips:

Once the whole octave is available, *a,b* forms appear quite naturally, because there is now a clearly defined distinction between a lower and a higher range. After we have played the entire scale it is divided into the two ranges. The dividing pitch, the 5th degree, is shared by both ranges, although some overlapping may occur:

I then play different phrases and have the children decide whether I have been using the lower, the higher, or the entire range. I do this to make them aware of what to listen for in the question, so that they can place their *b*-answers in a different range of the scale. Some examples of questions in the lower range, to be answered in the upper range:

Questions in the upper range, to be answered in the lower range:

Later, the entire range may be used for the question as well as for the response. In order to create *b*-phrases, the students must now hear whether the question originated in the lowest, the middle, or the highest range of the scale, and whether the general direction of the melody was descending, ascending, or curving. In the answers the directions can be reversed. An example of a question that begins high and moves in a generally descending direction:

A question that begins low and moves in a generally ascending direction:

A question that begins in the middle range (in the first example it first moves downward, then rises, and finally comes to rest in the middle; in the second example the directions are reversed):

The practice of *a,a¹* answers should, of course, be continued also with larger tonal ranges.

Once the students are fairly competent in improvising answer phrases, they may take over the role of the teacher in creating the questions. Finally, both questions and answers can be improvised as an entire form. But the teacher must still clearly define the improvisations in regard to form and melodic range.[6]

Notation.   Although Chapters 7 and 9 (pp. 189 and 236 respectively) deal with reading readiness and teaching procedures, at this point I will discuss some basic notation considerations in order to avoid giving the impression that Orff-Schulwerk delays unreasonably the teaching of pitch notation.

Script is a tool to preserve a formulated idea, whether musical or otherwise, so that it can be referred to again or made available to others. In his introduction to Volume I Carl Orff states that, in the beginning, musical notation should serve mainly the purpose of writing down musical creations. Formulation of musical ideas requires a conscious awareness of simple tonal relationships. There-

---

[6] Although the examples are shown only in the untransposed Do-mode, other pentatonic modes, as well as their transpositions, should be included in the improvisations once they have been introduced.

fore, a prerequisite to the introduction of notation must be a well-developed conceptualization of both partial scales and the pentatonic octave. Lower-elementary-grade children need at least two years to develop such conceptualization if they have practiced echo-play, improvisation, and singing on a regular basis.

Orff also stresses that "in order to achieve freedom in performance the children must play from memory." In other words, reading of instrumental parts serves no practical purpose as long as only the barred instruments are used, because the eyes are needed to focus on the sound bars. However, reading of pitch notation is essential for playing the recorder. Here the fingers are manipulated by the sense of touch rather than sight, leaving the eyes free to read the music. But once reading has been introduced, it is, of course, used not only for recorder playing but for singing as well.

Pitch notation may be taught along with the recorder, or it may precede it, provided the children have reached the state of reading readiness outlined above. I prefer to introduce the general concept of pitch notation and to practice reading and singing with a few notes before the recorder is actually taken up, which allows the children to master one major task before tackling another. This involves familiarizing the class with the entire staff and the placement of notes on lines and spaces according to their lower or higher sounds. The two leger-line notes that form the lower and upper limits of the barred instruments may also be included in this general introduction. With my younger students I use the terms "basement" and "attic" notes:

The next step is to concentrate on two or three specific pitches and to establish reading facility with them. Which pitches to start with depends on whether they are taught simultaneously with the recorder or independently from it. In the former case the first two notes will be C2 and A1, to be followed by D2—a transposition of the call and chant formulas to F (see also p. 230). When the notation is used in connection with singing, the choice is not as restricted. Thus, one can start with the untransposed Do-mode, introducing either the three lowest pitches or the call and chant pitches first. It is also possible to begin with the same pitches as on the recorder.

As soon as the first notes have been learned, ear-training activities should be extended to include dictation, rather than concentrating on instrumental imitation alone. As is the case with language, reading music is easier than "spelling"— that is, writing—it. The problem is compounded by the fact that not only the pitch but also the rhythm must be notated. Therefore, unless the aspect of dictation is included from the very beginning, when only a small number of symbols is involved, notating more complex musical ideas will be very difficult later.

SUMMARY

There are several important lessons to be learned from this chapter. The first one concerns the Do- or major pentatonic mode as it exists in traditional song literature, and its use with drone accompaniment. We have discovered that "pentatonic'' is not always what it appears to be. As the name implies, the major pentatonic rests firmly on the three pitches of the tonic (major) triad, the other two pitches being subsidiary. Put in practical terms, the three important scale degrees ought to be used on strong beats. However, the 6th scale degree, La, need not be ruled out completely. Because of its implied submediant harmony, which is closely related to the tonic triad, it is perfectly acceptable on strong beats even though it causes a dissonance with the drone. The supertonic, on the other hand, must remain a passing tone or an auxiliary note because in a stronger position it calls for a harmony change to the dominant. A strong supertonic must be avoided because the children are not ready for harmonization. This may be difficult to accept by anyone who has been brought up on the seemingly all-important tonic-dominant relationship and the cadence. However, at this point we are dealing with elemental music in its initial stage; traditional harmony simply does not yet have a place in it. As Orff-Schulwerk teachers we must readjust our thinking if we want to serve our students well.

The task is not easy. Although in improvisation we can teach the students from early on never to ''sit'' on the supertonic note, when it comes to traditional songs we have a problem because the majority of them belong to the pseudo-pentatonic variety, which demands harmonization. There are several solutions: (1) search for appropriate materials, (2) create new song tunes as Orff did, and (3) make small alterations in traditional tunes that will not distort their character.

The sequencing of tonal expansion and the development of melodic concepts connected with it are illustrated in the chart.

The second lesson of this chapter concerns instrumental playing and melodic improvisation. It can be summarized as follows:

1. Instrumental tunes need at least four, better yet all five pentatonic pitches to develop their own stylistic identity.

2. Range expansion may follow a different order and can proceed at a faster pace than vocal tunes. However, the structure of instrumental melodies must still adhere to the same vertical or harmonic considerations that apply to the vocal tunes.

3. Echo exercises, the beginning of ear training, need to be planned carefully to allow for the development of conscious pitch perception. They serve as the preparation and the basis for pitch notation, which should be introduced only when the children have acquired a sense of tonal relationships within the pentatonic.

4. Question-answer improvisations lead to the elemental form structures of a,a^1 and a,b. Basic terminology—that is, naming the phrases with letters—is the starting point of musical analysis and should therefore be used from the beginning. Musical ideas should be notated regularly and as soon as notational skills are available.

Having followed the development of melody to the point where it functions as a recognizable musical element, we will now turn to matters of harmonic development, namely drone and ostinato accompaniment. A complete, or ultimate, sequential procedure that combines both the horizontal and the vertical aspects can evolve only when each aspect has been contemplated individually.

6
FORMS OF
ACCOMPANIMENT

PART-MUSIC

Melody alone, or accompanied only by unpitched percussion, is called *monophonic* music (mono = one). The addition of one or more melodic lines or the addition of pitched accompaniment produces simultaneous pitched sounds. The terms "harmony" and "polyphony" are both used to describe this music.[1] The problem is that the same terminology is used in defining specific compositional techniques, "harmony" meaning the use of traditional harmony in a homophonic style, and "polyphony" meaning polyphonic writing or counterpoint. For this reason, I will speak in this chapter, whenever possible, of "part-music" when dealing with the *general* phenomenon of simultaneous sound.

Depending on the number of individual parts, their concurrent sounding forms intervals, triads, or larger chords. There are two basic designs according to which part-music in the Western musical tradition is constructed, *homophony* and *polyphony* (homo = same or similar, poly = many or different).

Early homophonic compositions (ca. 900 A.D. and before) are *homorhythmic* as well as *paraphonic*. This means that the (two) voices move in the same rhythm and parallel to each other; consequently, the same interval is retained throughout a composition. Paraphony is a horizontal or melodic concept, but at the same time it marks the beginning of the vertical aspect, harmony. *Diaphony*, the contrasting motion of two parts, seems a natural outgrowth of the former. By moving in opposite directions, the voices form different intervals; thus, diaphony constitutes a progression in the development of harmony.

---

[1] The term "polyphony" is used by ethnomusicologists to indicate simultaneous pitched sounds when referring to music of any world tradition. "Harmony" refers only to combined pitches based on the Western European tonal system.

Historical examples, as well as still-existing musical practices in folk and tribal cultures, show that paraphony may include triadic structures also, used in nonfunctional progressions. "Homorhythmic homophony" is also present in the chordal writing that evolved after the advent of traditional harmony. In today's usage, the term homophony includes all music in which a single melody line is accompanied by chords.

The simultaneous sounding of two or more melodic lines with independent rhythms (also called "polyrhythm") results in a polyphonic texture. As in early homophony, the linear (horizontal) design reigned supreme in early polyphony, and it is perhaps for this reason that polyphonic compositions of that period sometimes sound strangely dissonant to our ears. In time, the vertical aspect of simultaneous sound began to play an increasingly important role in composition. Mature polyphony may be said to combine the horizontal and vertical aspects of music.

Historically speaking, the chronological development of part-music has not always consisted of logical, next-step events. It is up to the music teacher to create an evolutionary sequence that is consistent, logical, and detailed.

Almost from the very beginning, the music of Orff-Schulwerk is part-music, as it uses pitched accompaniment in the form of drone and ostinato. These patterns of accompaniment represent the microcosmic counterparts of the designs found in all part-music, homophony and polyphony. However, since drone and ostinato are used in combination with melody, they form part of larger simultaneous sound units such as triads. In pentatonic music only two triads, the tonic and submediant, can occur in their complete form; all others remain incomplete, though they may be implied. Other simultaneous sounds occurring frequently are those that we define as dissonances. We will see later that they cannot be avoided when repetitive patterns of accompaniment are used.

OSTINATO ACCOMPANIMENT

The basic concepts of ostinato accompaniment are found in Orff-Schulwerk I (pp. 82–86) under the title "Ostinato Exercises for Tuned Percussion Instruments." As in the rhythmic section, the pitched ostinato examples are not meant to be presented in their entirety to the beginning student. They are an outline of and a guide to the whole range of possibilities in ostinato accompaniment. The fact that the exercises appear in the pentatonic volume does not mean that the concepts they illustrate cannot be applied to the diatonic modes and more advanced harmony as well. The whole idea of elemental music, its possibilities for improvisation, and the importance of sequential development are negated if these forms of accompaniment are abandoned too early in favor of more traditional types of harmonization.

Orff and Keetman very likely placed the entire developmental sequence in Volume I to give the teacher a sense of direction, and with it an ability to sequence in a consistent way by tying together specific stages in melodic-harmonic development. Although Books II–V contain some examples using the same concepts applied to diatonic and more advanced harmonic materials, they will be understood only if the ostinato exercises of Book I have been studied carefully.

In normal usage, an *ostinato* is a clearly defined phrase, repeated many times, usually in the same voice part. A pattern should appear at least three times in order to qualify as an ostinato.

Repetition in one form or another is a characteristic of elemental music. Although ostinato techniques are ancient and occur throughout the world, their use is not limited to elemental music. In Western art music the ostinato has appeared as a compositional device intermittently from the thirteenth century up into the present. Its longevity is due to the fact that it can be manipulated in many different ways and thus be adapted to various styles and techniques.

In Orff-Schulwerk the ostinato primarily serves the purpose of accompanying another part, be it metered speech, a rhythm, a song, or an instrumental tune. There are three basic types of ostinato accompaniment: speech ostinato, rhythmic ostinato, and the pitched patterns of accompaniment often referred to simply as "ostinati" (plural), which for clarity's sake we may call "pitched ostinato."

At first glance, the examples on pages 82–86 of Orff-Schulwerk I appear to be a bewildering variety of patterns, but actually these are only a few suggestions among many more possibilities. Because of this variety, we must first investigate the general organization of these pages in order to demonstrate sequential development within the categories.

The pitched ostinato exercises are organized in two ways simultaneously:

1. According to the rhythmic relationship between the two drone pitches,[2] which can be
   a. *homorhythmic*, which means both drone pitches move in the same rhythm— that is, both hands play at the same time;
   b. *polyrhythmic*, which means that the drone pitches have different rhythms—that is, the hands play independently from one another; or
   c. *monorhythmic*, which means that the drone pitches are placed in a successive, rather than a simultaneous, order, and the hands alternate in playing a pitch.
2. According to the "harmonic" relationship between the drone pitches. If one or both move to another pitch, different harmonies are created.

Thus, the exercises illustrate each harmonic development through homorhythmic, polyrhythmic and monorhythmic designs. In order to define and express this dual relationship of rhythm and harmony between the drone pitches, we can speak of homophonic, polyphonic and monophonic (= melodic) patterns. The three drone types representing the rhythmic relationship and requiring a different playing technique are of fundamental importance, as they represent the point of departure toward horizontal and vertical orientation. They should be introduced as soon as the children have the necessary playing skills. Along with the melodic-harmonic development, they prepare the way for monophonic, homophonic and polyphonic concepts.

---

[2] Chapter 4, p. 75–76.

The key ideas within these two main categories are as follows (the examples cited are from the "Ostinato Exercises for Tuned Percussion Instruments" in Part II of Orff-Schulwerk I, p. 82):

A. Rhythmic Relationship Between the Drone Pitches

1. Playing both hands at the same time (homorhythmic). Combined with pitch, this produces homophony and harmony.
   Examples: I/nos. 1–40, II/nos. 1–38.

2. Breaking the drone into successive pitches by playing with alternate hands. Used with changing pitches, this leads ultimately to the development of melodic patterns (monophony).
   Examples: I/nos. 41–48, 65–88, II/nos. 39–42, 64–75, 79–88.

3. Playing a rhythmically independent part with each hand (polyrhythmic). From these exercises, elemental two-part polyphonic patterns evolve when changing pitches are added. Here we find the horizontal and vertical concepts combined, as in all polyphonic writing.
   Examples: I/nos. 49–64, 89–96, II/nos. 43–63, 90–95.

B. Harmonic Relationship Between the Drone Pitches

1. *Simple Drone:* The two drone notes are stationary, although they may change to another drone note at a higher or lower octave.
   Examples: I/nos. 1–16 (both hands together, or homorhythmic), 41, 42, 75 (alternating, or monorhythmic), 49, 50 (independent rhythm in each hand, or polyrhythmic); II/nos. 1–12 (both hands together), 39 (alternating), 43 (independent rhythms in each hand). Certain variations in the basic simple drone structure are possible. They are used in the arrangements throughout the book, but are not mentioned in the "ostinato exercises." Such variations are:
   a. Only one tone of the drone appears, functioning much like a pedal point. Depending on the structure of the melody, either the root or the 5th of the drone is eliminated:

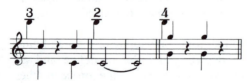

   b. One of the drone pitches, usually the root, is doubled in another octave: Both forms, the incomplete as well as the doubled drone, can be played in the three rhythmic designs demonstrated above.

2. *Simple moving drone*: One of the two drone notes moves to scale degrees other than 1 or 5, usually in stepwise motion.

Examples: I/nos. 17–24 (homorhythmic), 43, 44, 47 (monorhythmic), 51 (poly-rhythmic); II/nos. 13–18 (homorhythmic), 40 (monorhythmic), 44, 46, 47 (poly-rhythmic).

3. *Double moving drone:* Both drone notes are in motion. The movement may be parallel, opposite, or mixed.
Examples: I/nos. 25–40 (homorhythmic), 45, 46, 48 (monorhythmic); II/nos, 19–38 (homorhythmic), 41, 42 (monorhythmic).

4. *Ostinato (pitched)*: Although the "Ostinato Exercises" make a distinction between the three drone types based on whether the drone notes change (simple, simple moving, and double moving), we are not told at what point we should be speaking of an ostinato rather than a drone, because the transition from one to the other is not distinct. In his *Introduction to the Orff-Schulwerk*, Wilhelm Keller states (p. 26):

> When ornamentation and movement have expanded into independent figures we are no longer speaking of a "bordun" (drone), but of a "basso ostinato," in brief, "ostinato." The transition from bordun to ostinato is smooth and continuous: Therefore, there is no clear distinction between the two. In an ostinato the fifth need not always recur. It can be replaced by its complementary interval, the fourth. [This fourth, of course, refers to the inverted drone.]

Taking this ambiguity into account and keeping in mind that some patterns cannot be regarded as belonging to one specific category only, the following examples may be termed ostinati:
I/nos. 45–48, 52–74, 76–88; also 22–24, 27, 31, 34, 36–38. II/nos. 45–96; also 24, 27, 29–38.

Having now completed this overview of the general organization of the "Ostinato Exercises," I will attempt to break down the classifications into subcategories in order to establish a more sequential development. For this purpose I have adopted some terms that are not part of the original text. Let us remember that "development" implies a constant stage of flux. Often, starting points and directions used in developing an ostinato will determine grouping and, with it, terminology. Therefore, we must stay flexible at all times.

PRE-FORMS OF THE PITCHED OSTINATO

The Simple Drone

In Chapter Three we discussed the different types of unpitched ostinato. In that context I suggested that the pulse-beat accompaniment be considered a pre-form of the rhythmic ostinato, because although it has a pattern through recurring strong beats, there is no pattern in the evenness of these beats. The linear development of this pulse can create patterns with longer and shorter durations that we call rhythmic ostinati.

The linear development of the drone pitches into melodic patterns results eventually in "pitched" ostinato forms. The simple, simple moving, and double moving drones can therefore be regarded as pre-forms of the pitched ostinato.

The simple drone in its most basic design is a stationary pulse-beat:

No melodic development occurs in either of its two components. But this does not mean that we cannot create patterns. There are several ways to accomplish this:

1. *Through "relocation"*
   a. Relocating one of the two drone notes:

   Examples: I/nos. 9–12.

   b. Relocating the entire pulse-beat drone in its root position:

   Examples: I/no. 13; II/no. 7. Or by using inversions:

etc.

   Examples: I/nos. 15, 16.

2. *By forming rhythmic patterns*
   a. Stationary drone:

etc.

   Examples: I/nos. 3, 4, 6–8; II/nos. 2, 4–6.

   b. All forms under 1 can, of course, be rhythmically varied. In these cases, patterns are created through both relocation and rhythmic change:

Examples: Relocation of one drone note with rhythmic patterns: I/nos. 9, 11, 12.

Relocation of whole drone in rhythmic patterns: no examples are given in O.S.I.

Relocation using inversions and rhythmic patterns: I/no. 14; II/nos. 8, 10.

3. *By varying the playing technique* (mono- and polyrhythmic patterns)

a. Breaking the drone and playing in regular alternation, pulse-beat only:

Example: I/no. 41. (It is difficult to recognize the broken eighth-notes in no. 42 as a pattern because of the quick tempo.)

b. Broken drone, combined with rhythmic pattern:

No examples are given.

c. Independent rhythmic structure of the two drone notes. Such polyrhythmic patterns, even if only in pulse-beats, are difficult for beginners:

They should be prepared through slapping.

Examples with pulse beats: I/nos. 49, 50, 57; II/no. 43. (In examples using fast note values, such as I/no. 50 and II/no. 43, the actual patterns are, again, only one quarter-note count long.)

Simple rhythmic patterns:

Example: I/no. 58.

Improvisation of Simple Drone Patterns.   By now the infinite variety of patterns has become apparent, even though only the simple drone concept has been used. Improvisation works well in large classes because the patterns are short, and every student can have a turn without waiting too long. By having the whole class repeat each new pattern, the children will experience a broad range of variants. The teacher should set up these improvisational activities in a systematic way, concentrating on one idea only, until most possibilities have been exhausted. Improvisation will be more effective if it is focused. We may too easily skip from one idea to the next without following up on any one in particular. Such an approach might bring "instant success," but it will hardly produce the desired long-term result, that of extending the students' musical vocabulary. The gains are not only musical; after all, analytical thinking and the ability to organize are indispensable for all fields of learning.

In his *Introduction to Music for Children,* Wilhelm Keller states:

> The basic requirement for successful improvisation is *familiarity with materials and tools.* (Emphasis mine.) Playing techniques for the bar instruments must be developed to a sufficient degree so that they present no obstacle to free and spontaneous playing within a given range of tones.

For Schulwerk teachers this statement is of such fundamental importance that it should be framed and hung in a prominent place! Keller's words apply not only to the beginning stages of musical development but to all further levels as well. Each time we plan improvisation activities we must carefully review the possibilities and limitations. Initially, the choices may seem small indeed, but they can be expanded in a variety of ways.

With young beginners whose rhythmic vocabulary does not yet go beyond the four basic building blocks derived from words and names (♩ ♩, ♫ ♩, ♩ ♫, ♩), improvisation of simple drones may focus on aspects other than rhythm alone.

1. *Focus: Homorhythmic and monorhythmic playing.* The four building blocks are reviewed and notated on the blackboard. Whereas the homorhythmic drone will not produce new patterns, the broken drone certainly will. The children are asked to systematically explore each of the four rhythmic patterns. They will discover immediately that the half-note drone takes more than one "house" to be broken:

In order to stick with patterns no longer than two beats, we may want to temporarily set aside this particular pattern. Other possible solutions are:

a. Starting the drone on the root note while keeping the eighth-notes on the same pitch:

b. Starting on the drone fifth while keeping the eighth-notes on the same pitch:

c. Starting on the drone root and alternating on eighth-notes:

d. Starting on the drone fifth and alternating on eighth-notes:

Each new pattern should be played four times by the "inventor" and repeated in the same manner by the whole class. The possibilities under (c) and (d) may well prove too difficult to execute, even though the children may have invented them. Beginners seem to have trouble with patterns that start and end on the same note. Should this be the case, it is better to abandon the patterns rather than frustrate the children with a task they cannot yet handle.

2. *Focus: Combining two different drone patterns.* The improvisations can again by organized into more specific tasks, such as:

a. Combining homorhythmic patterns only, one of which is a pulse:

b. Combining a homorhythmic pulse with a broken pattern:

Here, all the ideas under 1(a) and 1(b), and possibly even those under 1(c) and 1(d), can be used.

c. Combining homorhythmic patterns with a broken drone in pulse-beat:

3. *Focus: Incomplete drones (root in octaves).* Although the idea of playing the drone root in octaves is not difficult to comprehend even for young children, the playing is not as simple because of the distance between the two pitches. Improvising in this new manner should wait until the instrumental skills are sufficiently developed.

After some practice in playing octaves, homorhythmic as well as broken, the improvisations can proceed according to the guidelines under (1). When combining two different drone patterns as under (2), it is musically more rewarding to keep to the complete drone in one of the two parts. The number of possible pattern formations doubles when the two parts are exchanged and placed above or below one another, respectively. Let me demonstrate this only with the first idea, the combination of homorhythmic patterns, one of which is in pulse-beat:

The foregoing suggestions are more than enough to keep a beginner's class of young children busy improvising simple drones for at least a year. Older students will naturally move faster. Whatever the age, though, I have learned to allow enough time for these initial steps in improvisation so that the children may understand better how the creative process functions.

The introduction of triple meter allows for a greater variety of rhythmic patterns. As a starter, the students might be asked to subdivide one of the three pulses of a homorhythmic drone. There are three possible patterns:

Next, two pulse-beats are subdivided, which results in another three patterns:

Now, we augment one of the pulse-beats:

Finally, the quarter-notes can be subdivided again:

There are now ten patterns, which, at some later time, may be turned into mono-rhythmic or broken drones.

Another improvisation may center around the use of three drone pitches:

The children may first explore the different ways in which the pitches can follow each other:

Then, the already familiar patterns with subdivisions and augmentations can be explored again.

The inversions of drones may become the focus of yet another improvisation. Both homorhythmic and monorhythmic patterns can be created.

In combined duple meter (quadruple meter), pattern formations multiply enormously and it is no longer feasible to explore every single possibility. By this time, though, it should no longer be necessary to lead the children through the same processes again.

In the first few years all improvisations should be done directly on the instruments, although the rhythmic patterns collected can be notated on the blackboard for referral. Sometime during the fourth grade, just before introducing the diatonic scale, I usually plan a comprehensive review of all drone types learned so far (including simple moving). Now the children begin to write their own patterns. As a new study I include simple forms of polyrhythmic drones.

The foregoing exercises find their ultimate application in the combination of melody and accompaniment. The improvisations include creating tunes to a given drone as well as finding drone patterns to an existing melody. From the beginning, emphasis should be placed on the rhythmic independence of one from the other.

The Simple Moving Drone

The moving drone brings us a step closer to pitched ostinato. The pattern of the moving drone is formed through a repetitive, short melodic progression by one of its components (see p. 128). The German equivalent, "schweifender Bordun," means "wandering" or "straying drone"; the Canadian version (by Doreen Hall and Arnold Walter) is "swinging bordun."

In the beginning, the moving part of the drone ventures no further than to a neighboring note. If this seems an insignificant developmental step, let us for a moment consider its implications:

As discussed earlier, the simple drone establishes the tonal center and at the same time introduces the most fundamental of all chordal structures, the tonic triad:

When one of the drone notes wanders off to a neighboring pitch, a change in harmony occurs. To be sure, such harmonic changes are only "side effects" of a melodic pattern; furthermore, in pentatonic they indeed are limited. Nevertheless, they represent the first step into the world of changing harmony.

Upper Drone Note Moving. In pentatonic, only two complete triads can be formed, C major and A minor, or to be more general, the triads of the tonic and of the submediant:

In spite of their different modal character, they are closely related, as they share two of their three pitches. (Sometimes, the submediant triad is called the parallel of the tonic triad; in harmony classes we learn that it can be used as a substitute for the tonic triad under certain circumstances—for example, in the chord progression I–vi–IV, or the deceptive cadence V–vi.) The drone fifth can accomplish the change from C major to A minor by merely stepping up to the 6th scale degree:

The example shows us, in effect, a tonic triad in root position followed by a submediant triad in first inversion.

More expansive movement possibilities of the drone fifth to nearby pitches lead back into the components of the tonic triad:

Improvisation of different moving drone patterns should again be structured carefully, making sure that the children follow one idea at a time. For example, the teacher will suggest a basic simple moving pattern, such as:

He or she might then pose the question: "How many different rhythmic patterns can you find by (a) playing both hands together at the same time? (b) breaking the drone? and (c) giving each hand a different pulse rhythm?" If the class has well-developed playing skills, the different pulses may be developed further into rhythmic patterns. As an alternative to having the whole class create together, small groups may work independently. After a reasonable period of experimentation, each group shows the patterns it was able to produce.

Aside from moving drones in root position, inverted forms should also be used as a basis for exploration and improvisation.

By doubling the note values of the first basic example, the possibilities in each category increase substantially because more rhythmic variations can be created:

Similar improvisations should be set up in triple meter also. The teacher, of course, must be well prepared, having worked through all possible variations in advance, in order to be of assistance to the children when they get stuck.

Considering the intervallic relationship between the upper moving drone note (5–6) and the melody, we find that the 6th scale degree is consonant with almost all the other pentatonic pitches. Only two dissonant intervals can occur, the major second (G–A) and its inversion, the minor seventh (A–G). These two dissonances are a characteristic sound in pentatonic; they cannot, and should not, be avoided.

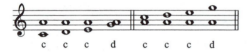

Improvisations of melodies over the simple moving bordun 5–6 are, therefore, not difficult. Parallel octaves, open as well as delayed, will occur frequently, especially when a chant formula is used:

There is no rule in elemental music forbidding parallels in improvisation. Such rules would stifle the creative flow; besides, they are meaningless to a beginning student, regardless of age. At a later developmental stage, when premeditated composition is practiced as another form of creative activity, such considerations perhaps may be taken into account.

Lower Drone Note Moving.   Matters are somewhat different when the drone root moves to the neighboring 2nd scale degree. Harmonically, this move cannot result in another complete triad (with melody), although it suggests a dominant (without third) in second inversion:

For this reason, it can have a mildly cadential effect when used to harmonize melodies that, though anhemitonic, are harmonically conceived. In my opinion, such melodies should not be part of the initial repertoire, as they presume more sophistication than the children possess in the early stages (see also Chapter 8).

In determining the relationship of the supertonic to the remaining tones of the pentatonic scale, we discern that the 2nd scale degree, "squeezed" between two other pitches, is not as compatible as the 6th, since it cannot help but be discordant with its neighbors. Within the pentatonic octave, it can form consonant intervals only with two notes:

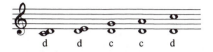

I explain consonant and dissonant intervals to my children by comparing them with a real-life situation: More disagreements erupt between people who live in crowded quarters than between those who have ample space around them. In musical terms, this lack of "living space" means that the supertonic creates frequent dissonances when its next-door neighbors appear as melody notes. For instance, in a call melody the interval of the fifth will be followed consistently by the second:

There is nothing intrinsically wrong with dissonances. We do not want to impose on the students our standards, which were acquired largely by accepting rules and working within their confines. The creative process is different. It consists of helping the children to find alternatives and make choices. These choices depend entirely on their experiences in discriminative hearing.

Here is an exercise for improving discriminative hearing: The call melody is tried out with each of the simple moving drone patterns, 5 moving to 6 and root moving to 2. The rhythm is confined to the use of pulse-beats:

Both melody and accompaniment are played on instruments of the same family and pitch—for example, two alto xylophones or two soprano xylophones—because the intervals will thus appear in their basic, close position and be easier to hear. The children are asked to listen carefully and to make a choice as to which pattern sounds better to them. Many, although certainly not all, will opt for the upper drone note moving. The teacher then demonstrates what actually happens between the melody and the accompaniment—how the E of the tune sounds at the same time as the A or the D of the moving drone, and how the distance between the two pitches affects their sound. Other intervallic relationships within the anhemitonic pentachord or hexachord are now examined and evaluated by placing each scale degree against all the other pitches:

Although this exploration need not become a formal study of intervals, it leads to a better awareness and discrimination of simultaneously sounding pitches.

Next, going back to the original song, the teacher might ask: "Is there any way in which we can allow the drone root to 'go for a walk' without colliding with the E in the melody?" The answer is, "Yes, there is more than one way." It can, for example, walk slower:

a.

Or, it can walk quickly, barely touching the D:

b.

c.

As always, the patterns found should also be tried in inversion.

The first time around, the children will not come up with these answers. But once they understand that there are alternatives and on what basis they are chosen, then they will be able to find their own solutions.

The exploration can be carried further in a different direction. Instead of making changes in the original drone pattern, we can widen the space between melody and accompaniment. The melody can be played an octave higher, or the accompaniment an octave lower, by using different instruments. A glockenspiel for the melody not only places it in a higher register but also changes the sound texture. These possibilities help to soften the somewhat harsh sound of the dissonance, although they do not eliminate it altogether. The insight gained from such explorations will help the students to understand the importance of instrumentation and scoring.

The moving drone root is apt to commit another "faux pas" in the eyes of traditionally trained musicians. When used with the chant, or with a tune containing the chant formula, it easily produces parallel fifths, either open or delayed:

Once again, there is no way to convince a child of the undesirability of parallels. One should distinguish between the musical efforts of a child and those of a trained musician; the same standards must not be applied to both.

All in all, the movement of the drone root is not as flexible as that of the drone fifth because it must be used with more discrimination. In the first few years of Orff-Schulwerk training, the children cannot be expected to adapt accompaniment patterns to melody notes, as vertical conceptualization of pitches develops later and only after horizontal pitch recognition is well established. For this reason the foregoing activities are not meant for beginners. The teacher should limit the use of this particular simple moving drone to patterns in which the supertonic note is a passing tone, appearing only on unaccented beats (see Chapter 7 for more information). The same applies to the use of double moving drones.

Double Moving Drones

When both drone notes are set in motion, we speak of a *double moving drone*. In its simplest form, the root and fifth step up to the next higher pitches. (For those not familiar with elemental music, it should be pointed out that parallels between the two drone notes are a characteristic compositional device. After all, parallelism is an elemental idea and has occurred widely in the global history of man's music.)

As with the simple moving drone, 1–2, the change of pitches results in a new triadic embryo, that of the supertonic triad without the third. Unlike the simple moving drone, the new implied harmony has no note in common with the tonic triad because both notes have moved up. Both pitches are dissonant with all three other pitches of the pentatonic scale, and therefore "sound collisions" cannot be avoided:

They are, in fact, part of the elemental sound picture; according to Wilhelm Keller, they "add flavor and intensity."[3] This does not mean, however, that they should be used indiscriminately.

[3] *Introduction to Music for Children*, p. 26.

If we carry on the ascending movement of the drone through the five pitches of the pentatonic scale, we will end up with five intervals: (1) the drone fifth, representing the tonic triad; (2) the supertonic fifth, representing the supertonic triad; (3) the interval of a sixth built on the 3rd scale note, which may be part of the tonic triad in first inversion or part of the submediant triad in second inversion; (4) a fifth built on the 5th scale note, belonging to the dominant triad; and (5) the submediant fifth, representing the submediant triad. The supertonic and the dominant triad will always stay incomplete in pentatonic.

We might argue that talking about triads makes little sense at the pentatonic stage. The argument is justifiable as far as it concerns our pupils, whose musical understanding grows only gradually. For the teacher, on the other hand, the entire developmental sequence must be clear; he or she must be able to recognize the origins of concepts in order to properly sequence their unfolding, step by step. Triads do not pop up all of a sudden; they are the result of an evolutionary process like everything else. That process begins the moment melody is combined with pitched accompaniment. For a long time, triads do not reveal themselves as such because they are for the most part embryonic—that is, they are mere intervals; and in accompaniment they have no function except as part of a pattern. Only the trained ear and mind are able to fill in missing tones and foretell future function. The untrained ear hears intervallic relationships and makes judgments on the basis of sound alone.

Double moving drones are difficult for two reasons: (1) they presuppose a fair amount of knowledge of harmonic concepts (unless used as "double passing tones"), and (2) they are difficult to play. Except for the basic move from tonic to supertonic (in root as well as in inversion), longer patterns moving farther away result in intervallic changes, even in parallel motion. In moving from an opposite direction, the two initial pitches must be far enough apart to allow for ample moving space inward (or vice versa). And finally, parallel and contrary motion combined is also a challenge to play.

In improvising double moving drone patterns, the students themselves are the best indicators of what they can handle at a given time. I have found that if children are interested in a project, they will take up a challenge and practice until they have mastered it. For the most part, however, such exercises are suited for older, more advanced children. Even then the improvisations must be structured carefully so that the essential not be lost among the maze of possible pattern formations. This is probably why the examples of double moving drones in the book are kept very simple rhythmically. Their structure and development follow certain harmonic patterns which indicate possibilities for improvisation without spelling them out. The teacher should analyze them carefully so that he or she can map out procedures and plan the extent of an improvisation.

In the first group of examples, three intervals among the possible five are singled out. The initial pattern, no. 25, reveals the basic formula:

I   ii   I   ii

By extending the parallel motion another step up, the interval of a sixth is reached. The formula may now be understood in harmonic terms as either I–ii–I–ii or I–ii–vi–ii.

I   ii   I (vi)   ii

The formula is demonstrated in both parallel and opposing motion.

As a first improvisation with double moving drone, only the parallel concept should be introduced and explored.

Exploration.   Examples nos. 26–28 show several basic versions of parallel movement, although not all:

1.   Starting with the drone fifth (no. 26);

2.   Same pattern inverted (no. 27):

3.   Intervals reversed, so that the sixth appears at the beginning and the drone fifth in the middle of the pattern (no. 28):[4]

4.   Same pattern inverted:

There are now enough patterns to use as "raw material." In the next stages of the improvisation these basic patterns will be varied.

At first, only simple rhythmic changes should be created. Since this idea is already familiar to the students from many previous improvisations, it is not

----

[4] An apparent printing mistake in pattern no. 28: D appears instead of C on the first count in the upper part.

necessary to go through all rhythmic possibilities. A few examples will do, such as ♩ ♩ ♫ ♩ or ♩ ♫ ♩ ♩. Whereas here one of the intervals will be played twice (because one beat is subdivided), in a rhythmic motif such as ♩ ♩ ♩ or ♩ ♩ ♩ one of the intervals must be eliminated.

Triple meter should be tried also. In a simple pulse-beat pattern, one of the intervals must again be dropped:

In order to fit all four intervals into three beats, eighth-notes must be used:

Two-measure patterns can be created by lengthening some of the note values:

(Such improvisations, aimed at "problem-solving," further the thought process.)

The next steps need not follow immediately; I will mention them here only in order to give the reader a complete picture of the possibilities.

5. The basic patterns can be played broken in a continuous eighth-note motion:

6. Lastly, polyrhythmic patterns may be tried:

Another time, improvisations should focus on the idea of contrary movement. Again, the possibilities must be studied beforehand by the teacher. The examples

I/nos. 29 and 30 (p. 82) offer some suggestions regarding the formula used so far, I–ii–I–ii. No. 31 is a I–I–vi–I progression. Since all preceding examples of double moving drones are based on a I–ii progression, I am inclined to think that there might be a printing mistake in that the third beat of the measure should read:

This change would also bring the movement of the upper voice parts in line with the other examples: all pitches, lower and upper, move to the closest note possible. There are no skips other than those dictated by the absence of the half steps:

In contrasting movement patterns, the initial interval must be spaced far apart. Instead of the drone fifth, we now find octaves on the tonic note (no. 29) or tenths (nos. 30 and 31). Each of the three examples can be varied to some degree. As before, intervals can succeed each other in different orders:

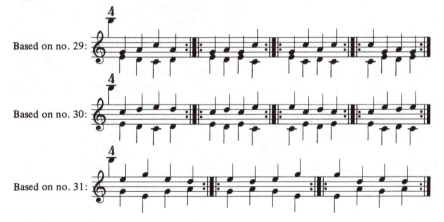

The improvisation of drones must never become an end in itself. It is an important preparatory step toward the goal of combining melody and accompaniment. Creative activities like the ones described provide valuable ear training. The students cannot help but absorb and internalize the sounds of the few intervals with which they have been working so intensively. This increased awareness and sensitivity will aid them when melody is added to the double moving drones.

In making up tunes over double moving drone patterns, we must remember that dissonances play a different role in pentatonic music than in diatonic. In pentatonic music they are not carefully prepared, nor are they carefully resolved, since there are not enough tones in the pentatonic scale to always move stepwise, and because patterns are used rather than harmonization. Therefore, dissonances simply appear and disappear; like hit-and-run drivers, they cause a collision and then leave the scene of the accident without explanation. There is not much we can do but try to use them with some degree of discrimination. The ability to do so will increase as more tones are added to the scale and as elemental harmonization begins to assert itself.

When adding melody to double moving drones, patterns should be selected that keep the clashes to a minimum. In the three-interval pattern used before, only the fifth built on the supertonic was somewhat incompatible. By delegating it to weak beats, the dissonances will be less frequent and only fleeting:

The children should also try their hands at finding drone patterns to given tunes. Here, it is helpful to add the visual picture to the sound. The melody can be written on the blackboard and analyzed as to form and melodic content. Then different drones can be tried out, and choices can be made by general consensus.

The exercise should not stop at this point. A discussion should follow concerning the reasons why certain patterns were chosen above others. This helps to bring to the conscious mind what the unconscious already knows, which results in learning.

We now return to the "Ostinato Exercises" Orff-Schulwerk I (p. 82) for a look at the remaining double moving drone patterns.

Examples nos. 32–35 introduce a new formation of three intervals, this one substituting the fifth built on the 5th scale degree for the one built on the supertonic note:

This combination is more difficult to work with for several reasons. First, because of its placement in the scale, it again does not lend itself to simple parallel or opposite motion in which each hand executes the same step or skip. The only exception is the descending pattern:

Second, in an ascending simple parallel movement the cadencing effect of a I–I (vi)–V–I progression becomes apparent:

It would be a mistake to dismiss such patterns immediately on the grounds that cadencing is not part of the pentatonic sound picture, since in the real world of pentatonic children's songs and folksongs we will find that many tunes are oriented toward a cadence (see Chapter 8). For this reason such double moving drones may be indispensable when the time comes; they lead toward cadential hearing, yet they remain elemental in that they are ostinato patterns and will not consistently adapt to the tunes.

The effect of a continuous I–V–I progression is weakened by inserting the submediant A-minor sound at least once between the intervals suggesting the tonic and dominant. (Within a four-beat pattern, not every I–V can have another interval interpolated.) Prior to any improvisation, the examples in the book should be analyzed in regard to the placement of the three intervals representing I, vi, and V, or their implied substitutes. Nos. 32 and 33 are based on a I–V–vi–V succession; no. 34 on I–vi–V–vi (I); no. 35 on I–V–vi–I. In all these patterns the submediant is used in such a way that it cannot be mistaken for the tonic interval:

In other words, the note A, together with C or E, is present at least once within a pattern, thus preventing it from becoming a mere I–V–I cadence. The following example may clarify this point:

In the first version, the I–V–vi–V pattern is clearly established, whereas it is questionable whether the corresponding interval in the second version (third count) would be interpreted by the ear as belonging to the submediant.

The last examples touch upon more possibilities. Numbers 37 and 38 begin with a submediant rather than a tonic interval. Since the oscillation between major and minor is characteristic of the pentatonic mode, such formulas are perfectly legitimate. In a number of examples an octave G occurs, leaving open an interpretation as to its harmonic affiliation. And finally, nos. 36 and 39 once more make use of the supertonic interval, revealing a I–ii–I–V and a I–ii–I–I formula, respectively.

Section II of the "Ostinato Exercises" (p. 84) shows double moving drones in triple meter, which can be analyzed in the same manner. Since all the patterns are two measures long, more extended harmonic formulas are possible. Even though most of them are based on intervals belonging to just three different scale degrees, some make use of four (nos. 25, 27, 36).

In conclusion I would ask the reader not to be discouraged by the apparent deluge of possibilities, but to keep in mind that with these examples the whole range of double moving drones is presented, and that many of the formulas cannot be used until a much later stage. This will become clear when the song arrangements and instrumental pieces of Orff-Schulwerk I are discussed in another chapter. The more complex forms of double moving drones can be fully utilized only when harmonic concepts are finally introduced through the study of triads.

PITCHED OSTINATO

Transitional Patterns

So far a discussion of "pitched ostinato" as a specific category has been avoided, although many of the examples analyzed obviously belong to that group of ostinati as defined by Wilhelm Keller (see page 129). I have not used the term because I want to make sure that the reader understands the unbroken developmental process leading from the drone to the ostinato. If this is clear, the vague borderlines between the two and a flexible terminology will not make us uncomfortable.

In my work with children I have found the need to make some allowances in regard to terminology anyway, especially for those patterns which are transitional between drone and ostinato. Let me illustrate my point.

From early on, my students are familiar with the practice of "relocating" a simple drone through inversion (see p. 130). When, some time later, simple *moving* drones are improvised, inverted patterns are inevitably created also. If one student has invented patterns such as those shown in (a) below, another one will certainly turn them, as in (b) around:

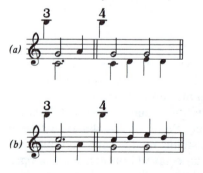

For this reason, to call the first version a simple moving drone and the other one an ostinato does not make much sense to the children. They see the second pattern for what it really is, a drone that has been inverted, and this is exactly what we call such patterns. The first two examples are simple moving drones, one moving 5–6, the other 1–2–3; the next two examples are *inverted simple moving drones*, moving 5–6 and 1–2–3, respectively (the root now on top and the fifth now the lower pitch). This terminology has the advantage of explaining the evolutionary process. The concept of intervals and their inversions is thus seen, experienced, and understood.

Double moving drones are named in the same way: As long as the complete drone occurs in the pattern, whether in root position or inverted, the students refer to it as a double moving drone pattern. However, once the drone is no longer complete because one of its components has been replaced by either the third or the tonic note, then the term ostinato is applied.

This is one way of dealing with terminology of transitional patterns; there are other possibilities, no doubt. Terminology can be flexible as long as the transitional nature of the patterns is clearly understood.

Homophonic and Polyphonic Ostinato

In this chapter I have spoken of the developmental stages in part-music and demonstrated sequential development through improvisation by moving from the pre-forms of pitched ostinati—the drones—to the transitional patterns. I also explained that the elemental patterns of accompaniment in Orff-Schulwerk exemplify counterparts in miniature of the two basic textures in all part-music, homophony and polyphony.

The homophonic concept is evident in the double moving drones and their transitional forms. All of these are paraphonic, and the drone fifth or its complement, the fourth, is always present. In an ostinato these intervals need not show up. This happens frequently when diaphonic motion of the two parts is used or when both paraphonic and diaphonic movement occur within a pattern. The basically homophonic texture is preserved even in the presence of rhythmic changes (see pp. 143–44). In order to distinguish such ostinati, I call them *homophonic ostinati*. In this group I count all homorhythmic patterns that have their origin in the double moving drone (including diaphonic and mixed patterns), and those in which the two components are broken in the simplest manner so that the underlying intervals are still clearly recognizable (for example, I/nos. 46–48, II/nos. 41, 42).

There are other patterns which I call *polyphonic ostinati*. Their beginnings may be found in the simple polyrhythmic drone, in which the two components are rhythmically independent. When to this independent rhythmic movement is added independent melodic movement of the two parts, simple polyphonic patterns evolve. The development is demonstrated sequentially in several examples on page 83 of Orff-Schulwerk I: no. 50, a simple polyrhythmic drone; no. 51, a simple moving, polyrhythmic drone, developed from the former; and no. 52, a polyphonic ostinato. In this last example both drone notes are now in melodic movement, retaining the same rhythmic patterns as the previous examples. One might argue that the drone fifth is still present on the very first count and that, therefore, the pattern is a "double moving, polyrhythmic drone with both parallel and opposing motion." This is, of course, correct, but the reader will agree with me that such a description is rather cumbersome.

In the next four examples, more melodic possibilities based on the same rhythmic design are explored.

Numbers 58–60 follow a different polyrhythmic pattern, which is first shown as a simple drone (no. 58) before it is developed into a polyphonic ostinato. The rhythmic figure is imitative, and the same idea is applied to the melodic motif in no. 60. The next example (no. 61) shows the same alternation of parts with a different rhythmic structure.

The ostinati in triple meter (II/ nos. 45–63) illustrate similar developments: no. 45, although shown in two measures, is actually only a one-measure polyphonic ostinato; nos. 46 and 47 are still simple moving drones, as one of the drone notes is kept stationary throughout the patterns (no. 46 again, only a three-beat pattern); but in no. 48 both parts move while the rhythmic structure is the same as before.

In general, the development toward more difficult patterns begins with the rhythmic design. Initially, the rhythm of one part is restricted to pulse-beats, whereas the other part moves in freer rhythms:

Next, the two voices alternate using the same very simple rhythmic design:

In the following two examples, each part has its own uncomplicated one-measure rhythmic pattern (the melodic motif, though, is two measures long):

The rhythmic pattern extends through the full two measures in nos. 57 and 58:

Finally, a more complex polyrhythmic design is demonstrated with no. 61:

Improvisation of polyphonic ostinati presupposes a fair amount of playing skill; for this reason alone, it cannot be a beginner's activity. When the time comes, though, the analysis of the rhythmic structure of the polyphonic ostinato examples will be helpful in the planning of improvisations in which polyrhythmic patterns are used as a starting point.

In every example but one (no. 49), tonic-triad pitches are in evidence on the strong beats of the measure. Thus, it is apparent how a polyphonic texture seems to lend complexity to even the simplest of harmonic designs. (Would that in our student days we could have learned to manipulate drones and tonic triads in this manner before being confronted with a bewildering assortment of chords, and the rules for using them!)

In their melodic interplay the two voices move frequently in contrary motion and stepwise. Leaps occur only on the natural gaps of the pentatonic, and between the drone pitches. Of the two possible dissonant intervals (second and seventh), only the seventh is found occasionally.

All these observations are guidelines for setting up improvisations. We have established three important factors in polyphonic ostinati: (1) the rhythmic structure, (2) harmonic simplicity, and (3) melodic movement of the two parts. We may want to start with polyrhythmic patterns in triple meter because they are long enough to express a melodic idea but short enough to keep it uncomplicated. The beginning interval, consisting of components of the tonic triad, is predetermined by the teacher in order to set the harmonic foundation. (Later, the students will be able to decide for themselves.) The movement possibilities of the two parts, whether in contrary or parallel motion, depend on the initial interval as well as the rhythmic pattern.

Examples

1. A simple polyrhythmic pattern in triple meter.

Starting on the drone fifth:

Starting on the octave:

[5]This pattern will produce parallel octaves when repeated.

Starting on the third E–G:

Starting on the third C–E:

Starting on the sixth E–C:

The examples show that with simple polyrhythmic patterns leaps cannot be avoided. To do so would allow for very few variations in pattern formation.

2. With longer rhythmic patterns it is helpful to set a motif in one part and improvise to it with the other voice. When no more ideas can be developed, the motif of the first part can be changed.

Polyrhythmic pattern in $\frac{4}{4}$

Starting on a drone fifth, with a melodic motif built on the root note:

The melodic motif is changed:

At this point, another starting interval, such as the octave, might be introduced.

When still longer and more difficult rhythmic patterns are used, it is not necessary to go through the complete sequence each time an improvisation is planned. It is much better to select a single starting interval that allows for many possibilities and to use it throughout the entire improvisation. But the teacher needs to think through these possibilities beforehand.

Another approach in developing polyphonic ostinati is to use homophonic patterns as the basis, and to create polyphonic designs through embellishment. The exercise is not easy, and the teacher must be sure to choose patterns that allow for independent melodic development of one or both parts. One should begin by simply filling small skips with passing notes in one voice only:

Example I/no. 31

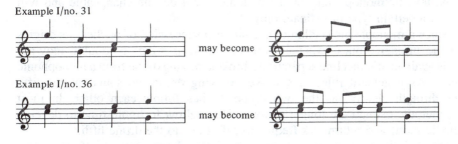

Example I/no. 36

may become

Then, the two parts may alternate in the embellishing:

Example I, no. 36, continued

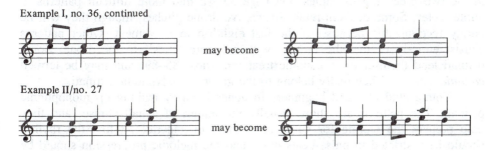

may become

Example II/no. 27

may become

In order to make longer embellishments possible, the teacher can prepare his or her own basic patterns or reduce polyphonic patterns from the book to homophonic skeletons. Naturally, the teacher should not expect the students to come up with the same solutions as the examples from which the basic patterns were derived.

For successful improvisations of melodies to given ostinati, one basic rule must be observed: The more complex the accompaniment, the simpler the tune; the more elaborate the melody, the simpler the accompaniment. (See also Orff-Schulwerk I, p. 142, "Instructions and Notes.")

The study of homophonic and polyphonic ostinati is an advanced activity for experienced students. In all likelihood, it will take place when the diatonic scale has already been introduced. However, there is nothing wrong in coming back to pentatonic; learning is at its best when it is combined with a review of already familiar material. Furthermore, improvisation of complex ostinato forms is made easier by working in pentatonic first. I would like to stress, though, that improvisation with advanced concepts must be prepared in the elementary levels through a thorough study of the basic drone concepts.

The Melodic Ostinato (Monophonic)

The very first and simplest ostinati belong in a category all by themselves, since they represent simply a melodic line or, more precisely, a melodic motif. In order to be consistent we may speak of "monophonic ostinati." Some may prefer the term "melodic ostinati"; however, in the Canadian edition of Orff-Schulwerk this term is used to designate *all* pitched accompaniment. In my discussion the terms "monophonic" and "melodic" will be interchangeable and will represent a certain type of ostinato only.

Since a monophonic (melodic) ostinato is a succession of pitches, its origins lie in the broken drones, whether simple, simple moving, or double moving. There is again no distinct line separating a broken moving drone from a monophonic ostinato. As a general rule, in a broken moving drone the sound of the fifth comes through clearly, as the two drone pitches follow each other. In most cases, melodic ostinati are longer patterns which allow for more time to develop a melodic motif and return less frequently, if at all, to the drone fifth.

Orff-Schulwerk I provides a number of melodic ostinati (p. 85, nos. 66–75 and 79–84) that clearly show their derivation from the broken moving drones in the two preceding examples. On page 83 we find more difficult patterns in duple meter. Some of them retain successive drone pitches, though they will be barely recognizable because of the fast eighth-note movement. Other patterns consist entirely of melodic motifs, with no more "ties" to the drone. Some ostinati lend themselves to canonic treatment (nos. 85–89) and may be termed *canonic ostinati*. They really belong to the group of polyphonic ostinati.

Young students, and beginners in general, enjoy making up monophonic ostinati. The patterns are short, usually the length of a half-phrase, and they help prepare the feeling for small form units in general. At first the rhythm should be restricted to pulse-beats only, and the melodic progression should be smooth and mostly stepwise. The patterns should begin on one of the drone pitches; later the third can be included as a starting point. In order to achieve melodic flow, I allow the motifs to be half of a phrase length (two measures in $\frac{2}{\rho}$ and $\frac{3}{\rho}$, one measure in $\frac{4}{\rho}$). Once subdivisions of the pulse are used (which means more pitches per measure), the patterns could possibly be shortened, at least in triple meter. Rhythmic patterns obtained through improvisation may again provide the basis for creating melodic ostinati. A simple stationary drone or a pedal point on the tonic note will help to retain the feeling for tonality.

The following improvisation sequences provide materials for several years. It must be kept in mind that these exercises, like all drone and ostinato improvisations, should include practice in the La-mode (A-pattern) as well as in transpositions of both the Do- and La-modes. (For more information on pentatonic modes, see Chapters 5 and 8.)

1. Mostly quarter-notes (pulse)

a. starting on the root

b. starting on the fifth

c. starting on the third

2. Subdivisions with two eighth-notes

3. Including longer note values

Aside from these few examples, many more patterns are possible, especially once the students' rhythmic knowledge goes beyond the most basic note values.

The improvisation of monophonic ostinati does not require great skill. The challenge arises when the ostinato is combined with another moving voice, such as a moving drone, a second ostinato, or a tune. In order to achieve a polyphonic texture, contrast in the rhythmic and melodic movement of the two parts is necessary:

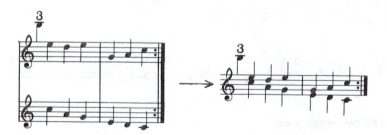

It is also possible to create two contrasting melodic lines (by two players) with the same rhythmic structure. In this case, the two parts, viewed as one, turn out to be a homophonic ostinato:

Such exercises provide good training for hearing intervals, and they lay a foundation for advanced improvisation of homophonic and polyphonic ostinati.

The exercises in Orff-Schulwerk I on pages 86–87, Sections III and IV, demonstrate many possibilities combining the various forms of drone and ostinato. They are also an indication of Orff and Keetman's belief that improvisation of accompaniment patterns in themselves is as important as the creation of melodies and of entire pieces or song arrangements.

Layered Ostinati

In her book *Elementaria*, Gunild Keetman acquaints us with an intriguing improvisational device that she calls "layered ostinati" ("geschichtete Ostinati"). Here many different patterns are stacked on top of each other to form a large "carpet" of sound. As one instrument after another enters, the dynamics build up in a steady crescendo, and may decrease in the same manner by having the instruments drop out gradually.

Layered ostinati of all degrees of difficulty are wonderfully effective in dramatic play and poetry. They can describe moods and feelings as well as underline actions. Because they are short patterns there are no timing problems, and they can be easily coordinated with the dramatic action.

DRONE PATTERNS WITH ADDED THIRD

The last examples of the "Ostinato Exercises for Tuned Percussion Instruments" suggest yet another idea: using the third of the tonic triad to fill in simple and double moving drones. This gives a rich chordal sound, swinging between the tonic and submediant triads. No harmonic function is implied by these triads; in fact, they need not even be viewed as triads, since for the children they are merely inverted moving drones with an added third. (See examples on page 83, nos. 89–91 and 93–96, and on page 85, nos. 90–95.)

SUMMARY

Part-music is not an invention of Western music culture. It has existed, and is still present, in various styles and degrees of complexity in many parts of the world.

In Orff-Schulwerk, the idea of coexisting pitches is used in such a way as to lay the foundation for the Western concept of harmony. Melody is supported by other pitches that establish a tonal and harmonic basis. The accompaniment consists of repetitive patterns, loosely termed ostinati.

The rhythmic relationship between the two basic pitches of these patterns (1st and 5th scale degrees) contains the germ cells of all musical texture, *monophonic*, *homophonic*, and *polyphonic*.

Harmonic awareness begins with the tonic triad. The *simple drone*, or *bordun*, in all its possible variations represents the tonic triad, even though incomplete. Until our students have developed vertical pitch perception, all melodies to be accompanied must be chosen to conform to this harmony.

The *simple moving drone* implies certain harmony changes, depending on which of the two pitches moves. However, as long as the movement occurs only on weak beats of the measure, no harmonic change is felt and the tonic-triad sound still prevails. For this reason it is possible to improvise and to use for accompaniment rather sophisticated patterns, provided the students understand their design and can play them.

The *double moving drone* and its variants is the most complex of the three bordun types. Its harmonic implications are far-reaching and can be understood only by a teacher trained in traditional harmony and by advanced students. Double moving drones should be confined to the simplest patterns (most easily played in inversion), in which the movement occurs on unaccented beats of the measure.

Since the "Ostinato Exercises for Tuned Percussion Instruments" in Orff-Schulwerk I do not supply us with a distinction between bordun and "non-bordun," I have adopted a terminology that classifies the drone types as *pre-forms* of the ostinato and the non-bordun types as *pitched ostinati* (even though the term ostinato is all-inclusive in a general sense). Since there is no distinctive borderline between the two, I designate the patterns that might be classified under either of the two categories as *transitional*.

In the pitched ostinato the ties to the two drone pitches are no longer recognizable. Because the three types of pitched ostinato involve melodic movement in all of their parts, the suffix "-rhythmic," as used with drones, is now replaced with the suffix "-phonic"—that is, *homophonic*, *monophonic* (melodic), and *polyphonic* (ostinato).

Other developments mentioned in this chapter, such as *layered ostinati* and filling the third of the drone, are not of great significance, but rather offer still more possibilities of varying and enriching the accompaniment.

I hope it has become apparent to the reader that the drone and ostinato exercises are of fundamental importance and must not be taken lightly or glossed over. Furthermore, creative and individual expression can take place only when there is a wealth of vocabulary; otherwise musical expression will remain limited to the use of a few stereotyped formulas.

7

SONGS AND INSTRUMENTAL PIECES IN ORFF-SCHULWERK I

GENERAL CONSIDERATIONS

We have mentioned earlier that the arrangements in the Orff-Schulwerk books should be considered illustrations of the elemental style rather than "teaching pieces." Elemental music is the *process* of making music, of improvising and creating. "Final" versions exist only insofar as the musical abilities of the children and the teacher set certain limitations. All "final" products are temporary because they leave open the possibility for change and for further development.

It is with this in mind that we should approach the study of the Orff-Schulwerk literature. The models we see in the books are the products of creative processes whose beginnings we must retrace. Analysis will help us to observe how musical concepts are applied and in turn will enable us to build sequence into the process.

Musical growth takes many years. Our students are not expected to play the music as it is set down in the book, nor are they expected to improvise on the same level of sophistication. But there would have been little reason for Orff and Kettman to write a whole volume of songs and instrumental pieces with just the simplest of drone accompaniment. They intended that such rudimentary pieces would be created by the teacher and the students themselves as part of the process. (See also Chapter 4, pp. 99–100.)

The published settings are important to the teacher because they demonstrate the entire development and the many possibilities of elemental composition techniques. The teacher who ignores Volume I will have a difficult time grasping the full meaning of elemental music and doing justice to Orff-Schulwerk.

At the same time, the children should be given opportunities to study and play selections from the books. As the title states, the music was created for them, and there are no better or more beautiful examples from which to learn than those written by the masters. We would be doing a great disservice to our students if we were to withhold the music from them altogether. The following analysis of the melodic and harmonic aspects of the songs and instrumental pieces will serve a twofold purpose: to suggest to the teacher how the pieces may be approached and ordered in a classroom sequence, and to suggest how existing models can be simplified. By understanding a composition it is often possible to come up with an easier version without sacrificing the essence of the original.

Let us begin by identifying some of the difficulties in Volume I that a beginning student will not be able to cope with successfully.

1. The sequential development of implied harmonic changes from simple drones to complex patterns illustrated in the "Ostinato Exercises" is not adhered to in the musical settings (for example, p. 4, no. 3b,c). In this area the teacher will have to make drastic changes, especially in the beginning, in order to lay a firm foundation for harmonic development.

2. Advanced playing techniques in many ostinati require a high degree of small-muscle control and coordination. Examples are: quickly repeated notes (p. 4, no. 3c, alto glockenspiel); continuous, fast pulse-beat in homorhythmic and monorhythmic patterns (p. 5, no. 4a); polyrhythmic patterns (p. 4, no. 3b); and double moving drones with intervallic changes (p. 7, no. 6, soprano xylophone). Difficult ostinati can be simplified while still maintaining the implied harmony changes.

3. Large instrumentations are more difficult to correlate. The ability to adjust one's own part to the rest of the ensemble presupposes rhythmic assurance and advanced listening skills, since the ear must be able to follow several simultaneous sounds. The advisability of reducing a large instrumentation depends on the piece. To an extent, the exuberance and excitement of some arrangements are created by the large body of sound. Adjustments might be made by simplifying individual parts rather than by eliminating them altogether. (See p. 37, no. 40.)

4. Pattern changes within a part are difficult to manage (p. 14/15, nos. 14, 15). In the beginning there must be none at all. In a next developmental step, they should be kept to a minimum, and enough time must be allowed for the change to be accomplished securely by the players.

5. Accompaniment patterns that are too long to qualify as ostinati belong to a later stage of development, as they result in nearly through-composed pieces (p. 20, no. 24). Patterns of up to half a phrase length (two meter patterns) are true ostinati and can be handled by children with relative ease. Since most texts used for melodic development have four lines, each line half a phrase long, an ostinato will be played at least four times. This pattern length is used most frequently in Orff-Schulwerk pieces. Still shorter ostinati (one meter pattern long) appear only rarely in any of the arrangements, but are demonstrated in the "Ostinato Exercises."

SONG ARRANGEMENTS

Call Songs (Falling Minor Third)

"Tinker, Tailor" is the only example in Orff-Schulwerk I of a call melody with pitched accompaniment. Three different arrangements are shown: the first for one instrument, the second for two, and the third for four, not counting the bass.[1] All the arrangements are far too difficult because they make use of advanced ostinato patterns that the children can neither comprehend nor play. (At this point they are just beginning to become acquainted with the barred instruments and basic playing skills.) Only the simple drone should be used, but it should be explored in all its basic variations:

1. The drone fifth can be played either simultaneously (homorhythmic) or broken (monorhythmic).
2. It can be played in slower or faster note values, and later also in rhythmic patterns.
3. It can be played either in root position or inverted.

In this way, the children will learn from the start the fundamental concepts that govern all further drone development. (The polyrhythmic drone has not been added to no. 1 since it is more difficult to play. The teacher should introduce it when he or she feels that the children are ready for it.)

If the rhythm in these patterns is kept to pulse-beats, two different drones can soon be combined. A new concept is then introduced, that of *contrast* or *complement*. It occurs most naturally as rhythmic contrast:

Other contrasts can be added to the rhythmic contrast:

There is no harmonic change in any of these drones; only the tonic-triad pitches are heard between melody and accompaniment. Some teachers might object to the monotony of sound and wish for more variety, but the use of simple drones in all their variants probably can keep the children challenged for a while. We must always allow enough time for our students to become comfortable with one idea or concept before moving on to the next.

---

[1] When Orff-Schulwerk I was first published, barred bass instruments were not yet available. Stringed instruments such as the cello or the viola da gamba were suggested as a bass foundation. Today, bass xylophones or bass metallophones can be used wherever the term "bass" appears in the score.

Chant Songs

The chant tunes in Orff-Schulwerk I all follow the same melodic and structural format, which, of course, is dictated by the text. Each text line is half a phrase long and thus represents melodically one chant pattern (see also Chapter 4, pp. 84–85). The form of each song is therefore a repetition of *a*-phrases (*a,a,a,* . . .), the number of which depends on the number of text lines. In Orff-Schulwerk I only one of the basic formulas is utilized (the one more popular in Germany, shown below), but this does not mean that the others should be ignored.

Although the arrangements are still unmanageable, we can extract from them ideas that point the way to harmonic development. A close look at the individual ostinato patterns reveals that the supertonic note D (Re) coincides frequently with the chant pitch A (La) in the tune

1. either as part of a melodic ostinato:
   no. 4b, "Bobby Shaftoe," soprano xylophone:

simplified:

2. or as the moving part of a simple moving drone:
   no. 4, last version, alto xylophone, measure 3:

simplified:

soprano xylophone, measure 3:

simplified:

3. or as inverted double moving drone:
   no. 8, "Ring-a-Ring," alto xylophone, measure 5:

simplified:

The simple moving drone 5–6, implying a change from C major to A minor, is hidden in the alto xylophone part of "Bobby Shaftoe," version b:

simplified:

The pattern adapts harmonically to the tune pitches in that the A (La) of the moving drone occurs simultaneously with the E (Mi) of the chant.

In "Wee Willie Winkie," no. 6, the harmony change is expressed in much stronger terms through the addition of E:

Without the E, the pattern turns out to be an inverted simple moving drone.

No harmonizing takes place in this example; on the contrary, the submediant triad is set consistently against the G in the melody. The effect is a mixture of major and minor modality, which is often used in Orff-Schulwerk.

If we now consider each setting in its entirety instead of extracting individual patterns, we find that the adaptation to melody is almost never carried through consistently in all accompanying parts. It is confusing and rather upsetting to discover dissonant clusters containing four or even all five pitches of the pentatonic scale. How are we to interpret these arrangements, and what are we to learn from them?

Orff and Keetman seem to be telling us: "Don't worry about dissonances, parallels, and all the things that made your life difficult as a music student. Worry instead about basic musical concepts, and do with them whatever can be done at a particular time with a particular group of students. Worry about your students! If they don't understand what you are trying to teach them, they won't be able to create and improvise and they won't enjoy themselves either. If they are not challenged, they will get bored!"

It seems as if all the important guidelines concerning the use of accompaniment are contained in these first few pieces. The guidelines I find most significant are the following:

1. Adaptation to melody through moving drones, although it is part of harmonic development, is not yet "harmonizing" in the traditional sense.
2. Not all accompanying parts need to adjust to melodic movement.
3. Patterned accompaniment has priority over consistent harmonization. Therefore, if an ostinato adjusts to one segment of the tune, it will often cause dissonances in another.
4. The dissonances caused by the supertonic appear almost always on the weak beats, which means that it is a dissonance we do not want to emphasize too strongly. On the other hand, the dissonances caused by the 6th scale note are in evidence on strong beats also. As a matter of fact, the tonic (major) and submediant (minor) harmonies are used interchangeably and often simultaneously.

The concept of simple moving drones is not difficult to understand. It can be introduced quite early and developed in as many ways as the children can handle (see also Chapter 6). During this stage, there is no conscious adjustment of the ostinato patterns to the tunes, although some patterns sound better than others. The simple moving drone 5–6, for example, is always compatible. Other moving drones, simple (1 to 2) or double moving (tonic to supertonic, for instance), are least disturbing if they occur as passing notes on weak beats, as in the soprano xylophone part of no. 6.

The ability to differentiate simultaneous sounds develops later than the ability to hear successive sounds. Therefore, implied harmony changes and the use of moving drones cannot be dealt with successfully for several years. The teacher should try to make the initial step as easy as possible. Here are some suggestions:

- Introduce only one specific implied harmony change at a time.
- Select tunes that lend themselves to purpose of illustration, even if this means going back to the most elemental call and chant pitches.
- Use small instrumentations consisting only of melody and one accompanying part (each part played by a group of children), in order to make the change easily discernible.

The implied harmony change in the simple moving drone 5–6 is illustrated most clearly through the call and the chant:

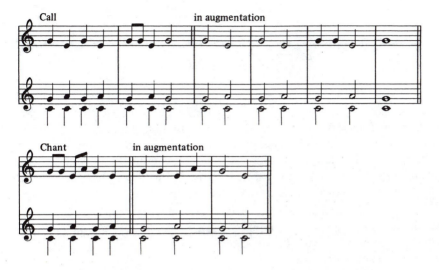

The students should explore, as an improvisation, different patterns of the same basic structure in root and inverted position, using homorhythmic, mono-rhythmic, and polyrhythmic devices:

Creative activities like these are very restrictive and serve only as an introduction to the concept of vertical pitch arrangement. Besides, since this particular moving drone is so compatible with all other pitches, we can hardly make a strong case for harmonization. This is clearly demonstrated in the arrangement of "Wee Willie Winkie." The drone pattern here is reversed, positioning the moving pitch A against the G of the call phrases. The resulting mixture of C-major and A-minor harmonies, mentioned earlier, lends a special flavor to the setting but doesn't serve to demonstrate implied harmony change.

Chant-Centered Songs

Continuing the melodic expansion, we will now extend the tonal limits downward and upward, using tunes with the range of a fifth (C–G), a sixth, and an octave. The added pitches C1 and C2, as well as the passing note D, will not necessitate any new harmonic developments. In keeping with the general idea of tonal expansion, the movement of the drone fifth may be extended a third up or down, resulting in longer patterns:

As we already discovered in Chapter 5, Orff-Schulwerk I offers very few examples of chant-centered songs. The only one in duple meter is no. 12, "Tommy's Fallen in the Pond." The melody is not typical, as the chant pitches are contracted so that the underlying harmony is the tonic triad throughout. In this setting, the continuous eighth-note movement of the simple drone (here designated "Bass," but usually played on a barred instrument) needs to be interrupted by longer note values to facilitate the playing, (as for example,   ). Likewise, the glissando must be simplified—for example, by having only the alto glockenspiel execute it, without any specific ending pitch. The soprano glockenspiel may play some filler notes:

The remaining songs in this category are no. 22, "The Baker," and no. 23, "The Day is Now Over." Surprisingly enough, the settings are much more transparent than any of the preceding ones and so reveal more clearly their harmonic implications. The new rhythmic ideas introduced here are triple meter and the upbeat. In Chapter 3 it was noted that the speech tempo in triple meter tends to be the eighth-note pulse; however, singing seems to slow down the pulse, so the quarter-note pulse feels perfectly natural here. We also learned that the rhythmic structure of the chant formula in duple meter, with its consistent subdivision of the second count, , turns into an even pulse rhythm in triple meter, . The succession of pitches in no. 22 follows the "American" chant formula.[2] Because we are in triple meter, the pitch A (La), though on a weak beat, carries more weight than it would in duple meter, since its note value is the same as that of the preceding pitches:

---

[2] That is, the chant formula used most frequently by children in the United States.

instead of:

The alto xylophone accompanies with a broken drone whose move from the tonic to the supertonic note coincides with the A of the chant.

In No. 23 the implied harmony change I–ii is expressed more strongly through the combination of a polyphonic ostinato (alto xylophone) and a melodic ostinato (alto glockenspiel). The tune here is more elaborate. The chant pitches serve only as a point of departure to the lower and higher ranges in the octave. The second scale note is also in perfect synchronization with the ostinato patterns.

These two song arrangements hint at a possible continuation in harmonic development. Chant-centered tunes in triple meter, with note values of the pulse or slower, lend themselves well to the introduction of the implied harmony change from tonic to supertonic. The first tunes with which to illustrate the new idea most clearly will have to be created by the teacher and should be structured along the same lines as the examples from the book. I know of no traditional songs that have such a clear melodic design.

Unlike the previous ostinato patterns, where a shift of the drone fifth sufficed to produce the implied change to A minor, the supertonic harmony can be stated only if both drone notes move. (A shift of the tonic note alone, with a stationary fifth, would cause an implied move to the dominant.) Thus, the introduction of a new harmonic sound is the result of the introduction of a new drone type, the double moving drone:

As always, the children should first be asked to vary the basic pattern (here, in triple meter, with the shift on the third count) by (1) keeping the drone homorhythmic, (2) finding polyrhythmic patterns, or (3) breaking the drone (mono-rhythmic patterns). The playing skills of the students may limit the choices at first, but the patterns will grow in complexity as their skills develop. At this time, the main objective is to expose the children to the double moving drone I–ii and to help them use it within the context of already familar concepts. The teacher should consider these factors:

1. The homorhythmic drone can be altered rhythmically:

etc.

2. The polyrhythmic type presupposes some coordination abilities. However, if prepared through slapping exercises, simple patterns will emerge which, once mastered, can be transferred to the drone:

3. Monorhythmic patterns are easier to play, but they revert back to the simple moving drone 1–2, since the A is not present in simple patterns such as the ones below. After first breaking the drone in the simplest fashion, rhythmic changes on the different beats should be developed:

etc.

Later, short melodic ostinati can be derived from these forms:

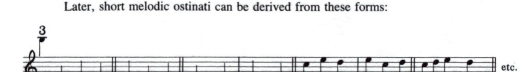

etc.

Once a few patterns have been found, any two can be combined to accompany a song. "The Day Is Now Over" thus might appear in a simpler version, yet with its basic harmonic structure. Most important of all, the arrangement has been created by the children themselves:

By the same token, if it is to have any lasting result, melodic improvisation over double-moving-drone patterns needs to be monitored by the teacher with great care and patience. Question-answer activities in an a,a^1 format, using only chant-centered phrases, can help the student to "step out" of the formula. Each phrase may begin with one or two chant formulas and then move on, either descending or ascending. For example:

Since new melodic motifs outside the formula are limited, it will take little practice to position correctly the two pitches compatible with the supertonic. In the beginning the teacher should supply the *a*-phrases, because they determine the style of the following answer.

Some readers might object that such a structured approach is too restrictive and allows for little freedom of choice. But freedom of choice comes only through the understanding of principles. The incorporation of the vertical sound aspect must be approached in a simple and limited way if it is to be understood. Besides, we do not look for perfect results in these improvisation exercises; like the first encounter with any new concept, they are intended primarily to open up a new avenue of thought.

Songs with Varying Ranges

In the last group of songs we shall discuss, the affiliation with the chant has been left behind. The tonal range of the melodies included here varies from an octave to a tenth (authentic) and from a sixth to an octave (plagal). (See Chapter 5, melodic chart.)

A further division according to the harmonic structure of the settings allows for two subgroupings. They are:

> Group 1: No new harmonic developments other than the ones already described.
>
> Group 2: Implied harmony changes I–V through simple moving drones with the root moving to the 2nd scale degree.

Songs Belonging to Group I. No. 15, "My Little Pony," a song well suited to dramatization, is based on the simple moving drone 5–6 throughout. The alto xylophone part can be replaced by an easier pattern, to be broken into eighth-notes only in the postlude. By the third grade most students should be able to handle continuous fast notes, as long as the pattern is simple. However, the alto glockenspiel part contains too many changes (and quick ones at that), and the patterns themselves are extremely difficult. After a rather lengthy introduction, the alto glockenspiel follows the melodic line of the song until the last two bars, where it ascends to a high G for a cadencing effect. To circumvent these problems, one might reduce the part to a melodic ostinato such as (*a*) below, or to simple harmonic fillers, such as (*b*), to be played only during the introduction and postlude.

(*a*)

(*b*)

A soprano xylophone might take over the melody part during the song, without the change at the end. Sleighbells worn by the dancers will contribute to the rhythmic variety. The whole form thus becomes a balanced *ABA*.

No. 13, "Unk, Unk, Unk," is another song children love to dramatize. The arrangement is not as difficult as it may seem, and it can be taught at about the fourth-grade level. Fermatas between the three sections help to prepare the players for the changes in their parts.

The harmonies implied in the accompaniment are, again, C major and A minor. At the beginning and end they appear simultaneously, and in measures 7–12 they appear as inverted simple moving drones in the alto xylophone part. Dividing the soprano and alto xylophone parts between two players or two groups of players (Sop. Xylo. I and II, Alto Xylo. I and II) not only provides for easier playing but also helps make clear the structure of the composition. After the children have learned the song, the accompaniment to the first portion of the B section (the song itself) can be taught vocally and with text and then transferred to the instruments. The toad's doleful lament on the tonic note appears simultaneously on the drone fifth in Alto Xylophone I. The few small differences may be simply ignored. The tune of Soprano Xylophone I is the children's mocking song heard later in measures 7–12. The short melodic ostinato of Soprano and Alto Xylophones II can be taught with the word rhythm "unk,unk,unk." (The eighth-note G's in the second half of the measures can be omitted since they are played by Soprano and Alto Xylophones I anyway.) Even the timpani conforms to the "unk" rhythm. In measures 7–12 both soprano xylophones change to drone notes, Alto Xylophone I to a melodic ostinato, and Alto Xylophone II to the inverted simple moving drone. (For more suggestions, refer to "Instructions and Notes," in Orff-Schulwerk I, p. 140.)

"Boomfallera," sections B and C, pages 45 and 47, a song-rondo, also seems to be a constant favorite with children. ("Boomfallera" in German is a nonsense term, perhaps synonymous with the English "Woopsy-daisy.") The songs in sections B and C, whose texts may be replaced by different ones, are again quite simple harmonically. The a,b,a,b^l tune of the rondo's B section, "The Cock's on the Housetop," spans only a sixth and is faintly reminiscent of the chant. The accompaniment is based entirely on the tonic triad. Its three pitches form a two-measure melodic ostinato for the alto glockenspiel. The homophonic ostinato of the alto xylophone is developed from a double moving drone in parallel motion. Since during the whole song the inverted supertonic fifth coincides only twice with the pitch D in the tune, it can hardly be called an implied harmony change. In section C, "Curly Locks," the melody (form a,a,b,b^l) expands to a tenth. As in section B, both accompanying parts consist of two-measure ostinati, one melodic (alto glockenspiel) and one the simple moving drone 5–6 with E added as a harmonic filler (alto xylophone).

In no. 39, "The Cuckoo," we finally encounter a tune with strongly emphasized 2nd scale degrees. However, the accompaniment with the combined C-major/A-minor harmonies does not acknowledge them. The main song is followed by a short, two-part lullaby ("Eia popeia," synonymous with "Rockabye") whose repeated melodic phrases suggest a polyphonic ostinato. The underlying tonic and submediant harmonies again sound simultaneously in the different instrumental parts. The lullaby ends with three soft cuckoo calls.

Songs Belonging to Group 2. There are only three songs in which the accompaniment adapts in varying degrees to strongly emphasized supertonic notes. The three tunes share certain similarities. The first three scale notes of the second octave are used heavily (two of the melodies are in plagal ranges, while the third one takes place entirely on these three pitches); the singing becomes two-part whenever these three pitches occur, with the following harmonization: E2 as tonic (a), C2 as submediant (b), and D2 as dominant (c). All three songs are in triple meter.

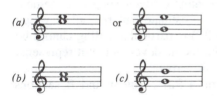

Lastly, the tunes are structured in such a way that the supertonic note appears at regular intervals—that is, always on the same count in the measure. This allows for the ostinato to adjust to the harmonic changes.

In no. 28, "O Lady Mary Ann" (form: a,a,b,b), all the instrumental parts of the a-phrases (excluding the bass) follow the alternating C major/A minor harmonies set by the melody—the alto glockenspiel with a homophonic ostinato developed from a double moving drone in contrary motion; the soprano xylophone with a pedal point on E, a pitch shared by both triads; and the alto xylophone with the inverted simple moving drone 5–6.

In the b-phrases the melody becomes two-part, its intervals forming the harmonic pattern I–V–vi–V. This harmonic change is reflected in the two-measure ostinato of the alto glockenspiel. The pitch E of the first measure adapts to the first and third bars of phrase b. The inverted dominant fifth harmonizes with measures 2 and 4:

The soprano xylophone likewise responds by shifting to a pedal point on G, a pitch shared by the tonic and dominant triads, and the seventh of the submediant. The remaining parts, alto xylophone and bass, do not adjust harmonically, although their patterns change.

In no. 41, "Boomfallera," the section A refrain is centered exclusively around the first three scale notes, and the supertonic occurs at phrase endings and at the cadence before the final. The entire accompaniment, except those instruments following the two-part melody, consists of a pedal point on the drone fifth, which falls to the tonic at the end. In traditional terms we would speak of a harmonization:

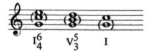

However, it would be a mistake to present it in this way to our students. For them, the G is the fifth of the drone, not the dominant. It happens to harmonize well with the strong supertonic, a fact they should be familiar with from their work with simple moving drones. Therefore, although this harmonization is actually traditional, it can be explained in elemental terms as well.

No. 40, "Old Angus McTavish," is the most difficult song arrangement in the book because of the numerous variations in ostinato patterns, all of which presuppose advanced playing skills. But even if this particular setting cannot be taught satisfactorily before the fifth grade, the harmonic development it represents certainly can, although in simpler and more basic terms.

The tune has the form a,a^1,b,b,a^2,a^2, or A,B,A^1. The A and B sections are separated by an instrumental interlude. As in the previous example, both melody and accompaniment contain the implied dominant, with the difference that here the changes occur independently from one another, not simultaneously. Although the instrumental parts coordinate harmonically among themselves, they do not do so with the tune, except in the last stanza. This lack of conformity of the ostinato to the melody seems related to the text and was probably intentional. As long as McTavish does not conform to the heavenly standards (symbolized by teams of his own choice), the ostinato goes its own way. Only when he finally assumes an attitude acceptable to St. Peter (symbolized by the team of six golden angels) does the ostinato harmonize with the tune. Students already familiar with techniques for harmonization should be made aware of this text painting. Learning to play this charming but difficult setting may be frustrating for the children if the instructor insists on simply telling or showing them what to play; they should instead be allowed to help create the accompaniment. It matters little if the final patterns chosen by the class do not exactly match those of the book. It is much more important that they learn to apply a new concept (here, that of using the simple moving drone, root to supertonic) and to combine it with already familiar concepts (the various ways a drone can be played). Once this task has been accomplished satisfactorily, the teacher may then, for comparison, illustrate Orff's own setting. The choice between the class arrangements and the original should be left to the children. In order for the improvisation to be successful, the teacher must be thoroughly familiar with the piece. All ostinati need to be analyzed and reduced to a basic pattern which, for the students, will become the starting point of the improvisations. The pattern is stated by both soprano and alto xylophone during the four introductory bars: a simple moving drone, root advancing to 3rd scale note. It can be reduced further to quarter-notes:

This formula, as well as its inverted position, will serve as the basis for developing homorhythmic and polyrhythmic patterns. For example:

As an exercise in fast reaction, the students might try to string together phrases of two or three different patterns. As another exercise, the moving pitches of the drone can be turned around, and explored along the same lines as before:

The formula used so far is the basis for all the soprano xylophone patterns, but not for all the alto xylophone ostinati. Here we find another pattern which, on the third count, implies the submediant rather than the tonic-triad harmony. The idea for this harmony change can be developed from a simple moving inverted drone the children have used before:

First, the drone fifth on the third count is moved to the sixth (a technique they are familiar with), which results in a double-moving-drone pattern with contrary motion, and already incorporates the harmony change (1). At this point the teacher may choose to stop; however, if the students have comprehended this much and are able to play the pattern, the final step may be taken—that is, replacing the drone pitch G on the first count with the drone pitch C (2). The teacher should point out that the implied harmony stays the same; however, the pattern, although it originated in a drone, is now a harmonic or homophonic ostinato, as the drone is no longer discernible.

Thus far, the improvisations have been conducted independently from the tune. For the last stanza, the children should be asked to adapt the basic simple moving drone as it was used in the beginning to the implied harmony change in the tune. Only two patterns can evolve, both with the pitch D on the third count:

1.   2.

These are essentially the ones appearing in the glockenspiel parts. The new patterns are used only in the *a*-phrases; in the *b*-phrases no change is necessary.

"Old Angus McTavish" represents a cornerstone in harmonic development and may serve as a gauge by which to judge our teaching achievements. Have we been able to instill into our students a basic understanding of the horizontal and vertical aspects of music? Have we succeeded in establishing the basic vocabulary of the three drone types, and in making clear the many possibilities for variants?

A final group to be discussed among the vocal arrangements is the rounds. In Chapter Two we learned how rhythmic and melodic echo-play leads into the improvisation of perpetual canons; also, how speech canons represent a different approach in that they are pre-set and must first be taught in their entirety before being performed in parts. Through many centuries vocal rounds have enjoyed great popularity among both art and folk musicians. In Orff-Schulwerk the round is a direct outgrowth of the speech canon. Not only is the singing of rounds a good preparation for part-singing in general, but children of all ages have great fun doing it. At my school, we begin all assemblies by singing a few rounds. The primary grades of the lower school benefit especially from this practice, as they are supported and carried along by the more experienced singers of the third and fourth grades. (The sound, of course, is not always the purest and most beautiful—but in assemblies, we sing for our own fun!)

The first rounds in Orff-Schulwerk I appear on page 24. Like most canons in this volume, their melodic lines are based in essence on the tonic triad. Despite their similarity the tunes have intrinsic differences for which the accompaniment accounts in varying ways.

In no. 29, "I Love Sixpence," which is based on the tonic triad, the 2nd scale degree appears on the strong beat in measure 2. Perhaps for this reason, the accompaniment consists simply of a pedal point on the drone fifth. The sixteenth-notes throughout need to be reduced to a simpler rhythm.

In no. 30, "Ding, Dong, Diggidiggidong," the combination of a homophonic and a melodic ostinato into a I–V–vi–V pattern adapts perfectly to the four-part round.

Another bell round, no. 31, "Ding Dong, The Bells Do Ring," is set entirely on a tonic-triad accompaniment to which the sixth is added on alternative beats, perhaps suggesting the gently dissonant sound of bell ringing.

No. 37, "Farewell to the Old Year," is a favorite among my lower-school students, and it has become a tradition to sing it just before we all part for the holiday break. The accompaniment is easy to teach because of the regularly spaced entrances of the parts.

THE INSTRUMENTAL PIECES

Differences Between Song Arrangements and Instrumental Pieces

Just as Orff's affinity for language finds expression through the speech exercises, speech pieces, and vocal arrangements, Keetman's affinity for movement evidences itself in the instrumental pieces. They are music inspired by movement and created for movement.

It is the elemental idea of a *purpose* that appeals to children. To them, instrumental music must not be abstract but must have an application. The most obvious and also most practical one is in dance. One short piece is all that is needed to create a little dance. There are other uses, though, especially in the area of play-acting, drama, and poetry.

In the early stages of Orff-Schulwerk training, instrumental playing correlates with vocal activities. Call and chant tunes are played along with the singing, or repeated afterwards, and simple drones keep the beat. Instrumental echo and question-answer activities mainly serve the purpose of helping to internalize these three word-originated pitches. A wider range is needed to develop truly instrumental tunes. Among the pieces in Orff-Schulwerk I there are none with a tonal range less than a sixth.

Melodies grow naturally from the instrument for which they are conceived. Children's songs evolve from recitation. They are syllabic, which means that there is one pitch per syllable (see also Chapter 5). As a rule, pitch changes occur on note values representing the pulse. Subdivisions of the pulse (such as two eighth-notes in $\frac{2}{\text{♩}}$, $\frac{3}{\text{♩}}$, or $\frac{4}{\text{♩}}$, or two sixteenth-notes in $\frac{3}{\text{♪}}$ or $\frac{6}{\text{♪}}$) are often sung on the same pitch. Longer durations occur almost entirely on phrase endings or final endings. Most of the songs in Orff-Schulwerk I and many traditional children's songs show these characteristics, reflecting the limitations of the child's untrained voice.

Once a few basic playing techniques have been mastered, such limitations do not exist in regard to instrumental melodies. Already the first examples in the book have a decidedly instrumental character. Although there are some in a rather slow tempo with sustained pitches (e.g., nos. 2, 5, 12), the majority move along at a brisker pace in successions of eighth-notes. A gradual development of playing skills can be discerned in the amount of melodic ornamentation used. In the beginning, pitch changes on single successive eighth-notes occur almost always when only two eighth-notes are played in a row (O.S.I, p. 95, meas. 5):

In longer successions, the same pitches repeat at least once (O.S.I, p. 95, meas. 6):

Examples of such tunes are nos 3, 13, 19, and 31. In an almost imperceptible next step, *one* change on single eighth-notes occurs while the other eight-notes in the same phrase still repeat the pitch (nos. 14, 15, 18). There are, of course, many other possibilities for melodic movement on different levels of playing difficulty. However, it seems a certain amount of pitch repetition on fast notes comes naturally to percussive playing; one might say that it is a characteristic of the elemental tune for barred instruments.

There is also a difference between vocal and instrumental pieces in regard to architecture and orchestration. Whereas most vocal arrangements are straightforward in form and in the division of parts between melody and accompaniment, the instrumental music seems more varied and complex. Melodies meander back and forth between different instruments, or complement one another in alternation. Tutti and solo phrases may suggest the idea of a concerto grosso in miniature. Canonic devices lend polyphonic texture. In short, the settings display a diversity of designs similar to those found in art music. One might say that they are elemental counterparts. There is no better way for students to comprehend musical architecture than by having them take on the role of architects and builders (see p. 42).

Part Three, "Instrumental Pieces," is divided into three sections:

  I.   Pieces for early ensemble playing,
 II.   Pieces for smaller but more advanced groups,
III.   Rondos, echo pieces, and canons.

Since we have already discussed melodic and harmonic development in the song section, we will now concern ourselves primarily with the formal structure and orchestration of the instrumental examples.

The Rondo

Of all instrumental forms, the rondo is the most fundamental. Its structure is clear and simple, and it supplies a formal setting for improvisation. Two easy examples can be found in Section III:

No. 32, with a text ("Solos Here for Everyone") for the A section, is an effective introduction to the rondo form in general. If used in this way, the arrangement may have to be changed to a basic simple drone and the simple moving drone 5–6 in quarter-notes (implied in Alto Glockenspiel II). The counter-melody (another new concept) of Alto Glockenspiel I may be simplified, played on recorder by the teacher, or deleted altogether.

No. 31 lends itself well to exploring movement in triple meter with a waltz-run or a waltz-step. The setting is uncomplicated and needs no adjustments.

No. 33 requires advanced playing skills, although the harmonic structure of the setting is quite simple. If necessary, all parts can be reduced to easier versions:

Soprano Glockenspiel I can be reduced to a simple moving, broken drone.

Soprano Glockenspiel II can be reduced to a melodic ostinato in quarter-notes.

Alto Glockenspiel can be reduced to a homophonic ostinato.

The melody can be reduced to

Even in this version the melody calls for good recorder players. However, glockenspiels might be substituted, which in turn would necessitate a change of instrumentation for the ostinato parts.

In all three rondos the interspersed sections need not be taught, as it is here where the improvisations should take place. Among the options for the improvisational sections are:

1. Division of parts:
   a. Echo (*a,a*): solo—solo
   solo—tutti
   b. Question-answer (*a,a¹*, or *a,b*): solo—solo
   tutti—solo
   solo—tutti
   (If the question is tutti, all play the same phrase, whereas, an answer in tutti will produce many different phrases, which does not matter in the least.)
2. Use of musical structure:
   a. stay in same meter and mode
   b. change meter
   c. change to another pentatonic mode
   d. use transpositions of the original mode
   e. combine c. or d. with b.

Part II, "Rhythmic-Melodic Exercises" (p. 88), offers further illustrations of the rondo form. A number of tunes on page 90 may serve as A sections and are to be worked out with accompaniment. But the teacher will find that, after the rondo form has been introduced and demonstrated with examples like nos. 32 or 33, the needs of the class are served best if new pieces are created entirely from improvisation.

One more rondo in the instrumental section deserves our attention. No. 39, especially favored by boys, is a piece clearly born from movement. The motoric and forceful drive of the A section is brought to a halt by the sharply accented rhythmic phrases of a woodblock (B, C, and D). The music consists entirely of two-measure ostinati for xylophones, all built around the tonic triad. There is no melodic development. The steady repetitions of the ostinati serve only to underscore the movement dynamics. The piece is not labeled a rondo, and the intervening woodblock rhythms are only half as long as the ostinato sections (six measures, as opposed to the twelve measures in A). In order to give the dancers more time to develop the B, C, and D sections the rhythmic phrase can be repeated; this also will bring about a more balanced rondo form.

Aside from the rondo, the other forms most often found in the instrumental section are *ABA* and *AB*.

Formal structure alone is not difficult to perceive and understand in relatively short pieces. Orchestration can add considerable complexity to an otherwise simple musical idea. In sequencing, we obviously must begin with uncomplicated and clearly defined designs. More intricate versions must never be imposed but should always evolve through experimentation with basic musical materials. Furthermore, exploration along these lines must wait until the children have fully mastered the craft of building straightforward *AB* and *ABA* pieces consisting of a melody and ostinato accompaniment. They also must possess enough playing skills to execute changes in ostinato patterns quickly and easily. In my experience, it takes the better part of the elementary grades to develop these skills. Consequently, not all of Keetman's suggestions can be taken up during the pentatonic stage. But we can always return to them when we introduce new aspects of elemental musical composition. Experimentation with new ideas such as orchestration or polyphonic design will be more successful if the musical framework is kept simple.

We will first consider designs in orchestration. Let us compare nos. 3 and 6. Both pieces use similar melodies with identical *a*-phrases but different forms: no. 3 is an a,a^1,b,b^1, no. 6 an a,a^1,b,a^1. The real difference lies in the orchestration of the pieces. The orchestration of no. 3 is simple, as each instrument is designated a specific role without change from beginning to end. In no. 6, the individual melodic phrases switch back and forth between soprano and alto glockenspiel. The accompaniment, reduced to a simple drone bass and drone fifths (timpani and alto xylophone) does not play straight through; instead, each instrument is assigned to accompany only *a* or *b*.

Explained in these terms, the orchestration of no. 6 seems rather complicated. But in reality the piece is in simple question-answer form, performed here with groups of players rather than with soloists. Experiments in orchestration work best if a piece is first presented in a basic version—that is, with all instruments playing their assigned parts without change or interruption. For example, in this particular piece the melody would first be learned in its entirety. After that, the basic version may be altered. Before changes in orchestration can be explored successfully each student must be familiar with all the instrumental parts, not just the one he is playing. Therefore, the original version that forms the basis for the improvisation should be extremely simple.

In nos. 12, 13, and 14, the orchestration is more advanced because all the barred instruments alternate between playing melody and accompaniment. In order to break down the pieces to their simplest structure, one must first trace the melody. In no. 13, for example, it begins in measure 3 with the alto glockenspiel (a,a), continues in this part, and is joined by the alto xylophone later on through bar 10 (b,b^1; the repeated measures of the *a*-phrase are counted as measures 3 and 4). After that, the *b*-phrases are repeated by the soprano glockenspiel. The form of the tune is thus a,a,b,b^1,b,b^1. When not playing the tune, all barred instruments take part in the accompaniment, which in *b* consists of a broken drone (timpani and bass) and the drone fifth, which is a harmonic adjustment to the strong supertonic in the melody. The ostinati of the *a*-phrases are all related to the simple and simple moving drone 5–6, in various patterns. The soprano glockenspiel adds a little dissonance. It goes without saying that the melody need not be played in octaves by one player.

No. 34, Section III, is a complex echo piece. The alternation between different instruments takes on the character of a miniature concerto.[3] Tuned glasses and soprano glockenspiel (with the melody) and two alto glockenspiels (with harmonizing patterns of their own) make up the "concertizing" group of instruments. (The first alto glockenspiel, however, joins the tune in the interludes also.) There is no bordun foundation, but timpani and bass help to indicate the implied harmony changes. The melody can be broken into ten phrases:

---

[3] The term "miniature concerto" is used by Werner Thomas in his commentary on the recording series *Musica Poetica*, I-V.

a,a^1,b	two measures each
b^1	extended by one measure
interlude c,c	one measure each
d	two measures
interlude c^1,c^2	(the phrases of the two melody instruments differ from those of the first alto glockenspiel)
d	as before

The distribution of the individual melody phrases among the instruments is demonstrated in the following chart:

	a	a¹	b	b¹	interlude c	c	d	c	c¹	interlude d
Glasses		x		x		x	x	x	x	x
Soprano glockenspiel	x	x	x	x		x	x	x	x	x
Alto glockenspiel I					x	x		x	x	

The parts of the two alto glockenspiels, as well as those of timpani and bass, are difficult to explain in elemental terms.

Even though this particular piece is beyond the capabilities of young students, the musical design it represents is not. Elemental group concerti can be made up just as well on more rudimentary levels. A melody is first created and learned by the class. Then, a chart similar to the one above is drawn up, and concertizing solo and tutti phrases are tried out. Once the children have found satisfactory solutions, they are blocked out in the chart and practiced. The accompaniment is best left very simple, but it may change for different sections of the piece.

Canons

Musical structures using canonic devices have evolved in various geographical locations around the world, independent of each other, and at different times. Only in Western art music, which possessed a means of precise notation, could these elemental practices develop into strict and consistent imitation. Because of its adaptability to different styles and techniques, the canon has never disappeared; instead, it has adjusted itself to polyphonic and homophonic style, to tonal and atonal techniques, as well as to vocal and instrumental treatment.

The oldest known canons date back to the early thirteenth century. They belong to the elemental type, the circle canon or round. Mostly in two or three parts, they were called *caca*, *chace*, or *caccia* ("hunt"). More elaborate types developed during the following centuries. The Ars Nova period (fourteenth century) produced canon at specific intervals. Guillaume de Machaut wrote the first retrograde canon. The culmination in development occurred during the second half of the fifteenth century, when the various types were systematically explored, such as double and multipart canon, inverted and retrograde canon, canon in diminution and augmentation. Although the later Renaissance brought no further developments, the seventeenth century produced new interest in canon composition through studies of contrapuntal practices and through the growing orientation toward harmony.

Music for Children abounds in rounds and canons. Among the five Schulwerk volumes, Book I contains by far the most numerous examples. While the vocal rounds are uncomplicated, the instrumental canons in section III display more complexity in their structure and are reminiscent of some of the canon types developed during the fourteenth and fifteenth centuries. The fact that intricate historical composition techniques and designs can be applied to the elemental style of Orff-Schulwerk never ceases to amaze me. There is no better way to lay the foundations for understanding art music than by acquainting students with these elemental correspondences. The following commentaries on the canons and canonic pieces in Orff-Schulwerk I are in order of difficulty, rather than in order of appearance in the book.

No. 41 (p. 132) A perpetual four-part canon over a simple bordun. It is possible either to end all voices at the same time or to let each complete the last phrase.

No. 42 (p. 133): A double canon with a total of four parts. Both canons begin at the same time, are of the same four-measure length, and have second parts that enter after two bars. All parts end together, with the first in both canons playing the complete phrase four times and the second playing only three-and-a-half times.

The next examples are not strict canons because, although they are imitative, noncanonic sections are interspersed with the canonic ones. Naturally, they are more difficult.

No. 7 (p. 99): This little piece is not in the canon section, but because of its simple design it serves well as an example of how to introduce the concept of *canonic devices* (as opposed to strict canons). Two phrases played in unison by glockenspiels ($a,a = A$) are followed by a two-part canon ($b,b^1 = B$). Both A and B are repeated, and the last canonic phrase is altered in one part so that the instruments end together. To make learning easier, a text may be invented to go with the melodic phrases.

No. 36 (pp. 120–21): An *ABAC* form with B as the canonic section. The A-phrases consist of imitative play between tuned glasses and alto glockenspiel. In B, the canonic voices are spaced at one-measure intervals; after two phrases this space is narrowed to half-measures. The piece ends with a delightful antiphonal exchange of echo phrases, with one or the other instrument leading. A melodic ostinato enhances the polyphonic texture.

No. 37 (p. 122): An *ABACA* rondo form with rather difficult instrumental parts. The A-phrases, in strict two-part imitation, are followed by echo phrases in B and C. It is interesting to note that C, with some exceptions, is the inverted version of B. There is no accompaniment at all. Although written for glockenspiels, the piece can be played on recorders; in this instrumentation, it brings to mind Telemann's sonatas in canon form.

No. 43 (p. 133): Before this canon can be analyzed clearly and taught successfully, some facts about imitational devices need to be reviewed.

The number of parts possible in a canon is determined by its form and by the length of its individual phrases. In our elemental form structures, the shortest unit consists of two meter patterns (a half-phrase). Thus, in a $\frac{6}{4}$ meter (the count of this particular piece), such a phrase will be one measure long. Voice entrances in elemental canonic structures often occur at half-phrase intervals. Therefore, a series of *a*-phrases of this length can be imitated by only one voice, because otherwise the parts will double up:

On the other hand, a melody in *a,b* form contains the possibilities for a four-part canon:

By the same token, if a phrase is extended to twice the most elemental length (four meter patterns), it can be set in four parts:

With this in mind, we can proceed with the analysis of no. 43. The piece, in *ABCD* form, contains two different canons (*B* and *C*). The first one is created with two melodic phrases, *a,b*, each two measures (or four meter patterns) long. This allows for four imitating parts. The second canon consists of a series of *a*-phrases in natural length (two meter patterns, or one measure) and for this reason is reduced to only two parts, which in turn results in a change of orchestration. After the *a,b* melody has been stated twice by all four parts in unison (section *A*, introduction), the canonic entrances follow each other at regular intervals of one measure, each voice playing the tune two more times. Immediately after the last instrument has finished, the second canon begins. Joined by tuned glasses, the two soprano glockenspiels now combine to form the upper voice, the two alto glockenspiels to form the lower. The melodic form of this section is *a,a* (one measure each), followed in the next two measures by a stretto with the same motivic material. The whole four-measure phrase is played twice, and both times the two parts end together, the last phrase of the lower voices (alto glockenspiels I and II) being shortened by half a measure. A coda (*D*) follows, consisting of the first phrase of the first canon played in unison, and of the second phrase of the second canon played in imitation as before. All parts end together.

Explained on paper and without the benefit of hearing the music (although I hope that the reader has followed the analysis with the score), the piece appears complicated indeed. In reality, it is not difficult to teach to a class. As with the orchestration examples discussed earlier, the students need only know well the basic musical materials of this piece, which are the melodies of the two canons, and their respective forms. Then, with the help of charts, the design of the entire piece can be illustrated. Middle-grade students who are old enough to work independently love to draw their own designs, inventing specific symbols for the various phrases. Activities such as these sharpen the mind and help to develop logical and analytical thinking. (Math teachers will love us for that!)

No. 40 (p. 131) is a similarly constructed piece, although shorter and less complex. It consists of two sections: *A*, the introduction, a unison statement of the "theme," and *B*, the canon. The simultaneous ending of all voice parts is achieved through repetitions of the last phrase by the instruments that entered first.

No. 44 (p. 136) is an instrumental version of the round "Diggidiggidong" (p. 24), and it can be used as an introduction and postlude to the song. In the accompaniment, the melodic ostinato of the vocal round reappears in a simplified form. The bass part, which should be taken by a bass xylophone, plays a simple moving drone, the timpani a simple drone. Both parts are broken and inverted. In order to simplify the piece, other accompanying parts (Soprano and Alto Glockenspiels II) may be omitted, since these instruments will join in the canon playing later in the piece anyway. The harmony-filling third of Alto Glockenspiel II can be played by a metallophone.

The canonic entrances of the four glockenspiels are not evenly spaced but occur instead in an accelerated manner, stretto fashion. In my experience, the following teaching sequence has worked well. First, everyone learns the tune and the coda. Then, the parts of the four canon instruments are studied individually. Alto Glockenspiel I begins by playing the canon four times and the coda for two measures (plus one note). Soprano Glockenspiel I makes its entrance after the first part has started over again. It plays the canon three times and the coda for one measure. In this fashion all parts are learned. Rather than counting measures, the children are asked to listen to the instruments immediately preceding their own entrances. A further help is to set up the canon ensemble in such a way that the imitating instruments face each other in a square:

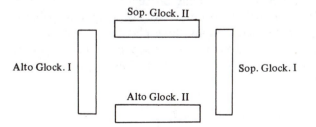

The reader will have noticed that, with the exception of the added bass foundations, the instrumentation of these canons consists entirely of glockenspiels. The effect is lovely, as long as the parts are performed as solos or by no more than two students respectively. In a larger glockenspiel ensemble the sound texture will lose its clarity and become blurred. (Besides, I can't imagine any music room possessing more than eight glockenspiels!) In order to accommodate a larger ensemble, soprano and alto xylophones may have to take the parts of the second soprano and alto glockenspiels.

In conclusion, it is quite obvious that most of these instrumental canons are not meant for beginners. Just as the more complex historical canon types evolved gradually with the growing conceptualization of composition, so will our students need time in developing the ability to grasp the advanced features of canonic structure.

Polyphonic Pieces

In Chapter 6 we discussed the origins of melodic and polyphonic ostinato, and we traced its development through the examples in Part II, "Ostinato Exercises for Barred Instruments." Gunild Keetman has provided us with a number of instrumental examples in which these forms of accompaniment have been utilized. All the pieces are short and rather pensive. Werner Thomas calls them "character pieces," and indeed music of this type has many applications in poetry and drama.[4]

The form is simple, the instrumentation sparse. The drone bass has been eliminated in most examples. This economy in all aspects allows for the polyphonic texture to come through with the utmost clarity. I cannot help but think of these pieces as elemental counterparts to Bach's two-part inventions and three-part sinfonias, or to Bartók's *Mikrokosmos*.

The examples illustrating best the characteristics of elemental polyphony are nos. 20, 21, 24, and 27–30. The exclusive use of $\frac{6}{\rho}$ meter (with the exception of no. 30, which is in $\frac{9}{\rho}$) may be due to the fact that this meter length allows more time to develop a melodic line for the ostinato patterns. Some of the pieces, such as nos. 20 and 24, still show a vertical orientation with clearly implied harmony changes (I–vi) in the lowest parts, only the middle part being a melodic ostinato.

The texture of no. 21 is entirely polyphonic, although the third voice (alto xylophone) consists only of a broken simple moving drone.

With the condensing of the two melodic ostinati into one polyphonic pattern, the division of the three instrumental parts among three players changes to only two players in nos. 27–30. The two components can be separated and played as individual parts. If this procedure is applied in no. 29, the lowest part of the *A-*

---

[4] Liner notes to recording series, *Musica Poetica*, record I, side 2.

section ostinato reveals itself as a broken simple drone. In no. 27 the ostinato extends over two measures, and a drone bass is added.

Nos. 29 and 30 have a more elaborate formal structure with middle sections. The *B* section of the "Tranquillo" consists of a short question-answer play between the two glockenspiels, whereas in the *B* section of no. 30 echo phrases develop into canonic imitation, the two voices following each other in quick succession.

We might ask ourselves what the possible applications for improvisation with children might be in the face of such masterly simplicity. Working on a strictly polyphonic basis is no more difficult than working from a harmonic basis. Both aspects are important, and we cannot concentrate on one alone to the exclusion of the other. Perhaps improvisation with polyphonic elements initially requires listening of a different sort. Instead of paying attention primarily to the harmonies, we are concerned more about the rhythmic motion in each part, since the interweaving of voices begins with independent and contrasting rhythmic movement (which brings us back to the importance of rhythmic improvisation). Resulting harmonies between the parts must be of secondary importance in the beginning.

As we have seen in Keetman's examples, $\frac{6}{}$ and $\frac{6}{}$ meter, because of the length of one unit, lend themselves well to melodic ostinato patterns. Furthermore, in $\frac{6}{}$ the pulse needs no subdivisions. The unhurried pace helps to avoid or minimize tensions that often manifest themselves in instantaneous creative activities. A sequential and systematic buildup of complexity will help the students in their improvisations. The following are some suggestions for creative activities. The reader must keep in mind that they represent a growth process of years.

Improvising in Two Parts.

1. Combinations of melodic ostinato patterns (for two players or groups).
   a. One simple broken drone combined with one melodic ostinato,
   b. One broken simple moving drone with one melodic ostinato,
   c. Two melodic ostinati.
2. Combinations of melody with one ostinato (for two players or groups).
   a. Broken simple drone with melody,
   b. Broken simple moving drone with melody,
   c. Melodic ostinato with melody,
   d. Two melodies, no ostinato.
3. Polyphonic ostinato patterns (for one player or one group of players).

In all the exercises, especially those under 1 and 3, rhythmic patterns for the broken drones and the melodic or polyphonic ostinati can be established beforehand, such as:

To begin with, only the rhythmic contrast should be stressed. When the students can achieve this without difficulty, voice leading also takes on importance.

Improvising in Three Parts.   A sequence may start either with three individual players, two of them improvising melodic ostinati as under 1a,b, and c, and the third creating a tune; or it may be a direct continuation of 3, involving only two individual parts, a polyphonic ostinato, and a melody.

In the three-part exercises, care must be taken to preserve lucidity. As a general rule, the busier the ostinato patterns, the simpler the tune should be, and vice versa.

SUMMARY

Sequencing Melodic and Harmonic Development

Unlike art music, elemental music has no real theory embodied in a set of rules. Instead of rules, Orff and Keetman have given us *guidelines* to procedure and sequencing, and models to demonstrate the application of concepts. These guidelines (Part II, "Rhythmic-Melodic Exercises") deal with the musical aspects of speech, rhythm, melody, and harmony separately and develop them in a sequential order. After one has learned how to augment and supplement this general outline, it is not difficult to adhere to a coherent sequence in the separate aspects. I have attempted to show these individual sequences in the previous chapters on speech, rhythm, melody, and ostinato accompaniment.

However, since melodic and harmonic aspects (as well as skill development) need to be considered together when teaching, sequencing them individually, though enlightening to the teacher, is only of limited value. In order to build a comprehensive sequence, we must consult the models in Parts I and III, because here we find demonstrated the order and manner in which the melodic-harmonic concepts should be introduced.

We have made the following observations concerning the order of introduction:

1. *Melody*: Melodic expansion takes place before harmonic expansion. The 2nd scale degree is treated as a passing tone in all but a few tunes.
2. *Harmony*: Implied harmony changes are introduced in this order:
    a. Simple drone, resulting in tonic triad,
    b. Simple moving drone 5–6, resulting in the implied submediant triad,
    c. Double moving drone 1–2, implying the supertonic triad,
    d. Simple moving drone 1–2, implying the dominant traid,
    e. Double moving ostinato patterns (homophonic ostinati), implying the tonic, dominant, and submediant triads (I, V, vi),
    f. Drone fifth by itself as pedal point, implying the dominant.

Both e and f have cadential tendencies and are used to accompany melodies with a strong supertonic.

If we now plan to outline an "ultimate" sequence, we must be guided by practical considerations concerning the readiness of the children in regard to (1) auditory discrimination, both horizontal and vertical, (2) conceptualization, and

(3) instrumental playing skills. Although here presented individually, the three aspects are interdependent. No definite guidelines can be established, as each teaching situation and each class of students differs from the next. The evaluation and subsequent suggestions given here are the result of my own observations in my particular teaching environment.

1.   We already have established that horizontal (successive) pitch awareness develops before vertical (simultaneous) awareness. This does not mean that moving bordun forms with implied harmony changes cannot be used from early on. It means that conscious adaptation to melody cannot be taught before the children have some ability to hear and identify simultaneous pitches.

   Ear-training activities incorporating the vertical aspect must start early. A first step in this direction is improvisation with moving drones, because the children have to deal with only two pitches at a time. Moreover, as they play the changing intervals on their barred instruments, the visual image of the pitched bars helps them to conceptualize the otherwise abstract sounds.

2.   Conceptualization and literacy are interrelated, as understanding is made easier if the concept can be expressed visually. The same holds for music. Musical notation makes visible, and therefore conscious, what the ear hears but cannot conceptualize. A multitude of sounds can be seen in their simultaneity in a musical score, and through this representation can be understood.

   Rhythmic notation alone already has been used during the first years of instruction. Pitch notation, on the other hand, is of no help when only the barred instruments are used because (1) the children can't read and play at the same time; (2) even if they could, their reading skills would still be less advanced than their playing skills and therefore would slow down the process of learning a piece of music; and (3) relying too early on notation will hinder the development of pitch recognition. Reading is needed for recorder playing, which I begin in the third grade. However, grade level is not as important as readiness. Before my students get their long-wished-for recorders, I make sure that they are proficient in the reading of rhythmic notation. At least another year goes by before they have gained fluency in reading melody. (See also section on notation in Chapter 5.) Sometime during the fourth school year, reading simultaneous pitches is begun. I do this through a comprehensive study of all drone types, most of which the students have used before but have not seen in writing. This study is combined with beginning adjustment to melody, through improvisations as well as notated "compositions." The progress varies from class to class, and only rarely do I get past the double moving drone. However, this does not disturb me. It is more important that the children understand the concept of harmony change in general and can apply it in a limited way with limited musical options. To expect more than that is to be unrealistic. Music curricula in schools should be kept rather general and should allow room for a certain amount of flexibility. To tie a teacher down to a detailed program that must be covered in a set period of time is to ignore the children's needs, to say nothing of the children themselves.

I venture to say that the child will be able to conceptualize anything he or she can hear *and* see: the root and inverted positions of the drone; homorhythmic, polyrhythmic, and broken drones; successive pitches (in melody and melodic ostinato), as opposed to simultaneous pitches (in moving drone forms). And all this before he or she can read music. The only concept that cannot be fully understood until musical literacy has been achieved is the relationship between melody and accompaniment—that is, elemental harmonization.

A careful analysis of the vocal arrangements in Part I of Orff-Schulwerk I brings to light the way in which harmonic aspects are treated. The general guideline here is to concentrate on one thing at a time. For instance, if the focus is on simple moving drones, do not at the same time be concerned with the vertical alignment of melody. If, on the other hand, adaptation to melody is the objective, keep the moving-drone patterns with the implied harmony changes very basic, and choose tunes that illustrate the changes in the clearest and most obvious terms. More specific guidelines include the following:

> Step 1: As many different patterns of moving drones and ostinati can be developed and used as the children can handle comfortably (see also Chapter 6). While the tonal range may be extended to an octave and beyond (see Chapter 5), or another pentatonic mode may be explored (see Chapter 8), all melodies must be noncadential. Improvisations consist of creating tunes and drone patterns. Whereas the implied submediant harmony is treated as a part of the tonic triad and used interchangeably with it, other implied changes occur only on weak beats. The predominant form is the rondo, and simple *A,B* and *A,B,A* forms round out the picture but are not of paramount importance. The orchestration consists of a simple division between melody and accompanying parts.
>
> Step 2: (a) Implied change I–vi through simple moving bordun 5–6: Introduce with call and chant tunes and continue with chant-centered tunes (see also p. 166).
>
> (b) Implied change I–ii through double moving drones: Introduce with chant and chant-centered tunes, using meters in which the supertonic note is equal to other scale notes, though not specifically accented. (Examples: "The Baker," "Day Is Now Over.")
>
> (c) Implied change I–V, through simple moving drones 1–2: Ideal tunes to work with are those in which the 2nd scale degree and/or the 5th appear regularly and on corresponding beats in each measure (example: "McTavish," A section).
>
> (d) Implied changes I–V–vi, through double moving drones and homophonic ostinati. Again, the melody is structured in such a way that the accented supertonic appears regularly. Two-part singing may be added to reflect the same harmonic changes as the accompaniment (example: "O Lady Mary Ann").
>
> (e) Cadential I–V changes, through the use of broken simple drone patterns (in which the 5th coincides with the supertonic in the tune), and through the use of the drone fifth as pedal point. The melodies may contain strong supertonic notes and may be cadential. Still, they are best structured in such a way as to make patterned accompaniment possible (example: "Boomfallera").

From the examples in Orff-Schulwerk I we see that in the larger settings only rarely do all instrumental parts adjust to the melody. Also, drone basses are added in most arrangements, no matter what the implied harmony changes might be. Longer forms and more sophisticated orchestrations are developed through instrumental pieces.

It is obvious that the entire sequence takes many years to develop. More advanced stages in harmonic understanding, as well as in the comprehension of complex orchestration, are not feasible in the elementary grades. To continue the harmonic studies in the middle school using only the pentatonic scale as demonstrated in Orff-Schulwerk I is neither necessary nor practical; after years of pentatonic the children are ready for further melodic development. Moreover, the expansion into the diatonic modes is a help, rather than a hindrance, in the understanding of harmonic concepts (see also pp. 147–48).

If I have been rather detailed in my explanations, perhaps to the point of exasperating my readers, I have done so because of a particular personal conviction. Even if none of us is ever able to make use of all the ideas offered in the first volume of Orff-Schulwerk, we must understand their purpose and meaning. Only in this way can we learn to recognize priorities and choose wisely in building our teaching sequence.

8

THE FIVE
PENTATONIC MODES

ANHEMITONIC SCALE STRUCTURES IN WORLD MUSICS AND IN WESTERN MUSIC

The anhemitonic tonal pattern is not restricted to the Do mode, 1–2–3—5–6—8. Any of the five pitches can serve as the starting point of a scale. Thus there are five scales altogether, each having a different pattern formed by the placement of the two minor thirds and the three major seconds:

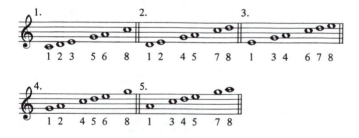

In order for us to better understand to what extent these other modes are applicable to Orff-Schulwerk, we will take a look at pentatonic music as it exists today.

Brian Brocklehurst, in the introduction to his *Pentatonic Song Book*, states: "In considering the structure of scales and their evolution it is important to remember that scales are the outcome of melody."[1] Musicologists and ethnomusi-

[1] (London: Schott, n.d.).

cologists attest to the fact that pentatonic music has appeared throughout all areas of the world, from Europe to Northern Asia, from Polynesia to Africa, and among the North American Indians, to name just a few. Pentatonicism is a tonal system, complete in itself. In its pristine and unadulterated state, as it can still be found in certain non-Western cultures, it is pure, horizontal melody, accompanied mainly by unpitched percussion. Pitched accompaniment, when it occurs, is not related to melody in the Western harmonic sense, although techniques such as ostinato appear, for example, in African music.

In the Western musical tradition, the anhemitonic scale formed the structural basis for the development of the diatonic system. Gregorian plainsong, which originated in the chanting practices of the Jewish synagogues, is the earliest Western music to be preserved through notation, and it can be considered the beginning of art music. It contains a great many pentatonic melodies as well as others in which the semitones appear as passing notes only, as if to form a bridge between pentatonic and diatonic. Gustave Reese says about Gregorian chant: "It has been asserted that in old melodies actually containing halfsteps the groundwork is still pentatonic and that the tones filling in the minor thirds are ornamental."[2]

Little information is available about the history of secular music in the Western hemisphere before the twelfth century, and none of the existing theories can be substantiated in the absence of written records. Bruno Nettl tentatively sets the emergence of European folksong during the Middle Ages, and he suggests that art music had a certain amount of influence on it.[3]

Curt Sachs raises an interesting point concerning the evolution of the folksong in Europe. He distinguishes two styles in melodic structure. The first style, occurring in the Mediterranean countries, followed the organization of the church modes. In the second style, which prevailed in Germany and the Northern countries, the melodies consisted of a series of thirds piled one on top of the other with no organization into scales ("tertial chains"). Thus, a tune with three consecutive thirds had the ambitus of a seventh! The 6th degree, Sachs continues, may have developed as a substitute for the triple chain (C–E–G–A instead of C–E–G–B) and was for a long time an upper auxiliary tone. Eventually the octave came into use, as it would often follow immediately after the 7th degree. In this way, Sachs concludes, "the third-fifth-octave skeleton of later Western music was established." Since the chains could be based on either a major or a minor third (i.e., **C–E–G–B** or **D–F–A–C**), they became the foundation for the later major and minor modes. By the same token, Sachs suggests that the use of the minor third instead of the leading tone below the tonic, seen in many fourteenth-century songs and referred to as the Landini cadence, may be a much older practice and a remnant of inverted tertial chains (see also Chapter 5, pp. 110–11); and that the tertial setup of these German and Scandinavian tunes is also at

---

[2] *Music in the Middle Ages*, (New York: W.W. Norton, 1940), p. 57.

[3] *Folk and Traditional Music of the Western Continents*, (Englewood Cliffs, N.J.: Prentice Hall, 1973), p. 38.

least partially responsible for the development of the Western Harmonic system based on triads.[4] Even if this theory cannot be proved, it contains much interesting food for thought. Incidentally, Sachs attributes the pentatonic song traditions of Scotland and Ireland and some Eastern European countries to a different scale structure which he calls "quartal chains." They are based on conjunct and disjunct tetrachords, and in this way resemble Gregorian chant. He offers no explanation as to their origins.

Although in central Europe all traces of pentatonicism have disappeared, in Eastern Europe and the British Isles it has prevailed far into this century. Since traditions are often better preserved among people away from their homeland, many songs brought to this country have been kept alive for many generations. A special case in point is the Appalachian folksong, in which British song traditions were preserved undisturbed by outside influences because the singers were isolated. And so it happened that Cecil Sharp, the English musicologist and folksong collector, and his collaborator Maud Karpeles, on their visits to the Appalachian region between 1916 and 1918 found a great wealth of virtually unchanged folk music whose roots could be traced back hundreds of years to England, Scotland, and Ireland. Since many of these tunes are pentatonic, we have an excellent source for the study of pentatonic modes. This may in turn help us to understand the extent to which they can be utilized in Orff-Schulwerk.

The research of Sharp and Karpeles is of importance to us in several respects:

1. Their analysis of the tunes and subsequent classification of scale structure attest that the different pentatonic modes exist not just in the minds of theoreticians but in living song as well (recall Brocklehurst's statement).
2. In the preface to the collection it is stated that the songs were rendered unaccompanied; only in a few instances was a dulcimer used as a drone instrument.[5] To my mind, the horizontal orientation in the conception of the tunes is unquestionable. We will see later that some of the pentatonic modes do not readily conform to patterned accompaniment, at least in traditional songs.

THE PENTATONIC MODES IN ORFF-SCHULWERK

Theoretical Aspects

Following this short and rather superficial overview, we now turn to the question of how the pentatonic modes fit into the framework of Orff-Schulwerk. We must begin with some theory (intended for the teacher, not the classroom student).

When Sharp classified the five pentatonic modes he established the beginning of a theory which, at that time, must have been of interest mainly to the scholar

---

[4] *Our Musical Heritage*, p. 56, and *The Wellsprings of Music*, pp. 154–163.

[5] The origins of the Appalachian dulcimer are uncertain. It is documented after 1870, and its use as a drone instrument to accompany singing developed still later, in the twentieth century.

rather than to the practicing musician and music educator. (Incidentally, his method of classification and terminology differs from that used in Orff-Schulwerk.) Not much later, and presumably unaware of Sharp's work, Orff and Kodály both recognized and utilized, though each in his own way, the tremendous potential the pentatonic offers for creative music-making and preparation for use of the diatonic system. Although the pentatonic volume of Orff-Schulwerk concentrates exclusively on the Do-mode, a systematic exploration of all five modes was undertaken by Gunild Keetman in her three books *Pieces for Xylophone*. Wilhelm Keller, in his fascinating and informative introduction, discusses the pentatonic scale built on C without the 4th (F) and 7th (B) degrees. Each of the remaining four pitches in this scale (D,E,G,A) becomes in turn the beginning of a new scale. Thus altogether five modes, each with a different scale pattern, can be built. Keller named them with solmization syllables (as in the Kodály Method), and this terminology has since become customary. The Do-mode, starting on C, is represented by the scale pattern 1–2–3—5–6—8; the Re-mode, beginning on D, by 1–2—4–5—7–8; and so forth.

It is also possible to use a terminology based on the fixed pitch letter names as they appear on the barred instruments; that is, the pentatonic mode based on C becomes the "C-pattern," the one on D the "D-pattern," and so on. However, such nomenclature makes sense only in a teaching approach that is based on fixed pitches entirely and does not make use of the solmization syllables.

The following chart illustrates the five authentic pentatonic scale patterns, and the teacher can choose a terminology best suited to his teaching approach.

	Do	Re	Mi	–	So	La	–	Do	Re	Mi	–	So	La
	C	D	E	–	G	A	–	C	D	E	–	G	A
Do-pentatonic, or C-pattern:	I	2	3	–	5	6	–	8					
Re-pentatonic, or D-pattern:		I	2	–	4	5	–	7	8				
Mi-pentatonic, or E-pattern:			I	–	3	4	–	6	7	8			
So-pentatonic, or G-pattern:					I	2	–	4	5	6	–	8	
La-pentatonic, or A-pattern:						I	–	3	4	5	–	7	8

It will be noted that the number system in itself does not give the major/minor qualities of the intervals. The numbers are, of course, meant to be used concurrently with either letter names or syllables. In this way the position of the five modes in their untransposed ("natural") form becomes readily apparent.

Sometimes the number patterns of the Re-, Mi-, So-, and La-modes are explained in terms of the Do-mode, each syllable retaining the same scale number as in that mode. Thus, the scale pattern of the Re-mode is 2–3—5–6—1–2, that of the Mi-mode 3—5–6—1–2–3, and so on. Although this system may be of great value when it comes to solmization and internalizing intervals, it is confusing from a theoretical viewpoint because it is not consistent with the usage of scale numbers from 1 to 7 in the diatonic modes.

The scale patterns of the five pentatonic modes are easy to understand, especially with the help of barred instruments. Yet the visual picture alone means very little unless it can be related to specific sound qualities.

Our own musical background and experience has predisposed us to hearing melody in diatonic terms, with clearly defined major or minor orientation and cadences. For this reason, it may be easier for us to understand the sound qualities of the pentatonic modes through our "diatonic ear."

The scale degrees that determine the major or minor character of a diatonic mode are the 3rd, the 6th, and the 7th. Together with the tonic note they form major intervals in major, and minor intervals in minor. A pentatonic scale does not contain all three intervals, and therefore the major or minor qualities are not as strong as in a diatonic scale. Thus, to our ears, the most outstanding feature of the pentatonic modes is their ambiguity, their lack of identity. They all seem to sound similar. A closer examination reveals, however, that there are indeed differences among the five modes which manifest themselves in their modal and harmonic propensity: The modes that contain two of the three characteristic major or minor intervals possess a stronger major or minor identity than those with only one of these intervals. Also, the modes containing the third scale note are more predisposed toward harmonic development than those without. Let us extend the chart to include these interval qualities:

	C	D	E	–	G	A	–	C	D	E	–	G	A	3rd	6th	7th
Do-pentatonic:	I	2	3	–	5	6	–	8						M	M	
Re-pentatonic:		I	2	–	4	5	–	7	8							m
Mi-pentatonic:			I	–	3	4	–	6	7	8				m	m	m
So-pentatonic:					I	2	–	4	5	6	–	8			M	
La-pentatonic:					I	–	3	4	5	–	7	8		m		m

The findings are interesting. The Do- and La-modes (C- and A-patterns) have a strong leaning toward the major and minor modality, respectively. The Re-mode (D-pattern), with only the minor seventh and the So-mode (G-pattern), with only the major sixth, are much weaker and resist a definite categorization into one or the other modality. The Mi-mode (E-pattern) is somewhat perplexing. Although all three indicative intervals are present in their minor form, the horizontal grouping of the pitches makes it difficult to establish a convincing minor tonality. A melody centered around the lower three notes (even if the subtonic is included) can easily be understood as the chant pitches in the Do-mode; the ear is likely to interpret the 6th, 7th, and 8th scale degrees as scale numbers 1, 2, and 3 of the Do-mode:

An accompanying pedal point on the tonic note (no fifth available) is necessary in order to establish a clear tonal identity.

The Do and La pentatonic modes have the strongest tendency to lead into our existing harmonic system. They are the only modes with a complete tonic triad, and it is this triad which stands at the beginning of all harmonic development. However, we must keep in mind that, without a drone accompaniment that establishes a tonality beyond a doubt, even the Do and La pentatonic modes are not always clearly defined.

The process of transposing pentatonic modes is identical to that of transposing diatonic modes. All scale pitches retain the same intervallic relationship among themselves as in their original scale patterns. The use of either relative solmization syllables or fixed pitch names serves the purpose of transposition equally well. Although it is possible to transpose the pentatonic modes to any key, the teacher should not use transpositions that need sharps or flats, because the children do not yet possess the necessary theoretical background. Although they know the names of the basic pitches, they have not yet learned about sharps or flats, and although they may be familiar with the basic intervals, they do not know about their classification into half- and whole steps, major and minor, or perfect, augmented, and diminished forms. In effect, they only work with the seven basic (diatonic) pitches.

A simple rule regarding transposition possibilities of the five pentatonic modes to keys without sharps or flats is the following: Any transposed diatonic mode with no more than one sharp or flat will, in its pentatonic correspondence, have no key signature at all. The reason, of course, is that the first sharp or flat in a key signature is always F or B. For example, G major and F major need F♯ and B♭, respectively. In Do-pentatonic there is neither a 4th nor a 7th scale degree; thus, Do-pentatonic on G will not use the F♯, and Do-pentatonic on F will not need the B♭. Therefore, Do-pentatonic can be transposed to G and F without the need of sharps and flats. The same is true of the other four pentatonic modes: all have a diatonic correspondent (Re-mode corresponds with Dorian, Mi-mode with Phrygian, So-mode with Mixolydian, and La-mode with Aeolian).

A more interesting and thought-provoking way to discover the answers we are looking for is the following: removing the pitches F and B is not the only way anhemitonic scales can be built. Instead, we can just as well omit one of the other two pitches that help form the half-steps, E or C. The three possibilities are illustrated below: (1) pentatonic scales without F and B, as we know them already; (2) without E and B; and (3) without F and C. A fourth possibility omitting both E and C, is not shown because it results in scale patterns not applicable to our studies.

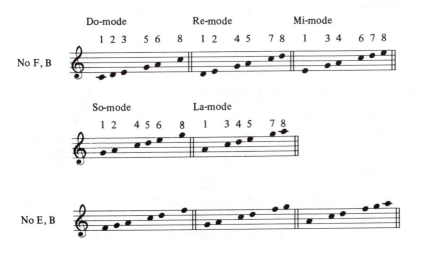

Looking at the results, we find that the two alternatives produce transpositions of the five basic (i.e., with F and B removed) pentatonic scale patterns:

The Do-mode, or C-pattern, is transposable to F and G.
The Re-mode, or D-pattern, is transposable to G and A.
The Mi-mode, or E-pattern, is transposable to A and B.
The So-mode, or G-pattern, is transposable to C and D.
The La-mode, or A-pattern, is transposable to D and E.

These, then, are the transpositions needing no pitch alterations and, therefore, no key signature. They are also the transpositions Gunild Keetman uses in her *Pieces for Xylophone.* Quite clearly, she believes that transposition to keys with sharps and flats, although possible on the barred instruments to some degree, exceeds the limits of elemental pentatonic theory. I also have observed that in virtually every song collection, songs in Do-mode transposed to G or F and songs in La-mode transposed to D or E bear the key signatures of their diatonic equivalents. In the absence of a diatonic accompaniment, this practice makes no sense at all.

Unclear, even incorrect, terminology in the identification of Do-pentatonic and its transpositions is also widespread. Again and again, one hears (and even reads) the terms "F-pentatonic" and "G-pentatonic" for modes that should properly be termed "Do-mode on F" and "Do-mode on G." The untransposed mode on G is the So-mode, with a different scale pattern, and there is no untransposed mode on F.

Deciding Short- and Long-Term Teaching Goals

So much for theory. By now some readers may be asking why we should burden ourselves with information that, in all likelihood, we will never be able to pass on to our students in the limited time allotted. The reason is that the student always possesses only partial knowledge, but the teacher must have a thorough understanding of his entire field, even if he or she teaches only a segment of it. Only then is it possible to give out small portions of carefully selected information which, over a long period of time, add up to form a large, organic unit in which, as in a puzzle, all the individual parts fit together perfectly. One cannot recognize teaching priorities unless one understands how music grows and functions along each step of development.

In regard to pentatonic modes and their transpositions, the teacher must decide where the priorities lie and what knowledge and skills need to be taught in order to build a firm foundation for future development. Designing a valid course of action involves some preparatory reflection. Long-term objectives, as well as the intermediary goals leading up to them, are sometimes lost in the maze of daily responsibilities and the fragmentation most music teachers face in their jobs. Each time I am about to begin a new and important study unit I have found it very helpful to clarify a number of points, which I will discuss here:

1. First, the teaching objectives of a new stage should be outlined in some detail. These objectives will in turn become the foundation of another development.

The study of pentatonic modes other than Do introduces new scale patterns based on different home tones (tonic notes). This in turn leads to the realization that bordun pitches are variable, as they must adjust to the different home tones. Finally, transposition as a means of moving certain scale patterns into a more convenient singing range will be studied and used or, if it was introduced earlier, reviewed and extended to include modes other than Do. The importance of this particular concept is that the children must learn to think in relative rather than concrete terms. Since the new ideas are developed with the help of the barred instruments, no real abstract thinking or knowledge of pitch notation is yet required. Like playing with Cuisenaire rods, playing with sound bars leads from the visual, and therefore "real," to a relative truth. A minimum of concrete information allows for a great variety of applications.

Unless our teaching objectives combine the understanding of musical concepts with skill development, we cannot hope to produce musicality in our students, to turn them into "musical musicians." Our most time-consuming task will be to familiarize the children with the sound essences of the various modes as they manifest themselves, not through scale patterns, but through melody. The students' ability to auditorily discriminate the modes is developed through melodic improvisation.

2. Next, the teacher needs to identify the concepts and skills that are prerequisites to the new concepts about to be introduced. Without a strong foundation, a smooth transition into the next developmental stage is not possible. Such prerequisite concepts and skills are:
    a. Authentic, untransposed Do-pentatonic, one octave minimum.
        Optional: Transpositions to the Do-mode on F and G; authentic range of five to six notes; plagal ranges of one octave or more. (See also Chapter 5, pp. 113–16.)
    b. Knowledge and understanding of the Do-pentatonic scale-pattern.
    c. Familiarity with simple and simple moving drone patterns.
    d. Improvisation: Use of the five pitches with an awareness of their "status" within the scale (i.e., home tone, 3rd and 5th as the most important pitches, supertonic as a "hot" note on which one does not want to sit for a long time, etc.).

e. Auditory perception, horizontal: hearing descending and ascending passages; discrimination between steps and leaps, and between smaller and larger leaps; identifying the intervals forming the tonic triad (thirds and fifths). (See also Chapter 5, p. 112–13.)

In addition, an awareness of vertical sounds should have evolved to the extent that the children are beginning to distinguish between more or less compatible, simultaneous pitches.

3. After having identified these prerequisites, the students' actual state of competency has to be evaluated. If there appear to be any gaps or omissions, they should be taken care of before going any further.

4. Now begins the detailed planning stage, in which the teacher decides on priorities and procedures.

As we have seen earlier, the Do- and La-modes possess the strongest identity among the five pentatonic modes, and lead directly into the diatonic major and minor modes. Because both are suited to drone and ostinato accompaniment, they have the best predisposition to harmonic development. It follows that they have priority over the other three modes. The Re- and So-modes are horizontally oriented. The creation of accompaniment demands in most cases an understanding of theoretical aspects whose complexity exceeds the ability of our students at this point. I myself am not at all convinced that one should attempt to put these horizontal modes into a vertical "harness." Be that as it may, the Re- and So-modes are of marginal importance to the development of harmonic awareness. Although they should not be ignored altogether, the extent to which they are incorporated is largely a matter of available teaching time.

Teaching Procedures

The initial step in the actual teaching procedure is to acquaint the children with the general concept of different modes. To this purpose, all scale patterns (including the Do-mode) are played, sung (where possible), compared with one another, and named. As an illustration of the scale patterns and their names, a chart similar to that on page 195 may be used. The students will notice immediately that the scales built on E, G, and A are in too high a singing range.

In order for the children to get a feel for these new modes, I usually follow up with some echo-play and instrumental improvisation. These improvisations are exploratory in nature and are entirely melodic, with no drone accompaniment. The only requirement is that the children be aware of the respective home tones to which they must return at the end of their improvisations. The rhythmic structure is kept extremely simple in that only quarter-notes are used, and half-notes at phrase endings. I do not even insist on a specific phrase length because I want the students to focus on the development of a melodic line. The next step in these exploratory improvisations is to impose some structure concerning the melodic range. Still using only the simplest rhythms and not worrying about phrase length, I now ask the children to make up questions and answers in an *a,b* form. The total melodic range should be limited to approximately one octave, and each of the two phrases should take up a different portion of its range. Both the authentic and the plagal range may be used for these improvisations:

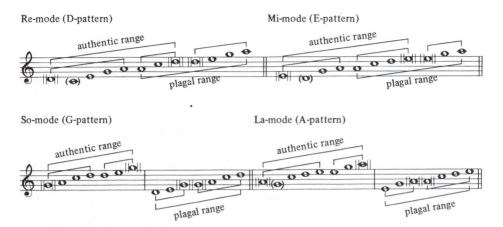

Re-mode (D-pattern)   Mi-mode (E-pattern)

So-mode (G-pattern)   La-mode (A-pattern)

Such introductory improvisations will give the students a general idea about the mode concept.

Moving from the general to the specific, we now concentrate on one of the new modes, the La- or A-pattern. Our aim is to familiarize the students with its sound qualities, which are distinctly different from those of the Do-mode. Since they can be experienced only through music itself, the time has come for singing and playing. In choosing suitable materials, the teacher must decide whether to start with songs or with instrumental pieces. Vocal tunes need to be transposed to D or E, whereas instrumental tunes do not. Unless transposition is already familiar to the students, it might be preferable not to burden them immediately with yet another new concept. Whether vocal or instrumental, all melodies should have a tonal range of at least a fifth, if not a sixth (by including the lower subtonic) or even an octave, in order to establish the minor modality in the strongest terms possible (minor third, minor seventh). In building a tonal range we need not proceed as carefully as was necessary with the Do-mode, since the students are already familiar with tunes of at least an octave in range.

The interval of the fifth is significant in all melodic development because of the polar relationship between its two pitches. The 5th scale degree represents a state of tension, and the tonic note the release. We feel it most naturally in singing (as the vocal chords tighten on the higher pitch), and it is not by accident that in Gregorian chant the 5th scale note is the most common tone of recitation. Even the simple childhood chant, which, like plainsong, is a form of syllabic singing, centers around the fifth. When the melody expands downward, the tonic becomes the note of rest, the cessation of motion. Thus, the pitches of the tonic triad are of primary importance in melody.

In comparing the tonic triads of the Do- and La-modes, we find that the two thirds forming them are reversed. In the Do-mode, the lower third is a major interval and the upper third (the call pitches) a minor one; in the La-mode the opposite is the case. In order to establish the minor character of the La-mode as different from Do, the tonic-triad pitches serve as "pillars" upon which to "hang" a tune. Inclusion of the lower 7th degree will further strengthen the tonality, and will help to produce a cadential effect, even though only a weak one. In this respect it serves a similar purpose as the lower submediant in the Do-mode:

The pitch D or Re is nearly as incompatible in the La-mode as it is in the Do-mode when used as an accented or otherwise strongly exposed melody note. In the beginning it is therefore best treated as a passing tone or an auxiliary note.

Summing up the comparison of the Do and La scale-pitches as melody notes, we find that both modes have a complete tonic triad which serves as the skeletal support for melody (nos. 1 in the following example). Next in importance are, in Do, the submediant and, in La, the subtonic pitch (nos. 2). Lowest in priority is D or Re, as the 2nd scale degree in Do and the 4th scale degree in La (nos. 3). Thus, the La-mode is in each of these respects the exact inversion of Do.

The same applies, of course, to the harmonic structure of moving drone patterns. The most elemental and useful simple moving drone in Do, 5–6, implies a change from major to minor or from the tonic to the submediant triad (the latter in first inversion). In La-pentatonic the corresponding drone movement is from the tonic to the subtonic note, from the minor tonic triad to the major mediant triad (in second inversion):

Again, an exact reversal.

The final analysis shows that in both modes the same pitches (though not the same scale degrees) form the basis for harmony. Combined, they are inversions of a seventh chord built on La. The slight dissonance caused by the interval of the seventh, most often occurring in its inversion as a second (because the seventh chord is inverted), is characteristic for both modes and need not be avoided:

Observations such as these are not meant to be shared with the children; their purpose is to help the teacher select or create suitable melodies for demonstration and to serve as a basis for improvisations. We will now examine what the discussion above means in terms of melodic and harmonic development.

As mentioned before, the first examples of La-mode melodies should have a range of at least a fifth (La–Mi), but a sixth (So below tonic–Mi) is even better because both minor intervals (third, lower seventh) lie within this range. The tonic-triad pitches occur on the more important counts of the measures, while the 4th degree remains a passing tone or an auxiliary note. A simple drone provides the foundation. (For singing, transpose to D or E.)

The Northwind

Instrumental improvisation starts with question-answer phrases in the form *a,a1*:

For *a,b* forms, the range is extended to an octave:

a) Authentic:

(Transpositions may be used also)

b) Plagal (Best used untransposed):

---

[6] Text from Opie, *The Oxford Book of Nursery Rhymes.*

The subtonic need not be avoided on strong beats. A song tune like the preceding example can also be adjusted to a plagal range:

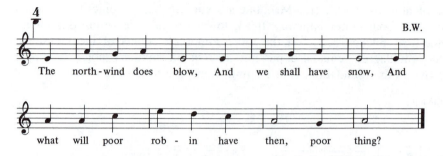

The north-wind does blow, And we shall have snow, And

what will poor rob - in have then, poor thing?

Along with the melody, the accompaniment will also be expanded.

1. *Simple drone*:
   a. Homo-, poly-, and monorhythmic forms are explored first:

   b. Auxiliary and passing tones may be inserted. They do not change the harmony:

   c. Melodic ostinati are first still linked to a broken simple drone:

   d. Later, this attachment is abandoned:

2. *The implied harmony change to major* (mediant) is effected through the simple moving bordun 1–7:

Again, many patterns can be created with the three drone types. However, the extent to which the children are able to use them for adjusting to the tune depends on their level of conceptual learning and vertical pitch awareness.

The basic guidelines to sequencing are the same in the Do- and La-modes. For suggestions concerning further harmonic development in La-pentatonic, the reader is referred back to Orff-Schulwerk I, ''Ostinato Exercises,'' and to Chapter Six of this book. As we already discovered in Do-pentatonic, how moving drones are related to certain triads can be understood only by the teacher who is well versed in traditional harmony and whose ear can supply the pitches not present in pentatonic. The student is not able to hear or conceptualize triadic configurations other than the two present in pentatonic, because such an interpretation is a question of musical experience and sophistication. The examples below are brief indications of implied harmony changes resulting from moving drones.

1. The components of the two triads in La can be interpreted differently in respect to their harmonic affiliation:

Tonic triad: i,   VI   i,   III   Mediant triad: III,   i   III,   v

2. Simple moving drones may imply different harmonic changes:

i - III   i - iv   i - v   i - VI

3. The implied harmony change i–VII can be accomplished only through the use of double moving drones:

This survey reveals the roots from which harmonic development grows later on in the diatonic realm, and will be helpful in dealing with folksongs.

ARRANGING TRADITIONAL SONGS[7]

Sources for Appropriate Materials

At the beginning of this chapter I mentioned that the pentatonic song has been especially well preserved in the Appalachian mountain region. When we talk about American folksong, however, we do not refer to the Appalachian song exclusively. The American song heritage has its roots in many cultures and folk traditions. Alan Lomax calls it a "melting pot": "Our best songs are hybrids of hybrids, mixtures of mixtures."[8] Thus, a search for tunes in the Re- and So-modes would be very successful if we turned to the Southern Appalachians. But to find songs in the Do- and La-modes, we need not restrict ourselves to this region.

Today there are many collections of American folksongs and children's songs, most of which contain pentatonic tunes. There are also collections that are entirely pentatonic. Unfortunately for us, many of them are furnished with diatonic accompaniment, thereby robbing the tunes of their pentatonic character. By far the best sources are those in which the songs are unaccompanied.

In order to search out appropriate materials, we must be able to analyze the melodies according to their modes. This is not always a simple task, especially when we work from collections in which the songs have already been harmonized. In order to establish the mode of a tune, one must first determine its tonic. It is usually the final, occasionally not. After having identified the tonic, one proceeds to build a scale with all the pitches appearing in the song. The scale reveals the mode, and whether or not it is transposed.

In Chapter Five we discussed the fact that the absence of the two semitones alone is not enough to make a tune suitable for ostinato accompaniment. Traditional pentatonic songs often do not comply with the requirements for patterned accompaniment because they are already harmonically conceived. The following is an attempt to examine pentatonic songs in respect to their compatibility with Schulwerk techniques, and to offer a few suggestions regarding their arrangement. The study is by no means exhaustive or conclusive, as it is not possible to cover the endless variants of melodic movement. The suggestions offered here are based on the objective of developing in the children a gradual awareness of harmonic considerations. This involves using moving drones and ostinati to adjust to specific pitches in the tune. There is, of course the possibility of entirely "droning" the songs, that is, never to change the drone fifths despite the resulting dissonances (as we find it in dulcimer accompaniment). But what sounds good on one instrument does not necessarily sound as good on another. The different sound qualities of

---

[7] All song examples are notated as they appear in the source books. Thus, some examples will bear key signatures because the author transposed to keys needing signatures. However, in transpositions where neither F♯ nor B♭ was needed, key signatures were eliminated even if they appeared in the source.

[8] *The Folksongs of North America* (Garden City, N.Y.: Doubleday, 1960), p. xvi.

dulcimer and pitched percussion instruments necessitate the use of different musical styles. Nevertheless, in arranging traditional songs, we must always use good judgment and sensitivity, in order not to destroy the essence of the folksong.

We will focus mainly on songs in Do- and La-pentatonic, as these are the modes best suited to our purposes. For a general orientation, I have grouped Do- and La-mode songs into several categories:

1. Those which accommodate easily to drone accompaniment, and can be set by the children.

2. Those which are harmonically conceived but can still be adapted to ostinato accompaniment, although by the teacher only.

3. Those which require harmonization rather than patterned accompaniment. These should actually be considered gapped diatonic songs.

Songs in Do-Pentatonic

1. Melodies with one of the tonic-triad pitches on the strong beats of the measures cause no problems with simple and simple moving drones 5–6. The 2nd scale degree remains a passing tone.
For examples of arrangements see the Appendix: "Mole in the Ground" (no. 1), "Farmyard" (no. 2), "I Heard the Angels" (no. 3).

2. The songs in this group are harmonically oriented as they contain the strong 2nd scale degree. However, the melodic form (such as *a,a1*) allows for evenly spaced supertonics, which means that patterned accompaniment is possible:

Run, Chillen, Run

Run, chil-len, run, The pat-ter-roll-er catch you, Run, chil-len, run, it's al-most day.

From Crawford Seeger, *American Folk Songs for Children*

One need only align the implied harmony change in the ostinato with the strong 2nd degree in the melody (and remember, not all the instrumental parts need to adjust). From the examples in Orff-Schulwerk I, we have learned that the supertonic may be interpreted either as part of the dominant or as part of the supertonic harmony. The drone fifth by itself suggests the former, the double moving drone I–ii the latter. Once a basic design has been decided upon, many variations in pattern formation are possible. It is here that the children can play an active role by creating the actual arrangement. Although the teacher may have to establish the fundamental harmony change, the students can build their own patterns around it and decide on instrumentation. Example in Appendix: "Run, Chillen, Run" (no. 4).

There are many songs with a phrase ending on the supertonic, which strongly indicates a change to the dominant harmony:

The Old Sow

What will we do with the old sow's hide? Make a good cush-ion as ev - er did ride. Coarse cush-ion, fine cush-ion, an - y such a thing, The old sow died with the mea-sles in the spring.

From Bradford, *Sing It Yourself*

Several solutions are possible to solve the problem in the example above. However, all patterns must be two measures long because the supertonic in question is in the fourth measure:

a. A simple drone can sound every other measure:

b. The whole song can be set over a pedal point on the drone fifth, with a drop to the tonic at the end. (See A-section of "Boomfallera.")

c. The drone can be broken in such a way that the fifth coincides with the phrase ending on the supertonic:

However, the pattern needs to be adjusted to the other, cadencing phrase endings. These and similar patterns can still be comprehended as broken drones rather than tonic-dominant harmonization. However, they are compromises whose use cannot be recommended wholeheartedly.

Example of an arrangement in Appendix (no. 5).

3. The last group of songs belongs to the pseudo-pentatonic or gapped major diatonic variety and is not suitable for ostinato accompaniment. These songs require harmonization for different reasons.

   a. The strong 2nd degree. In the following example one cannot help but hear very clearly a harmonization with V or V7, and one would not want it any other way:

Old Pompey

Old Pom-pey is dead and laid in his grave, laid in his grave, laid in his grave, Old Pom-pey is dead and laid in his grave, ho ho ho.—

From Bradford, *Sing It Yourself*

Button, Button

But-ton, you must wan-der, wan-der, wan-der, But-ton, you must wan-der ev-'ry-where. Bright eyes will find you, sharp eyes will find you; But-ton, you must wan-der ev-'ry-where.

From Kersey, *Just Five*

b. The 2nd scale degree is often quite prominent in plagal songs, because the upper range, consisting of the first three scale notes, may be used heavily:

That Lonesome Valley

When you walk the lone-some val-ley, you got to walk it by—your-self.—No one here may—walk it with you, You got to walk it — by your-self.

From Bradford, *Sing It Yourself*

c. In the next example, the same problem is compounded because of a lengthy form with many different phrases:

Night Herding

O slow up, do-gies, quit your rov-in' a-round, You've wan-dered and tramped all o-ver the ground. O graze a-long, do-gies, and feed kind of slow, And don't for-ev-er be on the go, O move slow, do-gies, move slow, Hi-yoo, hi-yoo oo. Hoo oo oo.

From Bradford, *Sing It Yourself*

d. An exposed and long-held 6th scale degree calls for harmonization with the subdominant:

Blow Ye Winds, Blow

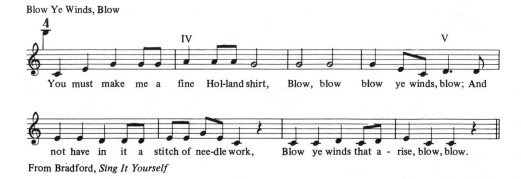

You must make me a fine Hol-land shirt, Blow, blow blow ye winds, blow; And not have in it a stitch of nee-dle work, Blow ye winds that a-rise, blow, blow.

From Bradford, *Sing It Yourself*

Songs in La-Pentatonic

1. As with the Do-mode, the easiest songs to arrange in the La-mode are those centered around the accented pitches of the tonic triad, leaving the other pitches (4 and 7) as passing tones.

    a. A good example is the well-known "My Paddle's Keen and Bright." The song, through accompaniment and instrumentation, gives much opportunity to convey the quiet and peaceful atmosphere on the waters. Interludes may be improvised. The song can also be rendered in canon.

    For an arrangement, see Appendix (no. 6).

b. The broken tonic triad occurs frequently in Afro-American songs. Often these tunes are clapping games, calls and responses, or other activity-oriented games:

Hambone

Ham - bone, ham - bone, pat him on the shoul - der, If you get a pret-ty girl, I'll show you how to hold her, Ham-bone, ham-bone, where have you been? All round the world and back a-gain.

From Jones and Hawes, *Step It Down*

Rosie, Darling

Ro - sie, dar - ling Ro - sie, ha ha, Ro sie; Ro-sie, dar-ling Ro - sie, ha ha, Ro - sie. Way down yon-der in Bal-ti - more, ha ha Ro - sie, Need no car - pet on my floor,— ha ha Ros - sie.

From Bradford, *Sing It Yourself*

In order to retain the percussive element so typical of these songs, pitched accompaniment should stay simple and merely reflect the pulse or the offbeat rhythms of the clapping. The example given in the Appendix does not end on the tonic note, but on the third; the final is still E, the pitch before the last note. The reason can be found in the speech accent of the text.

Example of arrangement in Appendix: "Rosie Darling" (no. 7).

2. In many La-mode songs, emphasis is placed on the 4th and 7th degrees. These pitches belong to the subtonic harmony and can be accompanied with a double moving drone. However, this device works only if the tune has regularly occurring 4th and 7th degrees that allow for patterns.

a. The following ballad tune illustrates this point:

Lord Thomas and Fair Ellinor, Version R (original on D)

Come rid-dle us all, our dear, good moth-er, come rid-dle us all __ as one, __ Wheth-er I shall mar-ry fair El - len-der, __ or bring the brown __ girl home? __ The brown girl she has hous-es and lands, Fair El-len-der she has none, __ So my ad-vice for you would be __ to bring the brown __ girl home. __

From Sharp, *English Folksongs of the Southern Appalachians*

For an arrangement of this song, see Appendix (no. 8).

b. There are songs in which the accented 4th appears regularly but is spaced farther apart. This may complicate the ostinato accompaniment. In the examples below, the 4th is placed in the third bar of the four-measure phrases:

John Brown's Coal Mine

The long-est train I ev - er saw passed by John Brown's coal mine, __ The en - gine passed at six o' - clock and the ca - boose went by at nine. __

Ama Lama

A - ma la-ma coo-ma la - ma coo-ma la - ma vee - stay. Oh, no no no no no vee - stay, Ee - nie mee -nie gyp - si - lee - nie, Oh ah oo

From Bradford, *Sing It Yourself*

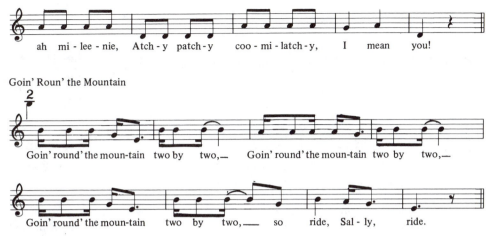

ah mi - lee - nie, Atch - y patch - y coo - mi - latch - y, I mean you!

Goin' Roun' the Mountain

Goin' round' the moun-tain two by two,— Goin' round' the moun-tain two by two,—

Goin' round' the moun-tain two by two,— so ride, Sal - ly, ride.

From Bradford, *Sing It Yourself*

For "John Brown's Coal Mine," a simple broken drone pattern will take care of the problem:

In the remaining two tunes—one a call-response chant, the other a circle game—a homorhythmic drone pattern again perhaps best reflects the rhythmic essence of a clapping accompaniment. The drone may follow the voice downward or execute other double moving patterns. Dissonances seem to enhance rather than disturb this type of melody.

Example in Appendix: "Goin' Roun' the Mountain" (no. 9).

3. In many songs the tonality floats consistently between major and minor without clear orientation toward one or the other. Often, only the final is an indication of the actual mode:

Nottamun Town

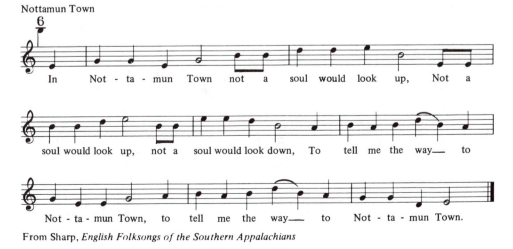

In Not - ta - mun Town not a soul would look up, Not a

soul would look up, not a soul would look down, To tell me the way— to

Not - ta - mun Town, to tell me the way— to Not - ta - mun Town.

From Sharp, *English Folksongs of the Southern Appalachians*

The Bird Song, Version B

Says the black bird to the crow: What makes white folks hate us so? It's
been our trade— of pull - ing corn, Ev - er since old Ad -am was born.

From Sharp, *English Folksongs of the Southern Appalachians*

Such melodies allow for simple moving drones, implying the harmonies i and III (A-minor and C-major), familiar to us in the Do-mode as vi and I. Often, the two harmonies can be used interchangeably, since the resulting dissonance produced by adding the tune will be one and the same 7th chord, only in different inversions (see also p. 202). For example, harmonizing a G in the tune with an A-minor, or an A in the tune with a C-major harmony, is not only permissible, but is a good device to underscore the harmonic ambiguity of the melody itself.

The following example illustrates how a basic simple moving drone can be developed into more interesting ostinato forms. Such patterns should be created by the students themselves in well-planned, step-by-step sequences. At first, ostinati can be improvised independently from the songs for which they are intended. Later they need to be tried out with the tune, so that the best patterns can be chosen. Depending on the texts, the ostinati of the final song arrangements may change from stanza to stanza, or new ones may be added.

Basic pattern for "Nottamun Town":

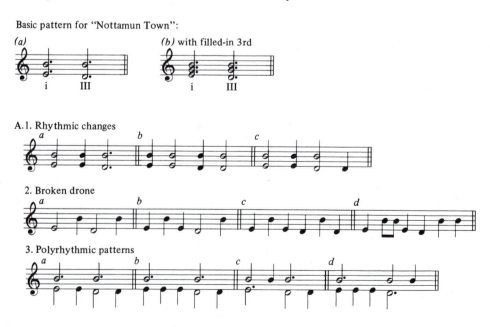

(a)

(b) with filled-in 3rd

i   III

i   III

A.1. Rhythmic changes

a   *b*   *c*

2. Broken drone

a   *b*   *c*   *d*

3. Polyrhythmic patterns

a   *b*   *c*   *d*

B. 1. Rhythmic changes

2. Broken into 1 + 2

3. Broken into 3 components

4. Some simple rhythmic changes

5. Skips filled in to develop melodic ostinati

The following melody also does not definitely establish a minor tonality, and the problem is compounded through the ending on F. Thus, the tune might be understood as a plagal Do-mode on F rather than an authentic La-mode on D:

Go to Sleep

Go to sleep, Go— to sleep - y, Go to sleep-y lit - tle ba - by,

Hush, li'l ba - by and don't you cry, — Go to sleep-y lit - tle ba - by.

From Library of Congress, AAFS 1324, A2 and A3. Sung by Aunt Florida Hampton. Collector John A. Lomax, 1937

It would be wrong to rule out an interpretation as major pentatonic, because the song can indeed be arranged in this manner. However, the predominance of the pitches D, A, and F on the accented beats of the measures makes a stronger case for the minor mode. The ending on F is not very significant, since it falls on a weak syllable. Whether the choice be Do or La, an arrangement should make the most of the modal ambiguity through the use of moving drones or by superimposing components of the D-minor and F-major triads on top of each other. Orff uses the same device in Orff-Schulwerk I, working from a Do-mode. A setting for this song can be found in the Appendix (no. 10).

Re- and So-Pentatonic

We will now examine some songs in the Re- and So-modes, which, though fairly common in Southern Appalachia, are difficult to use in Orff-Schulwerk. One problem with these songs is their textual content. It takes a mature mind to appreciate and understand the deeper concerns and universal problems that simple people express in these ballads of disappointed love and cruel deeds.

Songs in the Re-Mode.

The scale picture shows a rather disjunct order of pitches. There are no two steps in a row as in all the other scales (except when scale degrees 7, 1, and 2 occur in the same register). Neither of the two harmonizing intervals, the 3rd and the 6th, is present. And, of course, there is no tonic triad around which to weave a tune. All this has an effect on the shape of the melody. Songs in the authentic or near-authentic range tend to utilize the subtonic-triad pitches more than those of the other triad on the 5th scale degree. This can be seen clearly in the two examples below:

Old Betty Larkin

©1940, 1964 Jean Ritchie, Geordie Music Publishing Co. In the original the note values are twice as fast.

Betty Anne (original in F)

From Sharp, *English Folksongs of the Southern Appalachians*

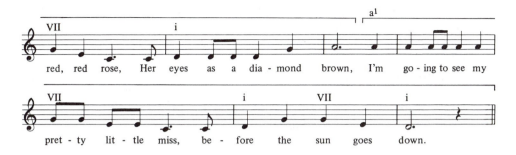

The form of the first tune is *a,b,c,d*, unsuitable for patterned accompaniment. But even if harmonization were used, the result would be unsatisfactory; the song is probably best left unaccompanied.

"Betty Anne" obliges with a good form, *a,a1,a,a1*, and with clear harmonic changes, i–VII. However, the patterns for these changes are four measures long for the *a-* and *a1*-phrases. Double moving drones can be used, but the accompaniment will still be a harmonization rather than an ostinato.

The next song, "The Rich Old Lady," is also in the authentic Re-mode. Instead of including the subtonic pitch, it adds the upper-octave 2nd scale degree. This brings in the minor triad on the 5th scale degree, and we find three harmonies, i, VII, and v:

The Rich Old Lady, Version C

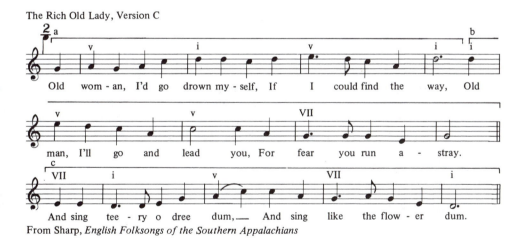

From Sharp, *English Folksongs of the Southern Appalachians*

The three (double) phrases show a harmonic picture, hardly fit for ostinato patterns:

> *a*-phrase: v–i–v–i
> *b*-phrase: v–v–VII–VII
> *c*-phrase: i–v–VII–i

Of course, elemental harmonizing techniques can be used. But we must keep in mind the difference between true ostinato accompaniment and elemental harmonization. The former makes patterns through regularly spaced harmony changes and through the manner in which they are played. The latter makes patterns only by playing in a similar fashion; the harmonies themselves have no regular, recurrent pattern.

The following melody is somewhat different. It moves in the plagal range of the Re-mode, and the emphasis on the 5th and 7th scale degrees makes possible an implied shift to the submediant with a simple moving drone. The effect is similar to that of the La-mode songs:

The Daemon Lover, Version V

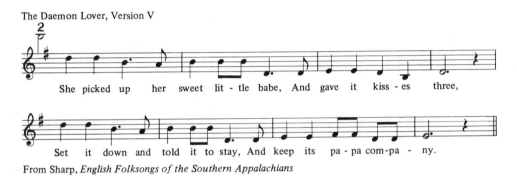

She picked up her sweet lit - tle babe, And gave it kiss - es three,

Set it down and told it to stay, And keep its pa - pa com-pa - ny.

From Sharp, *English Folksongs of the Southern Appalachians*

Basic drone patterns:

In summing up, it seems to me that the true essence of the Re-mode as exemplified in the folksongs is monophonic and horizontally conceived. In most cases elemental ostinato accompaniment does not work, and even elemental harmonization is not particularly attractive. Accompaniment should enhance a melody, rather than seeming superfluous. Our students will better understand the special beauty of the Re-mode songs if we present them in an authentic manner, not tethered to any kind of accompaniment.

Songs in the So-Mode.

Authentic So-mode

2   +   3   ii   IV

Plagal Do-mode

Final   vi   I

The So-mode is centered on the 5th scale note of the Do-scale. The two-plus-three grouping of its pitches is in reverse order from the three-plus-two grouping of the Do-mode. Thus, So-mode melodies tend to emphasize the scale degrees 4, 5, and 6, which our harmonically trained ears translate into the first three pitches of the Do-mode (plagal) and want to hear harmonized with the Do-mode's drone and dominant (on emphasized Re-mode pitches). In other words, the So-mode is often mistaken as a plagal Do-mode ending on its dominant rather than on its tonic. The two triads in the So-mode are on the 2nd and 4th scale pitches. Again, the subdominant triad is the tonic triad of the Do-mode, and strongly felt in this way.

The following song is an example of emphasized 4th and 5th scale degrees:

The Tree in the Wood, Version B (original in D)

From Sharp, *English Folksongs of the Southern Appalachians*

A full arrangement is shown in the Appendix (no. 11).

The second tune again centers around the subdominant. The strong 6th scale degree in measure 7 is the third of the subdominant triad.

The Old Grey Mare, Version A

From Sharp, *English Folksongs of the Southern Appalachians*

As before, there is no alternative to using a drone on G.

The following song makes possible the use of a simple moving broken So-drone with an implied harmony change to the subdominant:

Lord Thomas and Fair Ellinor, Version E

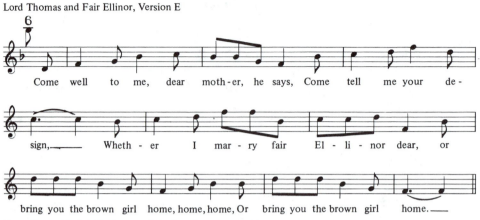

Come well to me, dear moth-er, he says, Come tell me your de-

sign,—— Wheth - er I mar - ry fair El - li - nor dear, or

bring you the brown girl home, home, home, Or bring you the brown girl home.——

From Sharp, *English Folksongs of the Southern Appalachians*

1. Simple moving drone on So (broken):

Or the tune may be set over a simple moving drone on B-flat, in which case we are again in the plagal Do-mode:

2. Simple moving drone on Do:

None of the solutions seems especially suited to the melody.

The last example appears in Ruth Crawford Seeger's *Animal Folksongs*, as well as in Doreen Halls's edition of Orff-Schulwerk I:

Daddy Shot a Bear

Dad - dy shot a bear,   Dad - dy shot a bear,

Shot him through the key - hole and nev - er touched a hair.

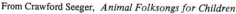
From Crawford Seeger, *Animal Folksongs for Children*

The melody encompasses the range of a fifth, again strongly accenting the 4th scale degree. Only a bordun based on the pitch C will sound satisfactory.

The question arises as to how far it is legitimate to use accompaniments that cloud, rather than clarify, the modal identity. If our purpose is to illustrate the So-mode in folksongs, we miss the point by using arrangements that more often than not must alter the mode in order to work. My own preference is to either sing the songs *a cappella* or use the tonic note as a pedal point, ideally played on a stringed instrument such as a dulcimer, psaltery, or *bordun*. In this way not only can the stylistic authenticity of the songs be preserved, but the unique melodic characteristics and horizontal orientation of the mode will remain readily apparent.

Milkweed Seed

This song was given to me many years ago by a student in one of my workshops. I have forgotten her name, and I was not able to fine a source for this lovely song.

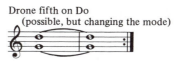

The Virginian Lover, Version C

From Sharp, *English Folksongs of the Southern Appalachians*

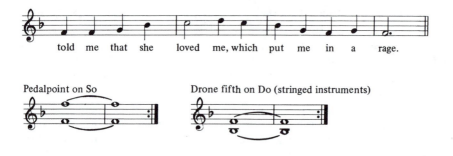

told me that she   loved me, which put me in a   rage.

Pedalpoint on So   Drone fifth on Do (stringed instruments)

The Mi-Mode

As mentioned earlier, the Mi-mode has little identity of its own because of the grouping of its scale pitches. No matter what the succession of pitches may be in a Mi-mode tune, the ear will interpret the lower three scale notes as the Do-mode chant-pitches and the upper three notes as the 1st, 2nd, and 3rd degrees of the Do-mode. The only way to establish a Mi tonality is by adding a pedal point on the tonic note. To my knowledge, there are no Mi-mode tunes in the American traditional song repertoire. The reason may very well be its lack of a unique tonal character. Therefore, it is a mode that exists in theory only.

SUMMARY

As we now come to the conclusion of our discussion on the pentatonic modes and the pentatonic folksong, let us once more review its main points:

1. To begin with, the pentatonic mode in its living expression through traditional unaccompanied song has no theory of its own beyond the fact that we can establish scales according to the placement of the finalis and the groupings of the pitches used.
2. A theory can be attached to the pentatonic modes only in retrospect, so to speak, by referring to harmonic aspects of the diatonic system. As soon as we apply this vertical point of view, some pentatonic modes begin to resist. Even categorization according to mode is difficult, as we have seen in the Re-, So-, and Mi-modes.
3. This does not mean that we need to limit ourselves to only those modes most suitable for ostinato accompaniment. It does mean, though, that each mode ought to be used to its best advantage, whether in traditional song or in improvisation.

The reader interested in learning more about improvisation and composition, especially in the more problematic pentatonic modes such as those on Re, Mi, and So, is referred to Gunild Keetman's three xylophone books.[9] All contain numerous pieces in the five pentatonic modes. The Re-mode tunes, excepting two, are unaccompanied. There are also many pieces in the So- and Mi-modes

[9] Stücke für Xylophone, by Gunild Keetman; B. Schott's Söhne, Mainz

for both one and two instruments. All are improvisations on a grand scale and are far beyond the comprehension of young students, but they illustrate how pentatonic can become a highly sophisticated and artistic expression of elemental music. In the elementary grades improvisation will not be possible beyond the building of simple melodies, with or without drone accompaniment, and the creation of melodic ostinati. There are many applications for the more unusual pentatonic modes in stories, dramatizations, and poetry. With the musically sophisticated and mature student, pentatonic improvisation can become more complex and much freer in design. But complexity and freedom grow out of understanding the essence of the various pentatonic modes.

9
RECORDER
PLAYING

THE RECORDER IN ORFF-SCHULWERK

In this chapter we will take a look at the role and use of the recorder in Orff-Schulwerk. The chapter is not a quick course in how to learn to play the recorder; rather, it is meant as a general guide to teaching procedures for the instructor who already knows how to play. The suggestions given here concerning these procedures refer to elementary-school children and any other students still working in the pentatonic realm.

The Instrument

It is not by mere chance that the recorder occupies an important place in the Schulwerk instrumentarium. With the exception of the human voice, it is the only nonpercussive instrument in the Orff ensemble and, as is the case with the voice, its tone is produced by means of the breath. Not only is it well suited to smooth and sustained melodic flow, a feat difficult to achieve on the barred instruments, it also lends itself naturally to playing fast passages and to embellishing (the latter being a direct outgrowth of improvisation). Thus, in Orff-Schulwerk the instrumental melody with a distinct style of its own begins with the recorder. (However, the differentiation between instrumental and vocal melodies will emerge only much later when playing skills are sufficiently advanced.) An elemental instrument, the recorder invites dancing and can even be played while dancing. In addition, its pure and light tone complements the sound texture of the barred instruments.

A few words about its recent history may help the reader to understand its use in Orff-Schulwerk. First mentioned in the fourteenth century, the recorder eventually became a popular instrument, adapting to different musical styles through the centuries until it fell out of use with the advent of the Classical period. After nearly 150 years of neglect, it was rediscovered at the beginning of the twentieth century in the wake of a new interest in early music. Arnold Dolmetsch was the first to construct new recorders after old models, soon to be followed by other instrument makers on the continent, especially in Germany. In his "Documentaria" Carl Orff recalls how, in 1926, he was searching for instruments that would serve for an elemental instrumentarium. Curt Sachs, his mentor and friend, persuaded him to try the recorder. Though reluctant at first, Orff ordered a set of recorders for the Güntherschule from Peter Harlan in Markneukirchen.[1] When the shipment arrived, there were no instructions on how to play these recorders. It was Gunild Keetman who experimented tirelessly and enthusiatically and soon developed a style eminently suited to elemental music-making. Her first publications with music for the recorder date from 1930.[2] They are as stylistically relevant to elemental music in our time as they were then, though for the most part too challenging for youngsters, since she worked only with young adults in those early years of Schulwerk.

Today we can hardly imagine an Orff ensemble without recorders. Experimentation in the making of instruments is now past. Handcrafted wooden models are reserved mainly for the professional or semiprofessional player. With the discovery of synthetic materials, it is now possible to manufacture recorders on a large scale, thereby filling the need for inexpensive but adequate classroom instruments. By far the best and most popular models nowadays are adaptations of the Baroque recorder developed in England. These instruments require the so-called English fingering, which differs only slightly from Baroque fingering and makes it possible (for those interested in historical performance) to follow, with just a few exceptions, the fingering charts shown in historical treatises such as Hotteterre's *Principes de la Flute* (1707). There are also recorders with a different boring that allows for a simpler fingering than the English and Baroque models. The early German-built recorders were of this type and can still be found occasionally. However, the so-called German fingering makes it difficult to play semitones and certain other pitches in tune, and its use is not recommended. (The recorder with German fingering should not be confused with the "song flute," a most inadequate-sounding plastic contraption still used in some schools.) English and Baroque recorders require cross-fingerings on the fourth note (F in C recorders and B-flat in F recorders), which is a bit more difficult to learn but well worth the effort.

The fingering chart by Hotteterre illustrates an interesting feature called the "supporting finger." The ring finger of the right hand keeps its hole covered for most pitches in the first octave:

---

[1] A "set" or "choir" consists of four principal recorders pitched at distances of fifths and fourths—bass, tenor, alto, and soprano. The lowest note on the bass is small F, on the tenor C1, on the Alto F1, and on the soprano C2. The set is extended further to include a sopranino starting on F3, and a great bass with small C as the lowest pitch.

[2] Gunild Keetman, "Spielstücke für Blockflöten und kleines Schlagwerk, Book I (Mainz: B. Schott's Söhne, 1952.

	IV	V	VI	VII	II¹	♯II¹	III¹
	●●	●●	●●	●●	●○	○●	○○
	●	●	●	○	●	●	●
	●	●	○	○	○	○	○
Supporting finger→	●	○	○	○	○	○	○
	○	○	○	○	○	○	○
	○●	○●	○●	○●	○●	○●	○●

Although not widely used today, the supporting finger is very helpful in teaching beginners. Since the first notes introduced involve only fingers of the left hand, the right hand as a support for the recorder will stay naturally in the correct position when the ring finger is kept on its hole.[3]

The Recorder in the Classroom

The question of when to introduce the recorder into the classroom ensemble cannot be answered in absolute terms because the time allotted for music instruction is not the same in every situation. However, the children should have had several years of basic Schulwerk training, should be conversant in the Do- and La-modes and their transpositions, and should be able to read rhythmic notation fluently and to improvise rhythmic and melodic phrases in duple and triple meter. The ability to read pitch notation is not absolutely necessary, as it can be taught along with the recorder pitches. Since movement training is another important and time-consuming aspect in the Orff program, recorder instruction is feasible no earlier than the third grade, but generally in the fourth grade, assuming the children began their basic Orff-Schulwerk training in their first year of school. We also should take into account that recorder playing requires home practice. Most youngsters below the third grade are not yet ready to add music assignments to their regular homework.

Because of large class sizes, the first recorder lessons are not always musically rewarding for either teacher or pupils. Nevertheless, teachers do find ways to cope. Many offer recorder instruction as a voluntary activity to those children who are willing to give up lunch periods or other breaks, or who are able to stay after school. Still, too many children will be excluded, and over a period of time their musical skills will noticeably lag behind those of the "recorder bunch."

I prefer an approach that gives equal opportunity to all children and keeps them musically on the same level of development. Granted, not all students will become expert players, but at least no one will be left out. Occasionally the class can be divided, and while the teacher works with one group on the recorder the others can be busy with different assignments. But most of the instruction should be directed toward the entire class. However, one should refrain from letting all of the twenty or more children play at the same time. Those who are

---

[3] Franz J. Giesbert, *Method for the Treble Recorder*, (Mainz: B. Schott's Söhne, 1937). English revised edition 1957. In this recorder method the supporting finger is called the "buttress-finger."

not playing can finger along without actually blowing; when their turn comes, they will have already done some silent practicing.

The instrument introduced at this level is the soprano recorder. Not only is it just the right size for small hands, but more importantly, like the barred instruments its natural scale is C. This means that recorder instruction can be treated as an integral part of the general Schulwerk program, rather than a separate entity which is stylistically and developmentally on a different level.

The first year of recorder playing is a crucial one. Future attitudes are determined to a great extent by the degree of motivation we can at this time develop in the youngsters toward a more serious commitment to musical study than was hitherto necessary. Although all are eager to play, some will lose their enthusiasm quickly when it becomes apparent that the recorder is more difficult to play than the barred instruments and necessitates regular practice. The teacher must be supportive and patient, extending as much individal attention as is possible in a given situation. He or she also needs to be imaginative and inventive in order to make practicing enjoyable and stimulating, all of which is a tall order indeed. Slogans such as "Learning is fun," which are designed to stimulate the children and in fact contain much truth, can be quite misleading to youngsters if they imply that things should come easily to them. The fun is not so much in the process of learning as in the results.

Since instrumental practice will be a new experience for most youngsters, they have to be taught how to go about it. However, I have found that, with each new piece, practicing procedures have to be demonstrated anew. We establish the form and rhythmic framework, the phrases and breathing spots. I explain to the children that it is more effective to practice each phrase separately than to struggle though the whole piece again and again. We pinpoint the more difficult passages or fingering combinations for extra practice. I constantly impress on the class that a piece may only be played as fast as one is able to play its most difficult passages. For this reason, we always first go over the most difficult spot in order to establish a tempo that everyone can hold when the whole piece is performed. A specific time limit for an assignment should be given, but in my experience one needs to check to make sure that the children not only practice, but practice correctly. It won't take long for the teacher to determine which students have problems with small-muscle control, with reading pitch notation and translating it into fingerings, and which ones do not practice at all. These are the ones who will need individual help and attention. But if we know our students, we know their potentials as well as their limitations, and we must expect no more and no less than they are capable of achieving.

For children, music-making is a sociable activity, and moreover they love—as we all do—the full sound of ensemble music. This is a fact we teachers can exploit. From the beginning, rather than isolate the recorder as a separate instrument with its own little tunes, I include it in the general ensemble. (A welcome by-product of this procedure is the fact that never more than a third of the entire class plays recorder at the same time.) This is possible even at the very beginning, when the children know only one or two notes. Another way to achieve a richer and more interesting sound texture is for the teacher to accompany the students' unison playing on a guitar, or with a challenging ostinato on a xylophone. As soon as four or five pitches have been learned, little canons or two-part pieces, with or without drone accompaniment, can be included in the repertoire.

If we are to provide the children with a solid head start on the recorder, its introduction is likely to preempt, to a considerable degree, other Schulwerk instruction. Thus it is important that we proceed in a manner compatible and consistent with Orff-Schulwerk concepts. In other words, we must find a way to teach the recorder without neglecting the study of musical concepts appropriate for this level and without giving up the many musical activities that are vital to the Schulwerk curriculum. In order to combine all these aspects without undue pressure on the children, I approach the "recorder year" as a time to review, reinforce, and deepen the musical knowledge and skills they have acquired so far.

The many good recorder method books on the market don't really serve our purposes, since we must stay within the framework of the Orff-Schulwerk studies and practices outlined in Chapters three and four, which deal with melodic development. (An exception is Isabel Carley's first book of *Recorder Improvisation and Technique*, which proceeds pentatonically.[4] The teacher will have to supply his or her own materials and make them available to the class on ditto or xerox copies. If this seems like a formidable task, there are certain advantages to it. For one, it allows for flexibility. No two classes are alike, and what works in one may not work in another. Adaptations and changes will be necessary from one year to the next. After having taught beginning recorder classes for several years, the teacher will have perfected his or her teaching techniques and accumulated a wealth of materials from which to choose, and preparation will become much easier.

In my music classes, the children collect their music sheets in a folder, illustrating and coloring the pages to their liking along the way. The notebooks contain not only materials supplied by the teacher but also the pupils' own musical creations. By the end of the year the children have their very own books, each a bit different from the next. They are very proud of them and love to read through the old songs again and again. They laugh at their first, easy pieces and never tire of tracing the progress they have made throughout the year. For the instructors, too, this approach will be a source of great satisfaction, even though it is initially time-consuming, since these notebooks are a mirror of their own creativity and pedagogical skills.

The sequencing of the materials for recorder instruction is not as difficult as it seems because it follows the same sequence established for melodic development in general, with the difference that now the musical concepts can be more fully explored and applied to a new instrument. Beyond this, it is certainly useful for the inexperienced teacher to have a good recorder method at hand from which to glean helpful ideas for teaching fundamentals such as tone production and correct breathing and phrasing.

---

[4] Brasstown, N.C.: Brasstown Press, 1970.

Planning the First Year

In the following outline for sequencing recorder instruction, I can neither deal with specific grade levels nor suggest definite time limits in which certain goals should be achieved. It is certain only that one may expect younger grade levels to progress at a slower rate than older ones because their small-muscle coordination and their capacity for understanding abstract concepts (such as transposition) are less developed. Much more important than grade level is their musical experience and preparation prior to the introduction of the recorder (see page 226).

As an initial step to sequencing, the teacher should project a goal for the year. I stress that this goal must be regarded as tentative, especially by the inexperienced instructor. Even an experienced teacher cannot foretell future development with precision. What matters is not the quantity of materials covered during the year, but rather the quality of skills and knowledge conveyed. Inflexible time schedules in which a certain amount of materials must be covered under all circumstances lead to pressure and frustration and undermine one's efforts to make recorder playing a positive experience for the youngsters.

The next step will be to divide the overall goal into sensible subgoals or units, again without setting specific time limits. This will give us a skeletal sequence that reflects the musical growth and skill development we anticipate.

Fleshing out the skeletal sequence constitutes the main part of our work because it specifies the actual teaching procedures through which we hope to achieve our objectives.

To this end it is helpful to prepare a list of activities and procedures to refer to while planning individual lessons. Some of the activities, such as echo-play, are appropriate at all levels; others will have a more limited use. Initially, such a list will not be complete because one cannot think of every possibility beforehand. Many successful activities will occur spontaneously during class; these should be added to the collection, along with other ideas one may have read about or picked up from a colleague or at workshops. In fact, the list should always stay open-ended. For the purpose of assembling these ideas, file cards do very nicely.

Our final task (another one that is never completed) will be a compilation of music to be used, which requires searching for songs and pieces appropriate to the recorder and to specific developmental stages (units), as well as creating new examples and exercises. However, the preparation need not be in a complete form with every detail already worked out at the beginning of the year. It is more efficient to prepare the materials at the outset of each new unit.

THE FIRST STEPS IN RECORDER PLAYING (CALL AND CHANT PITCHES)

What follows now is a discussion of the musical sequence and of skill development—that is, the order in which the first three pitches are introduced and how they relate to melodic concepts and their use in improvisation. Some examples concerning process and materials will be included, but by no means do they constitute an exhaustive treatment of the subject.

In my own teaching I see the children frequently enough to have them prepared for recorder early in the third grade. However, before the long-awaited instrument makes its appearance, all rhythmic and melodic concepts are reviewed thoroughly. My goal of the first year is to introduce the fingerings of the first octave plus three or four notes beyond, C2 to E3 or F3 (actual sound). The notation of the corresponding pitches (one octave lower) can be taught at the same time and in the same order as the fingerings. However, I prefer that the children already know how to read; therefore, I usually begin with pitch notation at the end of the second grade. If the recorder is to be introduced in the fourth grade, I would certainly recommend teaching pitch notation the preceding year. From the start, I familiarize the students with the complete staff, rather than adding one line at a time when needed, as some teachers prefer, since changing the picture of location each time a line is added keeps the pupils in a state of limbo. The fact that the soprano recorder is a transposing instrument sounding one octave higher than notated is not mentioned at this point because it is as yet of no consequence and would only confuse the class. In fact, the matter is never addressed until several years later when the alto recorder, a nontransposing instrument, is introduced. Only at that time is the information useful and therefore important.

The Fundamentals

In the first unit the basics of recorder playing are attended to, and two pitches, C2 and A1, are introduced. A third pitch, D2, follows somewhat later. The unit can be divided into two categories: (1) what one should know about the recorder, and (2) fundamentals of playing.

I begin by telling the students a little about the history and development of the recorder. (Links to the past are as important to children as they are to adults.) Naturally, the information should not be a dry acocunt of facts, but should be illustrated with little stories of interest. For instance, the children are greatly impressed when I tell them that King Henry VIII, "the one who had six wives," owned 77 recorders! We look at pictures of historical models and compare them with our modern instruments. Since I have available a complete recorder set, the students have the opportunity to see, touch, and hear the members of the whole family, and they quickly find where their own instrument fits into the set. Next, we listen to some examples of old dance music. The children are quite captivated by the beautiful, mellow sound. They identify readily their own recorder because its register is the highest in the ensemble.

We now examine our own recorders closely and learn how to take them apart and put them together again. (I prefer a model with three separate joints, because it can be adjusted to fit the little finger of the right hand.) We talk about the care of the instrument, in particular the need for regular cleaning and for using a protective case. In general, I try to instill a sense of attachment to, and responsibility for, their recorders. Finally, some ground rules are established for safety's sake and for keeping one's sanity, such as: Do not play while riding in a car or school bus, Do not play while walking unless it is a special assignment in class, Do not share your instrument with someone else, and In class, play only when asked.

With these preliminaries out of the way, we can finally turn our attention to the fundamentals of playing.

Music-making on the barred instruments involves two of our five senses, sound and sight. With the recorder a third sense, that of touch, comes into play. The holding position of the recorder makes it awkward to look down over one's nose at the fingers, and the eyes will be occupied more and more with reading the music. Therefore, the covering and opening of fingerholes to produce certain pitches relies more on the sense of touch than on that of sight. This brings up another point. Like most nonpercussive instruments, the recorder requires movement of individual fingers and finger combinations, and the ability to control the fingers depends on an acute physical awareness of them. Many children do not yet possess this consciousness to the degree needed in recorder playing.

Excluding the sense of sight sharpens the concentration. For this reason, exercises with eyes closed are very helpful in developing control over individual finger movement and the feeling for the location of the finger holes. The following activities are suggestions as to how recorder class might be handled in the beginning.

The teacher explains and demonstrates body posture, how to hold the recorder, and how to cover the finger holes. Common mistakes that should be discouraged from the very beginning are:

1. *Looking at the recorder.* This often results in bending the head down, which makes the recorder face downward also. Head and neck should be held straight, without being stiff, and the instrument should point a bit outward.
2. *Pressing down too hard on the finger holes.* I explain to the students that the soft, fleshy finger pads are full of tiny nerve ends which help us feel whether or not the finger holes are completely covered. There is no need for pressure because this would only make the fingers tense and keep them from moving lightly and quickly.
3. *Curving the fingers.* This is a result of pressing the upper arms and elbows against the body, forcing the wrists and fingers to compensate for the incorrect angle, the wrists by bending inward and the fingers by curving downward. In this position the holes are covered by the fingertips, but not completely. By keeping the upper arms slightly away from the body, elbows and forearms form a straight line down to the wrist, which is bent a bit upward. The fingers then need not curve, but can be brought down flat to cover the openings properly.

The children sit in a circle on the floor, eyes closed, resting their recorders on their chins, with each finger positioned on its corresponding hole. They are told to follow the teacher's directions as to which fingers to move. I impress on them that they must in their minds identify the finger in question before attempting to move it. My first directions deal with only one finger at a time; for example:

"Lift the index finger ("pointy finger") of your left hand"—"Put it back on the hole."

"Wiggle your right little finger ("pinky")"—"Lower it onto the hole again. Make sure you can feel that the hole is covered all the way."

After all fingers have been "called upon," there should be a brief rest period.

In the next round of concentration exercises two fingers are moved simultaneously, beginning with the corresponding ones of each hand, then progressing to different ones:

"Lift both middle fingers"—"Bring them back down"—and so on.
"Left thumb and right ring finger"—"Think"—"Lift"—"Down"—and so on.

In a reverse way, all but one or two fingers are lifted and then lowered again:

"Raise all fingers except for the left ring finger"—
   "Down"—and so on.
   "Raise all but your left middle finger and right ring finger"—
   "Think first"—"Now do."—"Bring them down again,"—and so on.

Each new set of exercises should be interspersed with rest periods or different activities. To prevent boredom, different body positions should be tried out, such as lying on one's back or on the stomach (with elbows propped up), kneeling on one or both knees, or sitting on the heels. The exercises can even be combined with movement (eyes open), such as walking to a pulse-beat.

The directions will become more challenging by omitting the "down" command that brings the fingers back into the original position. Instead, each new command results in a different combination of raised and lowered fingers. We again start with all holes closed:

"Raise your right little finger"—"Now raise the remaining fingers of your right hand, except for the ring finger"—"Raise your left ring finger and middle finger"—"Put down your left middle finger, but raise the index finger"—and so on.

Naturally, the sequence demonstrated so far presents a development over a period of time. The challenge is increased gradually by starting each class with a few of these exercises.

For our first recorder class, however, we do not go further than raising and lowering one finger at a time. We devote the remaining time to matters of tone production—namely tonguing, breathing, and blowing—and introducing one or two pitches.

Tonguing, the initial attack of every note, is a real problem for some children, and it is necessary to check them frequently and individually. I compare it to the pronunciation of the two consonants "dw." The "w" is not cut off, however, but is continued by a soft airflow passing through lightly closed lips. There is no voice sound. The air should flow gently and smoothly as if one were blowing dandelion seeds from a flower, a few at a time. We practice this attack combining it with breathing. A breath is taken and the airflow is sustained as long as possible. We then progress to executing rhythmic phrases using echo-play, question-answer improvisations, and reading. Now, the duration of the airflow is determined by longer and shorter note values, for example:

The breath has to last through the entire phrase.

For the actual tone production the same exercises are used again. The recorder is placed on the lower lip (without touching the teeth), and the upper lip closes around the mouthpiece so that no air can escape on the sides.

Before introducing the first note I familiarize the children with the fingering chart. I draw the basic fingering diagram, with circles representing the open holes. The positions of the two hands, the opening for the left thumb (which on the recorder is on the back of the instrument), and the opening for the supporting finger are identified:

Thumb→   ○ ○
(in back)   ○ } left hand
               ○

               ○
               ○ } right hand
Supporting finger→ ○○
               ○○

Then I fill several circles and have the children find out for themselves which holes they are to cover. I continue with this activity, arbitrarily filling circles and erasing previous "fillings." All this is done without playing. When I am satisfied that everyone knows how to read the chart, I finally draw the fingerings for the first two notes, C2 and A1:

We have arrived!

Reinforcement

The next classes are devoted to practicing with the new notes. I always make a point of asking my students the meaning of the word "practice." Although their answers differ in length and clarity, the essence of their responses is always the same: "Doing something over and over again till you get it." Repetition is essential to practice, but it must not deteriorate into mindless drill. A large part of "process teaching" is the many activities teachers invent to help the children work on a certain skill until they have mastered it. The secret of this kind of practice lies in its variety and challenge. For variety, there are at our disposal all types of Orff-Schulwerk activities, such as ear-training, improvisation, reading, movement, and ensemble playing. The challenge has to do with the way these activities are presented. They must be designed to spark interest and induce motivation, but at the same time the goal must stay within reach in order to prevent frustration. What follows here are some suggestions for practice activities for beginners. Later, this general order of procedure may change, steps may be omitted or other activities added, depending on the students' skills.

1. After introduction of the new note or notes, start with exercises involving only listening, not reading. Playing by ear is the most natural way and therefore the easiest.
   a. Echo-play
   b. Improvisation with texts (this works best with call and chant pitches only)
   c. Improvisation without texts (question-answer)

   Add bordun accompaniment whenever possible to enrich the sound and to keep a steady beat.

2. Reading: Since pitch notation is fairly new to the children, it is best to proceed in two steps:
   a. Transition: Use only rhythmic notation to which the children make up their own tunes. Again, the exercise is most successful when only two or three pitches are used.
   b. Use full notation.

3. Ensemble play: Add recorder parts to an instrumental piece or to a song arrangment the children are already familiar with.

Since examples of activities for melodic development have already been cited in Chapter 3 (pp. 43–49), I will briefly elaborate on only those points that have not been brought up before.

The earlier illustrations involved barred instruments, which are stationary. The recorder, on the other hand, can be played while moving around. Listed below are some activities, most of them using movement. (Needless to say, the teacher must be able to demonstrate everything he or she asks the students to do.)

I. Exercises involving listening (playing while moving):

a. Echo-play. *Stationary*: Begin with the most natural position, sitting: on chairs, on the floor, on the heels. Change to different positions: kneeling, lying on their back, squatting. Have the class invent positions, but rule out any that interfere with holding the recorder naturally. Play while standing, both on one foot and on two feet. Stress good posture in all positions.

Locomotion: Use only walking in even pulse rhythm. Start by moving on the accented beats only, then progress to walking on every pulse-beat. Prepare the walk by shifting the weight from one foot to the other, from side to side, and (in step position) from forward foot to foot in back. Start the walk in a forward direction, then add changes of directions (facing front), turns, and sidesteps (grapevine). Keep the same movement and direction for the duration of the phrase. Do these echo exercises in both duple and triple meter.

Although echo-play is ideally performed solo-solo, solo-tutti is a more practical and timesaving solution in large classes. Initially, the teacher will play the first phrase, which the children then repeat. Soon, however, the students can take over the solo, and little games can be devised to make practicing more interesting. For example:

> The children stand scattered throughout the room. One child, while walking around, echoes the phrase given by the teacher. At the end of the phrase he or she stops in front of another student. During the repeat (tutti), the two children walk and play together, while everyone else walks and plays by themselves. Then the child who was chosen as a partner becomes the new soloist to repeat the echo before the tutti.

> Or, three groups of players are stationed in free formations in different parts of the room, each with a leader at the head. The first leader repeats the teacher's phrase while at the same time moving to a different location; his or her group follows in the tutti echo. The second and third groups then take their turns. The challenge for the leaders is to evaluate quickly the changes of location and direct their groups accordingly. After one round, new leaders are chosen. Formations such as circles and lines can be used in similar ways.

b. Improvisation with Texts. The musical part of these improvisations is extremely simple, and instant success is almost guaranteed! The texts consist of rhymes that lend themselves to being sung on the call formula So–Mi. The teacher might want to revive some of the texts that were used when pitch was first introduced, such as "Tinker, Tailor" or "One, Two, Tie My Shoe." (See also Chapter 3, pp. 45–48.) The students are asked to find the call-tune on the pitches C2 and A1 and to create drone patterns (based on F). Simple dances in different formations are easily created to these elemental tunes. Texts for the chant formula follow later, when D2 is introduced.

c. Improvisations Without Texts (Question-Answer). (Activities in this group need not be limited to the call and chant formulas.) Since these improvisations are purely instrumental, the vocally and textually conceived call and chant formulas ought to be avoided. Rather, other combinations with the same pitches should be attempted. The phrases, however, cannot end on the final, because the two or three pitches available represent the 3rd, 5th, and 6th scale degrees of the Do-mode. For instance:

Recorder

Drone instrument

But it is possible to interpret these notes as scale degrees 1, 3, and 4 of the untransposed La-mode (on A). In that case, the final is represented by the pitch A.

Just as with echo-play, question-answer improvisations are difficult to accomplish in large classes because they require solos. One way to deal with the problem is to utilize the rondo form, each section consisting of only one phrase which is repeated: Question *aa* (tutti), answer *b* (solo), *b* (tutti), and so on. Movement can be included most effectively in a circle formation, for example:

> The first solo player stands inside the circle. While all play the question (*a*) twice together, the circle walks in one direction, the child on the inside in the opposite direction. Everyone stands still for the duration of the answer, which is improvised by the solo player and repeated by everyone. The soloist then exchanges places with the student from the circle who stands closest to him or her, who will improvise the *c*-phrase following the next *aa*.

If both question and answer are to be improvised, they can be repeated in tutti so that all children are involved: question solo-tutti, answer solo-tutti. With this arrangement other formations for movement are possible, as for example:

> Two concentric circles facing in the same direction are formed. One circle will repeat the question, the other one the answer. The solo players for the improvisations, one from each group and standing side-by-side, are predetermined. Each circle walks only while echoing.

2. Reading

Practice activities involving reading notation preclude movement.

a. Transition.   The teacher writes a number of rhythms in a column on the blackboard. In a second column to the right of the first one are staff lines, two for each rhythm. The first rhythm is clapped by the class. Then, one child creates a tune to it, which is repeated by all. The teacher notates the pitches on the staff to the right. The same rhythm is used for another improvisation and notated. The process is repeated for the remaining rhythmic phrases. Now the teacher erases the rhythms and the children play all the melodic phrases, reading from the pitch notation:

This exercise is useful also later on when the class has progressed to pitches beyond those of the call and chant.

b. Full Notation.   No specific examples are necessary, beyond the suggestion that reading and playing a new recorder piece ought to be prepared in carefully sequenced steps. It takes a long time for the children to be able to read rhythm and pitch simultaneously. When introducing a new recorder piece I always have the class first read and clap the rhythm by itself. When this has been mastered, I work phrase by phrase, asking the students to say the pitches rhythmically. We repeat the exercise, but now we finger the pitches as we say or sing them. Only after this preparation do we actually play the phrase.

3. Ensemble Play (Adding Recorder Parts to a Piece).

At the third- or fourth-grade level the students are already quite accomplished on the barred instruments, and the pieces we select should match their skills. On the other hand, the recorder part we plan to add needs to stay very simple. Let us assume that the students were taught at some previous time instrumental piece no. 6 on page 98 of Orff-Schulwerk I, but that on the recorder they are familiar only with the pitches C2 and A1. The piece was previously played untransposed, in Do-mode on C, as it appears in the text. In order for us to make use of the recorder, it needs to be transposed to Do-mode on F. Here, then, an excellent opportunity presents itself for reviewing the concept of transposition and for extending its use. The new learning experience for the children will be to transpose an entire piece.

For the procedure, notation is not necessary, but if the students are already familiar with the whole staff (as might be the case with fourth graders) it should be included. We first review the piece by playing all the parts individually and putting them together again. Then we review the scale pattern of the Do-mode on C and notate it on the blackboard. Next, we transfer the same number pattern to build the scale on F, writing it down also:

With this guideline on the blackboard, every instrumental part can now be transposed easily. (Perhaps it should be pointed out that we must transpose downward in order to stay within the range of the barred instruments.)

For an added recorder part, I have some children play their two pitches whenever they hear them in the melody, while the rest of the class performs the piece. Their part will turn out in this way:

We now can fill the measures of rest also and change the end. The *b*-phrase is given to a second recorder group while the soprano glockenspiels rest:

SEQUENCING PITCH INTRODUCTION IN ACCORDANCE
WITH THE MELODIC-HARMONIC DEVELOPMENT
IN PENTATONIC

At this point we might pause and ask ourselves: "Why do we begin with the pitches C2, A1, and D2, rather than, as in most recorder methods, with B1, A1, and G1? Doesn't it make more sense to allow the student to immediately grasp the basic idea of recorder fingering—"Add one finger to get the next lower pitch"?

When the recorder is taught as part of the Orff-Schulwerk curriculum, the order of pitch introduction is not based on what is easiest to play, but rather on what is most consistent in terms of musical development. By beginning with the first three pitches of a scale—for example, G–A–B (Do–Re–Mi)—the notes introduced next, C and D (Fa and So, or scale degrees 4 and 5), produce a pentachord containing a half-step.[5] To work within the framwork of the diatonic scale makes good sense as long as the children are already familiar with it, or are about to be introduced to it anyway. However, in my opinion, the pentatonic realm has not yet been explored enough to justify progressing into the diatonic, even by fourth grade. Moreover, most of the do–re–mi tunes contain a strong supertonic and therefore tend to suggest dominant-tonic cadences. The accompaniment to such tunes needs harmonization for which the students are not prepared because their vertical (simultaneous) pitch recognition is not sufficiently developed. (See also Chapter 6.)

In order to teach recorder according to the Orff-Schulwerk philosophy, which emphasizes that children not be rushed into concepts they are not ready for, we must stay with pentatonic for the time being. As I stated earlier, the first year of recorder instruction is an opportunity to deepen the students' understanding of the pentatonic modes, thereby giving them the necessary skills for improvisation within a framework they can handle, not only from the viewpoint of melody but from that of harmony as well. We must never forget that improvisation is one of the main objectives in Schulwerk training.

Approaching recorder instruction through the pentatonic scale calls for its own different order of pitch introduction, following the same sequence that was used for melodic development. We begin with the call and chant pitches So, Mi, and La (scale degrees 5, 3, and 6), adding as the next notes Re and Do (scale degrees 2 and 1). The sequence thus serves as a valuable review of the beginnings of melody. The difference between the earlier and the present studies lies in the fact that, instead of starting with the untransposed Do-mode, we now use the transposition to F. It will be followed by other pentatonic modes and more transpositions. The concept of transposition and of different pentatonic modes should not be altogether unfamiliar to the children, as they have worked with both already on the barred instruments, even if perhaps only to a limited degree.

With the call and chant pitches as the foundation, further development becomes simply a matter of proceeding in a logical order. The following chart suggests the sequence according to which new pitches may be introduced. Here

[5] *Pentachord* usually refers to the first five pitches in a diatonic scale.

we make the startling discovery that, every time one or two more notes are added, the possibilities in the use of modes increases substantially. This is cause for reflection: How much of this pentatonic wealth do we actually utilize in our teaching? There is no doubt that time, the music teacher's eternal adversary, allows exploration of only a fraction of the available possibilities. For this reason we must use good judgment in the selection of modes and give priority to those that are most important as a basis for future melodic-harmonic developments. (See also Chapter 7, pp. 188–91, and Chapter 8, p. 200).

In the chart the most important modes, are marked with double asterisks. Once a mode has been introduced, it is not listed again even though its range may have extended with the addition of new pitches. Rather, only the new possibilities available have been indicated, in order to keep the chart intelligible and useful. Basically, we deal only with the Do- and La-modes and their transpositions, since these are the modes most compatible with drone and ostinato accompaniment. Of the remaining, more horizontally oriented modes, those marked with one asterisk deserve at least some attention in improvisation, but only untransposed and in their authentic form. Finally, I have added some brief suggestions pertaining, for the most part, to improvisation.

The teacher is advised to study the chart with recorder in hand, to play each new development in scale construction and range expansion as it presents itself, and immediately to try some improvisation. In this way the chart will come to life and take on meaning.

THE SOPRANO RECORDER: A GUIDE TO THE SEQUENTIAL INTRODUCTION OF PITCHES DURING THE PENTATONIC STAGE

Explanatory notes:

"f" refers to the final of a mode.

The column to the extreme right shows the pitches and, underneath, the scale degrees they represent in each modes.

Plagal modes are introduced in the chart only once the circumference has reached an octave, with the exception of the Do-mode, where a range of a sixth is already useful. The same is true of authentic modes, except in the case of the Do- and La-modes, which in fact are utilized from the very beginning.

I. *Call and Chant:* C2, A1, D2:

**Do on F	(no f)	3 5 6
Modes possible: **La on A	(f = A)	1 3 4

Echo, question-answer over drone: *aa1,a,b.*

2. *Adding G1, F1:*

Modes possible: **Do on F, authentic (f = F)
                                  **La on A, authentic (f = A)

	1	2	3	5	6
	7	1	3	4	

Echo, question-answer over drone: *a,a1, a,b.*

3. *Adding E1, E2:*

New modes possible: **Do on C, plagal   (f = C)
                                 **La on A, plagal   (f = A)
                                 *Mi on E, authentic (f = E)

		5	6	1	2	3
5		7	1	3	4	5
1		3	4	6	7	1

Improvise as before using different modes; notate echo phrases as well as improvised phrases; use canons, transposed to F, from Orff-Schulwerk I, "Melodic Exercises."

4. *Adding B1:*

New modes possible: **Do on G, authentic (f = G)
                              **La on E, authentic (f = E)

		1	2	3		5	6
1		3	4	5		7	1

Improvise as before, adding rondo form and *a,b,a* form; (different sections may be in relative keys;) continue with canon exercises from Orff-Schulwerk I by adding transposition of Do-mode to G.

5. *Adding D1, C1:*

New modes possible:

			1	2	3		5	6		1	2	3	
Do on C, authentic (f = C)			1	2	3		5	6		1	2	3	
Do on C, plagal (f = C)							5	6		1	2	3	
Do on F, plagal (f = F)	5	6		1	2	3		5					
Do on G, plagal (f = G)			5	6		1	2	3		5			
La on D, authentic (f = D)	1			3	4	5		7	1				
Re on D, authentic (f = D)	1	2			4	5		7	1				
Re on G, plagal (f = G)	5			7	1	2		4	5				
Re on A, plagal (f = A)		5			7	1	2		4	5			
So on C, authentic (f = C)	1	2		4	5	6		1					
So on G, plagal (f = G)	5	6		1	2		4	5					

Improvise along same lines as before; in rondos, each intervening section may be in a different mode; create longer melodies in the following forms: *a,a,b,a; a,a,a,b; a,b,a,b; a,b,b,a.*

6. *Adding notes in the higher register: F2, G2, A2:*
   Introduce pitches as the need arises

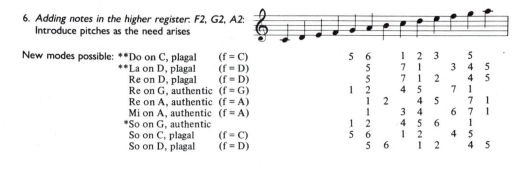

New modes possible:

**Do on C, plagal	(f = C)	5 6	1 2 3	5					
**La on D, plagal	(f = D)	5	7 1	3 4 5					
Re on D, plagal	(f = D)	5	7 1 2	4 5					
Re on G, authentic	(f = G)	1 2	4 5	7 1					
Re on A, authentic	(f = A)	1 2	4 5	7 1					
Mi on A, authentic	(f = A)	1	3 4	6 7 1					
*So on G, authentic		1 2	4 5 6	1					
So on C, plagal	(f = C)	5 6	1 2	4 5					
So on D, plagal	(f = D)	5 6	1 2	4 5					

Perhaps this exercise proved to be a struggle and you asked in exasperation, "If *I* had difficulties playing these scales and trying to improvise, what on earth will the *children* do? How long will *they* have to struggle before they have mastered these concepts and skills?" My initial response would be a question: "Are you sure you are ready to teach recorder?" But the matter does not end here. Another important issue may be that as teachers we must accept the fact that anything worth learning takes time. The value of a learning experience can often even be measured in terms of the time spent on it. Furthermore, what is difficult for an adult is not necessarily as difficult for a child. The music teacher trained in the traditional system has to rethink, readjust, and relearn; children brought up with Orff-Schulwerk do not face this problem. It is very tempting for the music instructor to teach what he or she feels comfortable with, and in a manner that demands less effort, but this attitude is not necessarily in the best interest of the child.

In my experience it takes about two years to work through the concepts and skills contained in the chart. Once the students have mastered them, they are ready to progress to the diatonic scale and concepts related to it, such as half-steps, key signatures, and fingerings for sharps and flats.

SUMMARY

The synchronization of recorder and Orff-Schulwerk instruction is the foundation for the methodology offered here. This means:

1. teaching within the framework of melodic-harmonic concepts relevant to the developmental stage of the students: basic pitches C1–A2, studies in all pentatonic modes and those transpositions that do not require sharps or flats.
2. process teaching: working with the recorder in all areas of Orff-Schulwerk: echo-play, improvisation, ensemble playing, movement, reading and notating.
3. helping the children develop positive attitudes toward practicing; staying sensitive

and responsive to their needs and capabilities; remaining flexible and creative, rather than relying on method books.

4. being a competent teacher who is able to demonstrate in all areas.

For many children, the recorder may well be the only traditional instrument they will ever have the opportunity to study. Even if only in a small measure, the recorder can help to fill a void and to give them a lifetime of pleasure.

10
WORD AND LANGUAGE IN ORFF-SCHULWERK

LANGUAGE AND CULTURE

Although the focus of this book has been the musical concepts of rhthym, melody, and harmony embodied in Orff-Schulwerk I, I would like to bring up another dimension which in the Orff approach cannot be separated from the music, namely the word. I do not refer here to its musical function as a basis for rhythm and meter, but rather to its primary function as a vehicle for communication. In short, I am speaking about the textual content of language appropriate for use in Orff-Schulwerk. Too often, Orff's true objectives and convictions concerning music education are so narrowly defined as to misinterpret and distort his true intentions. I readily admit that there is a barrier not easily overcome, the barrier of language itself. Language is intimately connected with a people's cultural background. That background can never be understood in its entirety through studies and readings about it alone, because language is the most important key to a culture's way of thought, to its soul. Furthermore, culture is absorbed and assimilated because one lives in it. For many people and certainly for children, it stays a subconscious, unsophisticated, and unrationalized experience because there is no need for it to be anything else. Articulation (which presupposes consciousness) is left to teachers, writers, artists, and philosophers. Werner Thomas, perhaps the foremost authority on Carl Orff and his works, sheds light on the particular cultural setting that gave rise to Orff, the artist and pedagogue:

> The idea of Schulwerk must first be comprehended through the creator's personality. Orff's individuality is founded on the fact that, on the one hand, he represents the consciousness of our times, but on the other hand, he has stored and developed within himself an acute sense of his spiritual origins. Orff is South German, through descent and spiritual propensity closely bound

to the old Bavarian lands. In this scenery there prevail still today simple human conditions in the existence of the shepherd and the farmer. . . . In the dialect are stored riches which hold memories of the magical origin of language. But also, the Latin-Romanic spirit radiating northward from the antique world has been particularly well received and absorbed in Bavaria. To these sources Orff has returned as artist and pedagogue. [Translation mine][1]

Over the millennia, only that portion of human thought has survived which is fundamental to our understanding of ourselves and the world in which we live. This legacy of the essential truths has been offered to future generations as the only truly important heritage. It is preserved, on the one hand, in the collective folk memory which is transmitted orally and knows no author, and on the other hand, in the written word of the Greek philosophers whose teachings became the basis of Western thought and culture. The "simple human conditions" Thomas refers to can be found, of course, not only in Bavaria but in other parts of the world also. They exist wherever geographic conditions have prevented penetration by outside influences, and this includes the English-speaking world. Because they are universal in spite of their specific cultural differences, we are able to gain entrance to Orff's thoughts. This then, is the area of immediate importance to Schulwerk teaching, on the beginning levels especially, and I will return to it later for a more detailed discussion.

Thomas's second point, however, about the assimilation of antique thought and spirit, calls attention to a unique situation which was produced by the close proximity of the German-speaking South to the lands of the Classical cultures, Greece and Italy. It is difficult to fully convey a unique cultural condition because the particular assimilation Thomas refers to is not merely a state of being, of instinctive knowledge, but also conscious knowledge instilled through education. For American Schulwerk teachers, it is difficult to gain access to Orff's thoughts in this area because their own cultural background cannot provide the instinctive knowledge, and conscious knowledge has been denied to most of them because the teaching of humanism through the humanities is not an important and basic aspect of higher learning in this country today. Nevertheless, as Schulwerk teachers we must concern ourselves with it, because Orff's choice of texts in the more advanced stages reveals his pedagogical intention on a deeper level. After all, Western thought and culture are based on Greek thought, interwoven with and nourished by the Christian faith. Even though the American continent harbors people of many cultures and faiths whose contributions continuously enrich and broaden our understanding of humanity as a whole, our cultural foundation remains unchanged. To ignore all this as a teacher means to deny our students access to the culture they live in and are a part of.

Orff the pedagogue and Orff the artist cannot be separated, because his message is his works. For the Schulwerk teacher it is not enough to familiarize oneself with just the small segment called Orff-Schulwerk; only through becoming

---

[1] "Wege und Stufen im Orff-Schulwerk," in Schäfer, W.E., K.H. Ruppel et al., *Carl Orff, ein Bericht in Wort und Bild*, 2nd ed. (Mainz: B. Schott's Söhne, 1960), p. 30.

acquainted with the whole scope of Orff's works can one hope to sense the depth of the message. However, gaining complete access to them poses some problems. His works are almost exclusively written for the stage. They are not "opera" in the traditional sense, but "scenic plays" in which the word is of prime importance, and this is where the difficulties arise. The texts are not easily translated, and for this reason his works, with the exception of *Carmina Burana*, are hardly, if ever, performed in this country. However, books and articles about Orff's works are available, as well as recordings, which can be found in libraries and in record stores carrying European labels, all of which contribute to at least a partial insight into his works. Furthermore, there is no reason why the less demanding scenic plays cannot be staged with students on the university level, even if only in translation.

Orff's stage works fall into two main groups. The first is often described as "world theatre"; the second consists of Greek tragedies. This latter group is the more difficult to assimilate, not only because of the language itself (texts by Sophocles and Aeschylus, either in German translation or in the original), but also because their content is hardly popular fare. Nevertheless, these plays are the essence, the ultimate expression of the same universal themes of mankind with which Orff deals in all of his works.

However, the "world theatre" plays (to all of which Orff wrote his own texts) have a direct connection with Schulwerk and, for this reason, should be familiar to the Orff-Schulwerk teacher. They are themselves divided into two groups. The first two plays, *The Moon* (*Der Mond*) and *The Peasant's Wise Daughter* (*Die Kluge*),[2] are folktales from the Grimm brothers and are, because of their more universal character, the actual "theatrum mundi." The second group, also called "The Bavarian World Theatre" because of its pertinence to the uniquely Bavarian scene, consists of four works: *Die Bernauerin*, a play based on a historical event in fifteenth-century Bavaria and written in the Bavarian dialect of the time; *Astutuli*, a satire; and two mystery plays, *Ludus de nato infante mirificus*, a Christmas play, and, *Comoedia de Christi resurrectione*, an Easter play. The texts are in contemporary Bavarian dialect. Since the various German dialects amount to almost different languages, one can see that Orff did not make it easy even for German-speaking audiences!

All the "theatrum mundi" plays are symbolic representations in which the world is seen as a stage and the people in it as actors. Humanity appears in its spirituality and its vulgarity, in its frailties and its humor, and we see ourselves as in a mirror. This, of course, was Orff's intent as a pedagogue. The symbolic forms of folktale, mystery play, parable, and satire are the same ones mankind has used to express the truth about itself since time immemorial. One might call them "folk psychology." The smaller forms in Schulwerk—the sayings, proverbs, riddles, as well as the folk- and fairy-tales—represent the same basic themes and concerns of mankind and serve the same purpose of instruction.

Carl Orff, then, is not so much a composer in the modern sense as a storyteller,

---

[2] The full German title of this fairytale is "Die Kluge Bauerntochter."

a minstrel. And no matter whether we think of him as the composer of many stage works or as the originator of "Music for Children," it is always the same man with the same deep sense of mission, which he himself expresses thus: "In all my work, my final concern is not with the musical, but with the spiritual exposition.[3] This concern, to nourish and build the spiritual qualities in the growing human being, manifests itself throughout Orff-Schulwerk. The textual content of his five volumes of "Music for Children" make quite clear that there is no room for the superficial, the flippant, the cheap, and the tasteless. His careful choice of materials is evident in a logical sequence ranging from the first childish ritual of name-calling to the last mature speech pieces of Sophocles' *Antigonae*, Goethe's *Faust*, and the religious dialogues.

SMALL FORMS OF ORAL LORE

Although a new consciousness of folk traditions has developed in this country during the past few decades, interest has mainly centered around folksong, folk-dance, and folk arts and crafts. This is, perhaps, not altogether surprising. The complexity of our lives isolates us from one another, and we feel the need to reach out for the simple and unpretentious relationships found in pleasures shared; amidst the new achievements of technology we yearn to create things simple and beautiful on our own. These folk traditions are alive in the sense that they are able to function in any setting, at any time, regardless of the prevailing cultural climate, as long as there are people who have a need for the simple pleasures such traditions afford.

However, song, dance, arts, and crafts are only a part of the complex of folk traditions. There are also the purely verbal forms of lore which, as the word "lore" indicates, have to do with "learning." Proverbs, weather sayings, riddles, cures, and spells belong in this group. More than any other lore, they have disappeared from our consciousness and from our active vocabulary. They have become obsolete because they seem irrelevant to contemporary life. For this reason, they only linger on as printed words in folklore collections.

The Proverb

By far the most often occurring short form in Orff-Schulwerk is the proverb. As a means of summing up one's experiences and giving advice, it held great educational value in the past. The conciseness of the stated word was especially effective in a time when the acquisition of knowledge depended on listening rather than reading. Moreover, many proverbs are metaphors or allegories which needed to be contemplated before they could be understood. But even today proverbs serve an educational purpose. Not only do they contain much universal truth and timeless advice, but they also help children develop the skills of observa-

[3] From Andreas Liess, *Carl Orff: His Life and His Music*, (London: Calder and Boyars Limited 1966), p. 74.

tion and an awareness of the world around them. Much depends on how the teacher makes these old forms of poetic wisdom interesting to the class.

Proverbs deal with the whole range of human experiences. For instance, philosophical observations about human nature are often expressed by means of a metaphor, such as, "Rats desert a sinking ship." Others are pragmatic and give straightforward advice on sensible deportment: "Keep your own counsel," or "Haste makes waste." Still others offer rules for good health: "An apple a day keeps the doctor away." Finally, there are the countless weather sayings which at one time were of enormous importance to farmers, fishermen, and anyone else whose livelihood depended on weather conditions. All in all, one might say that proverbs teach in a nutshell everything one needs to know about how to get on in life without the help of psychologists, weather forecasters, physicians, investment advisors, or statisticians.

The use of proverbs in Orff-Schulwerk need not be limited to certain age groups, although not every type is appropriate for all levels. To select the right proverb for the right age level, we should have at least a general perception of the mental growth processes of the maturing child and how these processes relate to speech expression. Although reading literature on this subject is important, the insight gained remains in a vacuum unless we relate it in some way to personal experience. Every adult has had these experiences, be they in teaching, in parenting, in one's own childhood, or ideally all three. However, just as written subject matter must be pondered in order to be understood, so too must personal experiences be analyzed in order to become valuable knowledge.

The acquisition of conceptual and communicative skills starts with the concrete and tangible and leads to the abstract and intangible. Young children first learn to understand concrete language because they are in the process of discovering and learning the realities of their world. Let me illustrate through an example. A mother tells her child not to touch knives, and some time later she warns the child about knitting needles. In order for the lesson to sink in she will not only have to repeat it many times but go through the same process with every new sharp object the child discovers. Soon the child is likely to turn a deaf ear to the constant refrain of "Don'ts." The language of a well-known proverb, however, not only concerns *all* sharp objects but also intrigues the child's ear because of its rhyme and rhythm: "Children and fools must not play with sharp tools." The child will say or chant it over and over again, delighting in the sounds, and like a deep secret the lesson will be remembered more readily.

Thus it appears that those proverbs giving simple rules that can be understood by every young child are the most appropriate ones to use in the lower grade levels. Other sayings, which condense human experience on a less elementary level or contain metaphors, are more appropriate for older students. I have found that children around the fourth grade or a little earlier are especially receptive to such proverbs. At that age they seem mature enough to think beyond the most obvious. They delight in deciphering metaphors, and, because the imagination of childhood is still within them, their sense of drama is strong.

Dramatization of proverbs is a very effective device to illustrate their meaning. The teacher may want to choose just one particular saying and have different groups of students create their own interpretations. Or several proverbs may be worked out simultaneously. I myself like to spend a small segment of the school year working only with proverbs (which does not mean that musical activities are not included). Once the students have an overall understanding of proverbs and how to use them creatively, they will be able in later years to do the same on more complex and abstract levels.

Before we start working on a specific text I discuss with the class what proverbs are all about. I ask the children to cite any they might know. The harvest is usually quite scant, but it increases when I point out the specific themes proverbs deal with, such as weather, time, or those which give general counsel. The children are encouraged to consult the library and their parents. When a number of proverbs have been collected we look at each of them and discuss their specific meaning. In weather sayings, for instance, the central subjects will be phenomena such as rainbows, fog, wind, rain, moon, frost, snow, and clouds. Since these phenomena are important to people like farmers and sailors, the proverb often suggests a course of action. For example:

> Rainbow in the east, sailors at peace;
> Rainbow in the west, sailors in distress.

The classroom discussion will center around the question why the sailors don't have to worry about a rainbow in the eastern sky, but should be concerned when it appears in the west. The answer is that the experience of our forefathers apparently has shown that storms often gather in the west and move eastward; therefore, a rainbow in the east means that the storm has passed, but a rainbow in the west indicates that a storm is brewing. The proverb does not spell out what action the sailors are to take, but it is implied. Obviously, if a storm is expected, the sailors have to prepare for it.

The dramatization of proverbs depends entirely on their contents. The preceding example does not warrant great physical activity; the movement might consist only of two rainbows rising slowly opposite one another, while between them a group of sailors assumes first a pose expressing peace, then one expressing anxiety. Here we may run into another obstacle, pantomine. We cannot take for granted that children are able to portray emotions and feelings through body posture and gesture. This is an area the teacher must explore with the students before improvisations can be attempted. Various possibilities should be discussed with the children. It is important that the teacher point out better solutions, but not without giving reasons. After all, we are trying to develop in the students an instinct for what is essential in order to create the beautiful. At the same time, however, we must be careful not to impose our adult standards and artistic expectations on the children.

Not every weather saying gives advice. Some merely are observations:

> Fog on the hill
> Brings water to the mill;
> Fog on the moor
> Brings sun to the door.

Here, the discussion will center around the question of how "fog," "water," "mill," "sun," and "house" might be depicted. Some of the nouns suggest action, others only a "sculpture." Again, the possibilities for interpretation should be explored together before the students create their versions of the whole proverb, because in order to express and describe a movement, an object, or an emotion, one must have an absolutely clear conception of it. Whereas objects like a house or a mill are not difficult to imagine and to interpret through a sculpture, natural phenomena like fog, sun, or water are not so easily perceived, because they are more like essences than objects. To this purpose, the children should be asked to describe in adjectives or verbs the nature of these phenomena. For example, "fog": soundless, colorless, moving slowly, changing shapes, rising and descending, opening up and closing in, and so on. With such descriptions the essence of "fog" is established and different movement interpretations can be explored by the whole class under the leadership of the teacher.

Metaphors counseling common sense may be illustrated by creating a specific situation or story around them:

> Count not your chickens
> Before they are hatched.

The obvious course of action would be to take the saying literally (as in Aesop's fable of "The Milkmaid", from which the saying comes). However, it is more instructive, as well as imaginative, to have the children transfer the meaning to a different situation. The stories can be told through pantomime, and when the different groups have created their own interpretations they can perform them for each other.

Our miniature dramatizations are not complete without music. Taken by itself, a proverb is very short. In musical form, its length may range from a half-phrase to two phrases, although longer forms exist. Proverbs often contain two aspects: on the one hand, the concreteness of matter and action, and on the other, the mysterious, elusive quality of something not immediately explainable— to put it more simply, the tangible and the intangible. Not every proverb involves both qualities, but those dealing with natural phenomena, like weather sayings, certainly do. It is these two qualities which we want to express musically, and for this reason it is important to discuss these aspects with the students, because musical interpretation can take place only when the underlying ideas have been understood. But comprehension alone is not enough. The children need suggestions and examples as to how tangibles and intangibles can be expressed in music.

The ostinato, whether rhythmic or pitched, serves well to underline the open-ended form of the proverb, because it can be stopped or started at any time. The difference between the ostinato describing the tangible and the one expressing the intangible can, for instance, be shown through different sound and rhythmic structures. Whereas the former may make use of the students' concrete musical knowledge, the latter can be more experimental and exploratory. The former may be based on a chosen tonality and metered patterns; the latter may use any sound combinations (including half-steps and sharps and flats) in free, unmetered rhythms, as well as isolated tone clusters. (Other possibilities need to be explored also. The setting of texts should never be approached through a formula, since no two texts are ever completely alike.) The choice of instruments is another matter that needs careful consideration. Improvisations in this area are very important and enough time should be reserved for them.

When the proverb is shaped into its final form, care must be taken not to let the music overwhelm the dramatic action. Only the essential needs to be said, in gesture as well as in music, because this is the character of the proverb. The unity of word, gesture, and music is retained only if the three aspects are properly balanced with one another.

One proverb alone is more a fragment than a complete form, like a picture without a frame or a precious stone without a setting. The addition of an introduction and a postlude will provide the necessary frame to achieve a complete musical form, *ABA*. There are a number of options as to the nature of the A-sections. They may be the proverb itself (either sung or recited), a short instrumental piece, or a combination of the two.

The study of particular types of proverbs, such as those dealing with weather, time, and health, can be concluded with the creation of a rondo in which the individual improvisations become the intervening sections. The A-part might be another proverb which contemplates the basic theme in general terms, for instance:

> Whether it's cold, or whether it's hot,
> There will be weather, weather or not.

The Riddle

Riddles are among the oldest and most widespread forms of oral lore. Just as with the proverb, the fundamental purpose of the riddle was pedagogical. Unlike the proverb, which gave counsel, the riddle's purpose was what contemporary language would call "problem solving." Mind-stretching games have always been part of people's lives, past and present, whether adults or children. Remnants of this once popular pastime are the quiz games, puzzles, and trick questions popular today. The true folk riddle, however, is quite different. The fact that it has always existed among people whose lives were closely bound not only to nature but also to their fellow man gives it a characteristic content and language. The riddle describes an object or a natural phenomenon in terms of association or comparison. It speaks in metaphors, in a mixture of mystery and fact, of deliberate disguise and truth; it contains humor and wit, as well as simple poetic beauty; it arouses curiosity; it is a game.[4] For all these reasons, the riddle has flourished as a source for entertainment among young and old since the beginning of time.

---

[4] In some cultures riddles are an important part of rituals. Also, the solving of riddles as a means to obtain a sought-after reward appears in many fairy tales.

The contemporary adult, however, is no longer interested in the true riddle; he has lost the ability to understand its language, and therefore he cannot solve it. With regard to children, the situation is not as hopeless. Even though the extent of their experience with riddles is more or less a casual acquaintance, they are not yet deaf to the mysteries of a metamorphic language that deals with simple and basic things. However, as with the proverb, we must help them to rediscover these things; we must open their eyes and ears and make them understand the mental and imaginative process that occurs when one thing is explained in the disguise of another, as for example:

> I have an apple I can't cut,
> A blanket I can't fold,
> And so much money I can't count it.
> (*The sun, sky, and stars*)

It is unlikely that any child will be able to solve the riddle, but it is this hidden mystery which captivates and fascinates.

Many riddles lend themselves well to dramatization with music and movement. They are, for the most part, longer than proverbs, so they can stand on their own as complete forms. At the same time, a number of them strung together in rondo form can be an effective and enjoyable way to sum up the creative activities of the students.[5]

Riddles are not always easy to interpret through gesture and movement, as the preceding example demonstrates. However, since the objective of the riddle is *not* to give away its secret, there is much freedom in the manner it can be presented. As with the proverb, discussion, contemplation and preliminary improvisation are an indispensable preparation for the actual process of creating. The same is true of the music to be added.

Once the students have understood the language of riddles, they often want to create their own. In many schools poetry writing is part of the language-arts curriculum. The riddle is a poetic expression, especially suited to the imaginative mind of the growing child. It is of great pedagogical value and should be a part not only of an Orff-Schulwerk program but of the language-arts curriculum.

Poetry

Although poetry is a literary art form, I have included it here because it is another creative expression in which word and music can form a unity.

Poems are usually not distillations of a collective lore whose beginnings are obscure and which, because of its universal value, speaks to everyone and is handed down orally from generation to generation. Rather, poems are often intensely personal expressions of an individual's inner self. They have an author and they can be preserved only through the printed word because their appeal is

---

[5] A riddle rondo can be found in the Hall and Walter version of Orff-Schulwerk I. Another example appears in the Murray version of Orff-Schulwerk III.

selective rather than universal. The following poem, written by an 11-year-old, sums up beautifully what poetry is all about:

> In poems, our earth's wonders
> Are windowed through
>> Words
>
> A good poem must haunt the heart
> And be heeded by the head of the
>> Hearer
>
> With a wave of words, a poet can
> Change his feelings into cool, magical, mysterious
>> Mirages
>
> Without poetry our world would be
> Locked within itself—no longer enchanted by the poet's
>> Spell.

> Peter Kelso, Australia[6]

The fact that Orff-Schulwerk I contains no poetry aside from the traditional forms of nursery rhyme and proverb does not mean that poetry should be excluded from our work. The selection of suitable material is not an altogether easy task because much literature written by adults for children is—though well-meaning—contrived, pseudo-childlike, and condescending in its content. On the other hand, there is also a wealth of truly fine poetry available which can be researched in school and public libraries. But even so, our choices are still based on our own, adult standards. How do we judge a poem's appeal to children?

The answer to this question can be found in the poetry children themselves write. In their own poems they reveal thoughts and emotions which otherwise they often keep hidden within themselves. Many years ago, I came across a book entitled *Miracles*, consisting of poems written by children and collected by Richard Lewis.[7] I was utterly fascinated by the quality of the poems and greatly humbled by their profundity of perception. I began to remember the little slips of papers I occasionally had come across when cleaning my own children's rooms. At the time, I had been amused and also a little proud of what I thought was precociousness in my children, but I never had attached much importance to these attempts at self-expression. I also recalled my own scribbles as a child which I had kept hidden away, but which I always threw out after a while, because I felt embarrassed at the thought of some adult gaining access to them. Only after reading *Miracles* did I come to understand the significance of children's poems. They are mirrors reflecting the child's view of the

---

[6] From Richard Lewis, ed., *Miracles: Poems by Children of the English-speaking World* (New York: Simon & Schuster, 1966). Copyright 1966 by Richard Lewis. Used by permission.

[7] See footnote 6 above.

world around him or her: observations of nature and people, thoughts about life and death, happy and sad feelings, dreams, play, and humor. An understanding and knowledge of children's poetry will help the teacher in choosing materials.

Most of the poems are unrhymed and unmetered, and this, I believe, contributes to their quality. Without the restrictions of rhyme and meter children are free to follow their thoughts and to express them in their own words. The formal structure is equally free; some poems are no more than a fleeting thought, others are longer, detailed formulations. But none are excessive in their verbiage; every word seems essential to the articulation of the poem. In his introductory note Richard Lewis says: "The children's very limitations of vocabulary and grammar served much the same functions as the deliberate restrictions of form that the adult poet uses to concentrate his vision."[8]

Poems written by children are understood by children. For this reason, I prefer to draw from this source every time I begin a poetry unit with elementary-school students. From there it is not difficult to advance to adult poems that deal with the same visions and thoughts the children expressed initially.

The criterion for selecting poetry for use with music and/or movement should be whether or not the addition will enhance and intensify the words. Many poems are best left alone, either because their content is too personal and fragile or because the poetic expression is so perfect that any augmentation would seem artificial.

I usually first sketch arrangements of the poems I have selected because it helps me to pinpoint the potential contained in them. Without this preparation it is difficult to help and guide the students in their own creations. There is always the danger of falling back on repetitive and unoriginal stereotypes of expression (such as the use of glissandi, which seem to be a favorite for all occasions and with all ages). The children need to be taught how to look at a problem from all sides and how to explore alternatives; only in this way will they become truly creative. Ultimately, the quality of an improvisation reflects the teacher's own depth of thought.

Poems fall into two main categories, metered and unmetered. Aside from the content, this may be a decisive factor in their treatment. Consider the following poem:

Household Problems

Tick-tock, tick-tock,
The sound of a clock.
You turn to the door
To answer a knock.
The children are fighting
Oops there goes a sock.
Tick-tock, tick-tock,
The sound of a clock.

---

[8] *Miracles*, p. 000.

The chair needs mending.
The hinges need bending.
The boys are still fighting,
Now two things need mending.
Tick-tock, tick-tock,
Times goes with the clock.
                    Larry Haft, age 11, USA[9]

The text is structured and humorous as well. There are all sorts of possibilities for rhythmic recitation and movement, alternations of soli and tutti, rhythmic or speech ostinati, and special sound effects. An unmetered example:

Breeze

Gentle as a feather
Cat quiet
Snow soft
Gentle, gentle as a feather
Softer than snow
Quiet as a cat
Comes
The evening breeze.
                    Marie Hourigan,
                    age 11, Australia[10]

The character of this poem is like the adjectives it contains: quiet, gentle, soft. Here, a choral recitation would not do at all, although the individual lines may be spoken by different children. Whether or not to add music, movement, or both is a decision the children have to make. A floating feather, falling snow, and a strolling cat are analogies describing the soundless and unseen breeze. These analogies may be made visible through movement without music, or their essences, though actually soundless, may be suggested through sounds alone without any movement. Of course, a third possibility is to use both sound and movement.

In sum, no two poems are alike, and each one must be looked at individually for its potential.

The children are asked to choose a poem from the selection I offer to them. However, before making their choices, we read all the poems and discuss both their content and the possibilities they offer for music and movement. Before the students separate into their individual groups to work on the poem of their choice, I give the following guidelines as to how they should proceed:

1. Decide the medium you want to use: music, movement, or both.
2. If you decide to limit your improvisation to only one of these, simply work as one group.

[9] From Lewis, *Miracles*. Used by permission.
[10] From Lewis, *Miracles*. Used by permission.

3. If both will be used, discuss and explore first each aspect separately with the whole group. This is important, because music and movement are an entity. Once you have agreed on the general movement and sound interpretations, divide into two groups to work on the details. After that, practice together to "remove the wrinkles."

3. Discuss and decide with your group how the poem should be recited: If it is short, you may want to have it spoken before the action. With a longer poem, each phrase may be recited separately, during or before the action. Consider options such as solo, tutti, and antiphonal speech. You may want to sing rather than speak. Decide whether you want the dancers to recite, or whether you want a separate speaker or speaking group.

One final thought on the subject: It may seem that the ultimate goal would be to have the children use their own poems which they may have written just for themselves or, perhaps, in a creative writing class. Although they certainly should be encouraged to do so, I have found that they are often reluctant to share their own, intimate thoughts and feelings with others. If that is the case, I believe that we must respect their need for privacy.

STORIES

The Importance of Traditional Sources

Stories are as old as mankind, and storytelling has always been an important part of our existence. Every country and culture on earth possesses a rich store of folktales and legends; storytellers were greatly honored because they were the transmitters of a people's origins, history, and spiritual consciousness, as well as being teachers of the young and the old. Whereas proverbs and sayings taught the practical aspects of life, stories were the symbolic expressions of the deeper strata of human needs.

Our age substitutes the certitude of scientific and technological knowledge for the mystery of spirituality, and fairy- and folktales are no longer considered serious literature for children and adults. Certainly, a few stories are standard fare in nursery books and motion pictures, but it is doubtful that any pedagogical value is intended with their presentation. In his book *The Uses of Enchantment*, Bruno Bettelheim, the noted educator and therapist of disturbed children, says:

> For a story to truly hold the child's attention, it must entertain him and arouse his curiosity. But to enrich his life, it must stimulate his imagination; help him develop his intellect and clarify his emotions; be attuned to his anxieties and aspirations; give full recognition to his difficulties, while at the same time suggesting solutions to the problems which perturb him. In short, it must at one and the same time relate to all aspects of his personality— and this without ever belittling but, on the contrary, giving full credence to the child's predicaments, while simultaneously promoting confidence in himself and in his future.
>
> In all these and many other respects, of the entire "children's literature"— with rare exceptions—nothing can be as enriching and satisfying to the child

and adult alike as the folk fairy tales. True, on an overt level fairy tales teach little about the specific conditions of life in modern mass society; these tales were created long ago before it came into being. But more can be learned from them about the inner problems of human beings, and of the right solutions to their predicaments in any society than from any other type of story within a child's comprehension. Since the child at every moment of his life is exposed to the society in which he lives, he will certainly learn to cope with its conditions, provided his inner resources permit him to do so.[11]

Dramatization is a natural outgrowth of storytelling, and it too is an old tradition as widespread among the various cultures and peoples as the strictly oral presentation itself. Dramatizations occur in many forms; they may be stylized dances with masks and costumes, pantomimes, puppet shows, or more realistic plays with spoken dialogues. Although such plays are entertainment for an audience, many of them serve a pedagogical purpose as well. The person benefiting most, perhaps, is the actor himself, who must be deeply involved with the story in order to present it convincingly. I believe that the same is true for children as actors. By recreating a story on their own, they rise well above the superficial level of "acting out," since they must probe the story's meaning first and then identify with the specific problems it represents. In this manner they come to understand the fundamental concerns of mankind, which are always present in these folk stories. The creating of the dramatization is the process by which they learn. This process is much more important than the actual performance of the play, the quality of which can only be judged in relative terms anyway.

I would like once more to recount some childhood experiences, because they illustrate and complement the foregoing discussion.

I had a grandmother who was a living storybook. She had spent most of her life in the rural areas of Franconia, a region rich in local lore, all of which she had stored in her memory and which she shared generously with her many grandchildren. She also was able to recount Grimm's and Bechstein's fairy tales, the stories from *The Arabian Nights*, Andersen's tales, and legends traditional in other parts of the country. Later, when I had learned to read, I recognized many of the stories I had heard from her. My love for folktales is a result of her tireless storytelling.

Then there were the vacations I spent with other relatives in the Franconian Alps. Our frequent mushroom- and berry-hunting hikes in the forests with my uncle were like journeys into a remote and mysterious region of the earth. We explored spectacular rock formations, caves, and castle ruins, and through him we learned many legends about dwarves, fairies, princes, and princesses that once had populated those secret places.

When I was a little older, perhaps ten or eleven, I began telling and reading stories to my little brothers. Often, I would collect neighborhood friends and we would play "theatre," improvising dramatized versions of fairy tales and

---

[11] Bruno Bettelheim, *The Uses of Enchantment* (New York: Vintage, 1976), p. 5. Used by permission.

performing them (complete with background music from the piano) for the younger children. Other than sliding glass doors for a curtain, we had neither a stage nor fancy costumes, but we had our imaginations and we saw what we imagined.

My childhood experiences have been invaluable for me in my work with children because they have kept alive the child within me. I still feel connected to that preschool learning environment of mine and to the magic and mystery of my first encounters with folk- and fairy tales. I realize now that those spontaneous dramatizations I created in my early youth represented an intuitive working-through of the problems posed in the stories. The sum of those initial experiences laid the foundation—just as Bettelheim said they would—for my understanding of the universal problems mankind faces, and eventually for my learning how to deal with these problems in my own life. "Old-fashioned upbringings" may be old, but they are never out of fashion; "Old World values" may be old, but the world never really changes.

Telling or reading a story to the children is the first step toward dramatic play. Oral transmission not only allows but forces the listener to transform the word into a mental picture; thus, the listener confronts his own imagination rather than someone else's, which is the case when we actually see a play on stage or on screen or when the students memorize a given script.[12] The initial narration should be rendered in a lively and expressive way though naturally and without sounding artificial, so that the children will form their own mental image of the characters, places, and events. Once a story has come to life in the child's imagination, it is ready for the outside world of dramatic play.

Creative Play-Acting

Play-acting differs from formal acting in that the actors are involved in creating the play. Isabel B. Burger, a well-known authority on children's dramatics, states: "[Creative dramatics] is the expression of thought and feeling in the child's own terms, through action, the spoken word, or both."[13] Furthermore, the purpose of dramatic play is to help the children develop an awareness of themselves and others, rather than to prepare a play for an audience. (This is not to say that performances should never be planned. As a matter of fact, they are a natural outgrowth of the creative activities.)

Good play-acting does not happen spontaneously; like any other skill, it has to be developed in carefully sequenced steps. Acting is a combination of pantomime and the word. Body language is the more elemental of the two; it can be used by itself and does not need the word to be understood. Isabel Burger describes a series of developmental steps that she uses in her teaching approach.

---

[12] This is not to imply that movie or stage dramatization should be withheld from the children. But in order to exercise their own imagination, it is better to find stories that have not been professionally performed.

[13] Isabel B. Burger, *Creative Play Acting* (New York: Ronald Press, 1966), p. 6.

I have found them very helpful for folktale dramatizations within the context of Orff-Schulwerk.

Step I: Pantomime. She begins with "activity pantomime," in which the children act out familiar activities, first by themselves, later with a partner. She then progresses to "mood pantomime," in which the students are asked to express moods and feelings. The last step, "change-of-mood pantomime," leads directly into dramatization, because a change of mood is brought about by some dramatic event even in the shortest story. (One only need think of the nursery rhyme "Little Miss Muffet," in which the drama unfolds when the spider approaches and she flees in fear.) Ms. Burger stresses the importance of developing in children the ability to concentrate and to observe others, and of discussing their improvisations with them.

Step 2: Dialogue. Spoken dialogues are introduced with only single words or short phrases used in everyday life, such as "Come here!" or "Wait!" As with the pantomime exercises, the children are asked to "set the stage" by imagining a specific scene in which the word or phrase is spoken in a manner fitting the circumstances. Ms. Burger emphasizes to the children that they must "be" a character rather than "act" a character.

Step 3: The Play. Short plays based on stories are also approached through improvisation. There is no set dialogue. The scenes, or smaller sections thereof, are improvised, analyzed, and tried out again. Through this creative process of exploring, improving, and finally choosing good solutions, the play eventually takes shape and format, although it will never be cast into a rigid, unalterable frame regarding the details.

Although the music instructor has neither the time nor the skill to substitute for a teacher of dramatics, there is much to be learned from the sequence outlined here, because it reaffirms the Orff-Schulwerk philosophy in regard to a natural teaching and learning sequence.

The textual materials in Orff-Schulwerk are taken from traditional sources. As was pointed out in the beginning of this chapter, folklore is a means of learning fundamental truths universal to all mankind. The plots and characters in a folktale are symbolizations of humanity and the world, as it was and always will be. Thus, the process of analyzing oneself and finding an identity begins with the universal and constant and leads to the individual and changeable. Modern psychology approaches the process from the opposite end by starting with the individual and helping him or her to adjust to the existing world. I believe the former process, however, leads ultimately to a deeper understanding of self and others because it establishes a connection between a universally shared past and the present existence of the individual. The process used by psychologists takes place in a vacuum because it isolates the individual from a universally shared past. Without a sense for the deep-rootedness of his or her life, the individual has no hitching post to which to fasten his or her individuality. Consequently, he or she will remain trapped in the present with little inner strength to adjust to its ever-changing face.

Stories and Dramatic Activities for Different Age Groups

First Grade (Six- and Seven-Year-Olds). The rate of mental and emotional growth varies widely among children. For this reason it is not possible to establish absolute guidelines regarding the textual materials to be used and the dramatic abilities one may expect at specific age levels. The following suggestions, therefore, which are the result of my own observations and teaching experiences, must be regarded as adaptable.

First-graders have not yet outgrown early childhood altogether. Since they themselves are still small, all that is small appeals to them. Thus, the large living things of the real world are reduced in their playworld; they love their stuffed animals, dolls, and puppets, and these miniature characters act and behave in accordance with a six-year-old's experience in the world. They also delight in things not ordinarily alive, but which in the imaginary world take on life, such as the pancake that jumped out of the frying pan. The children have experienced feelings like happiness, sadness, fear, anger, and love, but they are not capable of analyzing the often complicated causes of their emotions. Their world is, or ought to be at any rate, still simple.

In the first year of school the child must make great social adjustments. This is especially true for the Orff-Schulwerk child, who must learn to interact and cooperate with others in the music room in many different ways. Musically, too, he is only at the threshold of development. Basic skills and knowledge emerge only slowly during the course of the year. When considering dramatic play, the music teacher must be mindful of these limitations and must not overtax the children's emotional development and social skills, or their musical abilities.

Nursery rhymes. The simplest form of activity pantomime is the representation of people performing everyday actions familiar to the children, and such actions have the best chance of being recreated in a true-to-life manner. Nursery rhymes such as "Little Jack Horner" or "Tommy Tittlemouse" lend themselves well to this purpose. Since only one character is involved in the rhymes, the whole class can experiment simultaneously. "Simple Simon" is an example of a series of actions and interactions, because the first two verses include a second character, the pieman. "Little Miss Muffet" allows for a simple change-of-mood pantomime. First, she enjoys her cereal ("curds and whey"); her mood changes to fright when the spider comes near. The rhyme can be developed into a mini-play, with actions leading up to the point of crisis and then to a definite conclusion. For example, she might fix her breakfast before sitting down to eat it, and after she has fled, the spider (if he actually appears in person) may sit down to eat her food (or whatever ending the children prefer). I beieve that this is the extent of play-acting a first-grader can handle successfully.

The music must likewise remain very simple. It should draw from the students' actual musical experiences. For instance, during the first year they become acquainted with simple rhythmic patterns and small percussion instruments. These can be incorporated in rhythmic ostinati to describe the spider's approach. Barred instruments are useful in creating little songs on the call or chant pitches. Special sound effects, such as a gong or maracas, may mark especially dramatic moments.

Stories. Because of their greater length and complexity, stories are best left in their narrational format, without dramatization. However, the storytelling can be enhanced by having the children add music. Tales such as "The Pancake," "The Gingerbread Man," or "The Little Red Hen and the Grain of Wheat" (a fable) afford plenty of opportunities for rhythmic as well as pitched ostinati to describe continuous movements like walking or rolling, and for other effects to illustrate a single sound or action, such as the sizzling fat in the pan or the pancake jumping. Stories like these often have repeated short dialogues which, after several tellings, the children know by heart and like to speak themselves. In this way dialogue is introduced into the narration. Since no acting is involved, full attention can be given to clear speaking and good voice inflection.

Storytelling with music need not be confined to the lower grades. In older age groups the students can take over the narration and the music will become more sophisticated, reflecting their level of competency.

Second Grade (Seven- to Eight-Year-Olds). During their second school year children seem to grow by leaps and bounds. They begin to develop self-awareness. Friendships spring up which go beyond a momentary teaming up with playmates. They acquire a keen interest in the world around them and become sharp and accurate observers. Their sense of right and wrong becomes well defined. They are full of enthusiasm and imagination and they enjoy learning. It is an ideal age to assimilate the morals of simple folktales and fables.

Now the pantomime exercises focus more and more on interactions with a partner and within small groups. Feelings and emotions begin to play an increasingly important role because they are present in every story. The children should be asked to think about and discuss in their small groups the characters they represent and the reasons for their actions. Roles may be traded around so that everyone has a chance to play a favorite character. The various groups can perform short scenes for each other, which are then critiqued in a friendly, positive way by the whole class with the teacher leading the discussions. In this way, the dramatization of a short story can be developed over a period of time. It is also possible to spread out the different scenes of a tale over the whole year. As the year proceeds the children gain better skills in all areas, and scenes created earlier can be improved upon during the review. Also, the children will not tire of the story if only a little bit at a time is practiced. The music may be created at the same time as a scene, or after the whole play has assumed its final shape. In any event, care should be taken to limit the number of different musical pieces in order to keep the play manageable. The use of recurring motifs or "themes" not only simplifies the creative process and saves time but also gives cohesiveness to the play. Sometimes a proverb expressing the moral of a story may form the prologue or epilogue to a play. Songs and short dances may be included also, but only if they are an organic part of the story. I know from experience how quickly a production can become too difficult for children to handle because too many different musical ideas have been injected. Music should enhance and intensify the play, but should never interfere with the simplicity and clarity of its presentation.

Text Sources. I have mentioned earlier that seven- and eight-year-olds find great delight in animal tales. These are either fables teaching moral lessons or "why- and how-stories" which explain the reasons for the character traits or physiognomy of certain animals. Such folktales can be found in every culture. They contain wit and humor which the children understand and appreciate. Before work on a story can begin, the teacher must decide which scenes are most important and should be acted out, and which ones should be narrated. (Narration is always part of the dramatizations even with the older children, because to put together a whole play, complete with dialogues, is beyond their skills.) Spoken dialogues usually don't work very well yet, and for this reason it is advisable to stay with pantomime. The story and the animal characters should be thoroughly discussed with the children. Since people cannot change their looks (unless elaborate costuming is used), the pantomimers must convey the physical essence of the animals they portray through movement. The typical action of a cricket, for example, might be seen in its quick, nervous movements and in its continous rubbing together of its forelegs to emit the characteristic chirping sound (which the actors might try also). Aside from the physical, there is the moral aspect to be considered. The animals are humans in disguise and depict certain familiar character traits. This, too, needs to come through in the pantomime. The children profit enormously from discussion, even though their pantomimes cannot yet be as perfect as the teacher might want them to be.

In primal folklore why- and how-stories focus not only on animals but also on natural phenomena. Among these, the moon with its changing phases and its dark spots has held the greatest fascination. Stories about the moon are full of primeval imagination, although they unfold in a realistic, factual manner without any moral meaning attached to them. These and similar tales have great appeal to second-graders, and they are easily portrayed through activity pantomime. Dramatization of other why- and how-stories dealing with less tangible phenomena, such as darkness or light, are best left to older age groups.

Nine- to Eleven-Year-Olds.   In my experience, the age between approximately nine and eleven is a prime time for creative dramatizations of folk- and fairy tales. The children's world is rapidly expanding as they learn about other peoples and other lands. Their power of observation and their ability to ponder what they see and hear gain in accuracy and depth. Although their emotions are by no means mature, they begin to understand them better, and this in turn helps them to perceive other people and peoples. Their verbal and musical skills are expanding, but at the same time they retain their powers of imagination and their love for the mysterious.

Although the alternation between narration of segments of the story and pantomime is still the fundamental approach to dramatizations, improvisation with dialogues are now practiced also in a step-by-step progression. The teacher should not be disappointed if these improvisations turn out poorly in the beginning. After all, it takes much experience to a) invent on the spot a dialogue which is clear and to the point, b) articulate smoothly and intelligibly, c) interpret the speech through inflections and modulations in the voice, and d) accompany the spoken word with gestures. The addition of dialogues leads into the realm of acting, a skill that takes many years to develop. There is a great danger at this point that the teacher will abandon creative dramatics in favor of the formal play, thinking that it might save time and trouble. If he or she does so, the children's creative growth will be stunted and distorted because adult ideas and standards will be forced upon them. We must always remember not to try to imitate Walt Disney or Broadway or encourage stardom in individuals, but rather to be concerned about all children and their natural maturing process. The adult-conceived world will have its turn in good time, but it has no place in the child's world.

Text sources. The growing maturity of the students allows for a wider choice of materials. Fables are still a favorite with the children, and teachers may want to choose them because they are short. But now they should include stories from many different cultures, as well as the classic Aesop fables, which are a product of Western literary culture. The introduction of fairy tales and legends teeming with witches, goblins, elves, and fairies opens up a new avenue to familiarize the children with the cultural background of the Western world. At the same time, simple tales like the why-stories are enjoyed by all age groups. What matters most is not the degree of sophistication in a given story but the degree of refinement with which a play is approached.

Many fairy and folktales are too lengthy for dramatization and need to be compressed into a manageable format. It is the teacher's responsibility to select the scenes that are vital to the unfolding drama and to arrange a narration that connects the scenes smoothly yet concisely. After a time and with some experience behind them, the children should have a hand in the process of molding a story into a play.

As the play gains in sophistication, so does the music. Depending on the story, songs and dances should be incorporated in appropriate places; different pentatonic modes can now be used to express various moods. In order to keep things simple and manageable, one single instrumental piece may serve as introduction and postlude, as well as an interlude between scenes. It is not necessary or possible to have the students create every single musical number. I frequently utilize pieces and dances that the class has already learned. Even songs can sometimes be supplied with a different text to suit the situation. The children's main task is to create "mood music" to describe an atmosphere or an emotion, and ostinati to accompany actions.

Within a given school year the teacher should work out with the class at least two very short dramatizations, such as fables, and one longer play. This is not an impossibility if he or she plans wisely. The plans should be laid out at the beginning of the year and coordinated with the musical and movement studies. In other words, instrumental pieces, songs, and dances should be selected with an eye to their usefulness in the planned dramatic activities.

Although a music teacher has few opportunites to introduce the youngsters to mankind's spiritual heritage, nevertheless, if he or she maintains a consistent and sequential teaching approach over a period of years, the effect will be seen in time. This is especially true if this particular approach is reinforced in other areas of learning and is supported by fellow teachers. Ultimately, such an approach will contribute decisively to the students' lasting interest in, and appreciation for, great literature, the beginnings of which are to be found in folklore.

SUMMARY

Since the beginning of time the word, whether spoken or written, has been the primary means of educating mankind to the art of living in a world which is at once fathomable and unfathomable. Although different ages and societies have produced their own, unique lores and literature, they all have concerned themselves with the same two fundamental questions: "What is the nature of reality?" and "Who are we?" In the past the answers inevitably were anchored in the spiritual.

Today the questions are still the same and they are asked by the young in every stage of their development, whether on the subconscious level in childhood or on the conscious level in young adulthood. The answers are, perhaps, more difficult to find than ever before. As we rely more and more on our scientific knowledge, we seem to come ever closer to the "nature of reality." At the same time, the answer to the second question becomes more elusive because we neither address it soon enough nor approach it in the right manner. To have an identity is to have self-knowledge. This knowledge is the basis for emotional stability and self-confidence. Every young child longs for an identity even if only subconsciously, and this longing must be addressed, the sooner the better. Self-knowledge begins with the understanding of universal truths and values which, in my opinion, have their roots in the spiritual. Chidren enter the realm of universal truth through the symbolic language of primal lore and folklore.

From proverbs and sayings, however, children learn to become skilled and competent in the art of day-to-day living. To be sure, very few of us need to know when to "sow peas and beans"[14] nor do we speculate on future profits from hatching eggs.[15] But as with the fairy tales, beneath the overt meanings more fundamental advice lays hidden. In a deeper sense we are lectured gently on values, attitudes, and deportment, on a general modus vivendi which allows us to become competent at the things we must do. These rules are simple and are repeated in many disguises: Develop and use your mind, your senses, and

---

[14] "Sow peas and beans in the wane of the moon, Who soweth them sooner, he soweth too soon," (Orff-Schulwerk V).

[15] "Count not your chickens till they are hatched," (Orff-Schulwerk I).

your sensitivity; Don't waste your life or that of others; Be useful; Do what you do as best as you can; Be content.

Lessons like these are much more readily accepted and absorbed by children if expressed metaphorically rather than by means of a list of do's and don'ts. The process of creating a musical form or of dramatizing a proverb will imprint its meaning on the students far more effectively.

Finally, acquainting our young students with the manner in which people of the past expressed themselves may aid them in their own verbal and writing skills, both of which are highly important in our society. A certain skill with words, a glibness for coining phrases (which I sometimes encounter even among Schulwerk teachers!) is not good enough, because in the end nothing can mask the shallowness hidden beneath such fluency. Here then, we also can learn from our forefathers and, for that matter, from many "less advanced" cultures which somehow mastered the discipline of expressing the essential and important in a succinct manner.

Thus, in Orff-Schulwerk the choice of texts is as important as the choice of musical materials. Only if we use the right words can we hope to fulfill the purpose its creator had in mind.

CONCLUSION

During the many years of my involvement in Orff-Schulwerk teacher training, the one question most often asked of me has been: "How can I teach my children everything they need to know when I see them only once or twice a week?" The same question will be raised by many of my readers, because it will be obvious to them that the teaching steps and learning experiences outlined in this book presuppose a rather intensive music program, which most school administrations do not support today. Moreover, many music teachers are so used to taking the backseat in education that they accept this situation without questioning. On the other hand, however, why have they chosen to be music teachers? Because they know how much music enriches their own lives, and they want their students' lives to be enriched as well.

What I am talking about is commitment, the first and foremost prerequisite for a teacher. Anyone who teaches music to children has this commitment. Anyone who continually searches for better ways to teach and who is ever willing to learn more has this commitment. Anyone who has read this book and taken courses in Orff-Schulwerk teacher training has this commitment. And only the committed can bring about change because, ultimately, only the committed have the competence against which the forces of the status quo cannot stand.

Although Orff-Schulwerk is one of the most enjoyable ways to teach music, it is probably one of the most difficult as well. This is so because we constantly learn and create as we teach our children. But creativity in teaching calls for discipline in organization and planning. In closing, I would like to share with my readers just a few ideas which may help them establish a successful Orff-Schulwerk program.

- Be a competent teacher who knows his or her field. This means you must never stop learning and discovering.

- Be consistent and sequential in your teaching. (Since this book was all about sequence, I will say no more.)
- Have confidence in yourself and your own teaching style. Every person is different, and what works well for one does not necessarily work well for someone else. Stay away from "recipes." Your teaching ideas are born within yourself and take shape through the response of the class. Sometimes your ideas won't work, but that is part of *your* learning experience. A teacher need not be perfect. You will appear much more human to the children if you make a mistake once in a while, too.
- Stay flexible. Sometimes a lesson will turn in a direction different from what you had planned; if the direction is worth pursuing, you should pursue it.
- Reevaluate your teaching frequently. If a class has not gone well and the children had problems following, examine your teaching process to find whether you left out a step in a particular sequence.
- Take your time in building a program in your school, step by step. Do not try to convert all grades to Orff-Schulwerk at once; a comprehensive program is best built from the bottom up. Start the first year with, perhaps, grades 1 and 2. In the second year, as these children advance to the next level, a new first grade is added. Proceed in this way until all grade levels you teach are involved. It will take several years to build a program, but the advantage is that you can build your curriculum organically on what you taught the previous year. In this way, you have the best chances to design a successful sequence and to get some teaching experience. The curriculum will have to be adjusted and corrected more than once before you will be satisfied.
- Your curriculum is the sequence itself and it should be designed broadly. How you teach the various developmental steps need not stay the same all the time; here is where your creativity should come into play.
- The curriculum should address itself to the various aspects of Orff-Schulwerk, such as movement, rhythm, melody, accompaniment (drones, or preharmony, if you will), and recorder. Do not set your goals too high. It is easier to add than to cut back.

Nothing more needs to be added at this point except to remind the reader that it takes many years of experience to master the craft of teaching.

Schulwerk, of course, does not end with pentatonic. It is only the beginning of a musical journey which becomes more exciting as it continues into the diatonic modes and elemental harmony. Along the way, and to an increasing extent, the music teacher will find him- or herself on familiar ground but at the same time will make many new and interesting discoveries. What music instructor would want anything less? Teaching Orff-Schulwerk is a theme with endless variations, and this is the challenge as well as the glory of being an Orff-Schulwerk teacher.

BIBLIOGRAPHY

AMERICAN ORFF-SCHULWERK ASSOCIATION. *Orff Re-Echoes*. Isabel McNeill Carley, editor. Book I (c) 1977, Book II (c) 1985.

BETTELHEIM, BRUNO. *The Uses of Enchantment: The Meaning and Importance of Fairy Tales*. New York: Vintage, 1976.

BOATRIGHT, HOWARD. *Introduction to the Theory of Music*. New York: W.W. Norton, 1956.

BÖHME, FRANZ MAGNUS. *Deutsches Kinderlied und Kinderspiel*. Leipzig: Breitkopf & Härtel, 1897. Reprint Nendeln, Liechtenstein: Kraus Reprint, 1967.

BRADFORD, LOUISE LARKINS. *Sing It Yourself: 220 Pentatonic American Folksongs*. Van Nuys, Cal.: Alfred, 1978.

BROCKLEHURST, BRIAN. *Pentatonic Songbook*. London: Schott & Co., h.d.

BROWN PATRICIA. *The Mountain Dulcimer*. Woodshole, Mass.: 1979.

BURGER, ISABEL B. *Creative Play Acting*. New York: Ronald Press, 1966.

CARLEY, ISABEL MCNEILL. *Recorder Improvisation and Technique: A Teacher's Workbook*, Book 1. Brasstown, N.C.: Brasstown Press, 1976.

CHEIFETZ, DANIEL. *Theater in My Head*. Boston: Little, Brown, 1971.

COOPER, GROSVENOR W., and LEONARD B. MEYER. *The Rhythmic Structure of Music*. Chicago: University of Chicago Press, 1960.

COURLANDER, HAROLD. *Negro Songs from Alabama*. Published through a Grant by the Wenner-Gren Foundation for Anthropological Research. New York, 1960.

CRAWFORD, RUTH SEEGER. *American Folksongs for Children*. Garden City, N.Y.: Doubleday, 1948.

CRAWFORD, RUTH SEEGER. *Animal Folksongs*. Garden City, N.Y.: Doubleday, 1950.

CRAWFORD, RUTH SEEGER. *American Folksongs for Christmas*. Garden City, N.Y.: Doubleday, 1953.

EMRICH, DUNCAN. *American Folk Poetry: An Anthology*. Boston: Little, Brown, 1974.

EMRICH, DUNCAN. *Folklore on the American Land*. Boston: Little, Brown, 1972.

FOWKE, EDITH. *Sally Go Round the Sun: 300 Children's Songs, Rhymes and Games*. Garden City, N.Y.: Doubleday, 1969.

GERHEUSER, FRIEDRUN. "Gunild Keetman's Contribution to the Schulwerk." In *Orff Re-Echoes*, Book I p. 10, American Orff-Schulwerk Association, 1977.

GERSDORF, LILO. *Carl Orff in Selbstzeugnissen und Bilddokumenten*. Hamburg: Rowohlt, 1981.

GIESBERT, FRANZ J. *Method for the Treble Recorder*. Mainz: B. Schott's Söhne, 1957.

HALL, DOREEN, ARNOLD WALTER. *Orff-Schulwerk Music for Children*. Vol. I, Pentatonic. English (Canadian) adaptation. Mainz: B. Schott's Söhne, 1956.

HALL, DOREEN. *Teacher's Manual*. Mainz: B. Schott's Söhne, 1960.

JONES, BESSIE, and BESS LOMAX HAWES. *Step It Down*. New York: Harper & Row, 1972.

KEETMAN, GUNILD. *Elementaria. First acquaintance with Orff-Schulwerk*. Translated by Margaret Murray. London: Schott, 1974.

KEETMAN, GUNILD. *Erstes Spiel am Xylophon*. Mainz: B. Schott's Söhne, 1969.

KEETMAN, GUNILD. *Spielbuch für Xylophon*, Book I. Mainz: B. Schott's Söhne, 1965; Book II, 1966; Book III, 1966.

KEETMAN, GUNILD. *Spielstücke für Blockflöten und kleines Schlagwerk*, Book I. Mainz: B. Schott's Söhne, 1952.

KELLER WILHELM. *Introduction to Music for Children*. Translated by Susan Kennedy. Mainz: Schott's Söhne, 1974.

KENNEDY, MAUREEN. *Circle Round the Zero. Play Chants and Singing Games of City Children*. St. Louis: MagnaMusic-Baton, 1975.

LANDECK, BEATRICE. *Songs to Grow On*. New York: Edward B. Marks Music, 1960.

LEWALTER, JOHANN. *Deutsches Kinderlied und Kinderspiel*. Kassel: Carl Victor, 1911.

LEWIS, RICHARD. *Miracles*. New York: Simon & Schuster, 1966.

LIESS, ANDREAS. *Carl Orff*. Translated by Adelheid and Herbert Parkin. London: Calder and Boyars Limited, 1966.

LOMAX, ALAN. *The Folksongs of North America*. Garden City, N.Y.: Doubleday, 1960.

LOMAX, JOHN A. and ALAN LOMAX. *Our Singing Country*. New York: MacMillan, 1941.

MURRAY, MARGARET. *Orff-Schulwerk, Music for Children*. Volume I, Pentatonic. English adaptation. London: Schott & Co., Ltd., n.d.

NETTL, BRUNO. *Folk and Traditional Music of the Western Continents*. Englewood Cliffs, N.J.: Prentice Hall, 1965, 1973, 1989.

OPIE, IONA and PETER. *The Oxford Book of Nursery Rhymes*. London: Oxford University Press, 1955. Reprinted with corrections 1957, 1960, 1963.

OPIE, IONA and PETER. *The Lore and Language of Schoolchildren*. London: Oxford University Press, 1959.

ORFF, CARL, and GUNILD KEETMAN. *Orff-Schulwerk, Musik für Kinder*. Band I, Im Fünftonraum. Mainz: B. Schott's Söhne, 1950.

ORFF, CARL, and GUNILD KEETMAN. *Orff-Schulwerk, Music for Children*. Volume I, Pentatonic. English version by Margaret Murray. London: Schott & Co., Ltd. (n.d.)

ORFF, CARL, and GUNILD KEETMAN. *Orff-Schulwerk, Music for Children*. Volume I, Pentatonic. English (Canadian) adaptation by Doreen Hall and Arnold Walter. Mainz: B. Schott's Söhne, 1956.

ORFF, CARL, and GUNILD KEETMAN. *Paralipomena.* Mainz: Schott's Söhne, 1977.

ORFF, CARL. *Carl Orff und sein Werk, Dokumentation; III Schulwerk, Elementare Musik* (''Documentaria''). Tutzing: 1956.

ORFF-INSTITUT. *Year-Book 1962.* Edited by Werner Thomas and Willibald Götze. English translation by Richard Holburn and Anton Flossmann. Mainz: B. Schott's Söhne, 1963.

ORFF-INSTITUT. *Jahrbuch 1963.* Edited by Werner Thomas and Willibald Götze. Mainz: B. Schott's Söhne, 1964.

ORFF-INSTITUT. *Jahrbuch III.* Edited by Werner Thomas and Willibald Götze. Mainz: B. Schott's Söhne, 1969.

PETER, HILDEMARIE. *The Recorder Its Traditions and Its Tasks.* Berlin-Lichterfelde: Robert Lineau, 1953 and 1958. English translation by Stanley Godman. Berlin-Lichterfelde: Robert Lienau, 1953.

PISTON, WALTER. *Harmony.* 4th edition. Revised and expanded by Mark DeVoto. New York: W.W. Norton, 1978.

REESE, GUSTAVE. *Music in the Middle Ages.* New York: W.W. Norton, 1940.

REGNER, HERMANN, Coordinator. *Music for Children. Orff-Schulwerk American Edition. Volume 1. Pre-School.* n.p.: Schott Music Corporation, 1982.

REGNER, HERMANN, Coordinator. *Music for Children. Orff-Schulwerk American Edition, Volume 2. Primary.* n.p.: Schott Music Corporation, 1977.

REGNER, HERMANN, Coordinator. *Music for Children. Orff-Schulwerk American Edition. Volume 3, Upper Elementary.* n.p.: Schott Music Corporation, 1980.

SACHS, CURT. *Our Musical Heritage.* Reprint edition: Westport, Conn.: Greenwood, 1978.

SACHS, CURT. *The Wellsprings of Music.* Edited by Jaap Kunst. The Hague: Martinus Nijhoff, 1962. Reprint edition: New York: Da Capo, n.d.

SACHS, CURT. *The History of Musical Instruments.* New York, London: W.W. Norton, 1940.

SACHS, CURT. *Real-Lexikon der Musikinstrumente.* New York: Dover, 1964.

SAYRE, GWENDA. *Creative Miming.* London: Herbert Jenkins, 1959.

SCHÄFER, W. E., K. H. RUPPEL, GUSTAV RUDOLF SELLNER, and WERNER THOMAS. *Carl Orff. Ein Bericht in Wort und Bild.* 2nd expanded edition. Mainz: B. Schott's Söhne, 1960.

SCARBOROUGH, DOROTHY. *On the Trail of Negro Folksongs.* Cambridge: Harvard University Press, 1925.

SEUSS, DR. *One Fish, Two Fish.* New York: Random House, 1960.

SHARP, CECIL J. *English Folksongs from the Southern Appalachians.* London: Oxford University Press, 1932.

STEVENSON, BURTON E., EDITOR. *The Home Book of Proverbs, Maxims and Familiar Phrases.* New York: MacMillan, 1948.

SMITH, W. G., and JANET HESELTINE. *The Oxford Book of English Proverbs.* 2nd edition. London: Oxford University Press, 1948.

STRINGHAM, MARY. *Orff-Schulwerk, Background and Commentary.* Articles from German and Austrian Music Journals. Collected and translated by Mary Stringham. St. Louis: MagnaMusic-Baton, 1976.

THOMAS, WERNER. *Musica Poetica. Gestalt und Funktion des Orff-Schulwerks.* Tutzing: Hans Schneider, 1977.

THOMAS, WERNER, "Wege und Stufen im Orff-Schulwerk." In *Carl Orff. Ein Bericht in Wort und Bild*, 2nd expanded edition, p. 30. Mainz: B. Schott's Söhne, 1960.

THOMAS, WERNER, "Orff's Schulwerk." In *Orff Re-Echoes*, Book 1, p. 3. American Orff-Schulwerk Association, 1977.

TOWNSEND, JOHN ROWE. *Written for Children: An Outline for English-Language Children's Literature*. Philadelphia: J.B. Lippincott, 1965.

WALTER, ARNOLD. "The Orff-Schulwerk in American Education." In *Orff Re-Echoes*, Book 1, p. 14. American Orff-Schulwerk Association, 1977.

WARNER, BRIGITTE. "The Development of Canon in Orff-Schulwerk." In *Orff Re-Echoes*, Book 2, p. 77. American Orff-Schulwerk Association, 1985.

WOLLITZ, KENNETH. *The Recorder Book*. New York: Knopf, 1982.

ADDITIONAL TEXT SOURCES FOR CHAPTER 10

This list of books may be helpful to the teacher who is looking for suitable stories and poetry for creative play-acting and dance improvisation. The list is by no means complete; rather, it is meant as a point of departure for the teacher to do his or her own research into the great wealth of folktales and myths from all parts of the world.

ARKHURST, JOYCE COOPER. *The Adventures of Spider*, and *More Adventures of Spider*. New York: Scholastic, 1974.

BELTING, NATALIA. *The Moon is a Crystal Ball: Unfamiliar Legends of the Stars*. New York: Bobbs-Merrill, 1952.

BARING-GOULD, WILLIAM S. and CECIL. *The Annotated Mother Goose*. New York: World Publishing Company, 1967.

BAYLOR, BYRD and PETER PARNELL. *Desert Voices*. New York: Scribner's, 1981.

CURTIS, NATALY, EDITOR. *Songs and Legends of the American Indians*. New York: Dover, 1968.

DORSON, RICHARD M., GENERAL EDITOR. *Folktales of the World. Folktales of Chile. Folktales of China. Folktales of England. Folktales of France. Folktales of Germany. Folktales of Greece. Folktales of Hungary. Folktales of Ireland. Folktales of Israel. Folktales of Japan. Folktales of Mexico. Folktales of Norway*. Chicago and London: University of Chicago Press.

DUNCAN, LOIS. *From Spring to Spring*. Philadelphia: Westminster, 1982.

FELDMAN, SUSAN. *African Myths and Tales*. New York: Dell, 1963.

GRIMM, JACOB and WILHELM. *Grimm's Fairy Tales*. New York: Pantheon, 1944. Reprint, revised and corrected: New York: Random House, 1972.

GRINNELL, GEORGE. *The Story of a Prairie People*. Reprint edition: University of Nebraska Press, 1962.

HACKETT, J. W. *Haiku Poetry*. Volume IV. Tokyo: Japan Publications, 1968.

HARLEY, REV. TIMOTHY. *Moon Lore*. Reprint edition. Boston: Charles River, 1976.

HAYES, JOE. *Coyote: Native American Folklore*. Santa Fe: Mariposa, 1983.

JACOBS, JOSEPH. *Celtic Fairy Tales*. New York: Dover, 1968.

KAVANAUGH, JAMES. *Walk Easy on the Earth*. New York: E.P. Dutton, 1979; Toronto and Vancouver: Clark, Irwin & Company Limited, 1979.

KOMAROFF, KATHERINE. *Sky Gods: The Sun and Moon in Art and Myth*. New York: Universe Books, 1974. (Myths of the world: Indian, Eskimo, Egyptian, North American Indian, Aztec, Japanese, African, Inca, Chinese.)

LEACH, MARIA. *How the People Sang the Mountain Up: How and Why Stories*. New York: Viking, 1967.

O'DELL, SCOTT. *Sing Down the Moon*. New York: Dell, 1970.

PAXTON, TOM. *Aesop's Fables Retold in Verse*. New York: William Marrow, 1988.

SANDBURG, CARL. *Rainbows Are Made*. San Diego: Harcourt Brace Jovanovich, 1982.

WOLKSTEIN, DIANE. *The Magic Orange Tree and Other Haitian Folktales*. New York: Knopf, 1978.

APPENDIX

Mole in the Ground
(Do-mode on C)

Arr. by B. Warner

wish I was a   mole   in the ground,   I

From Crawford Seeger, *Animal Folksongs*

The Farmyard

Arr. by B. Warner

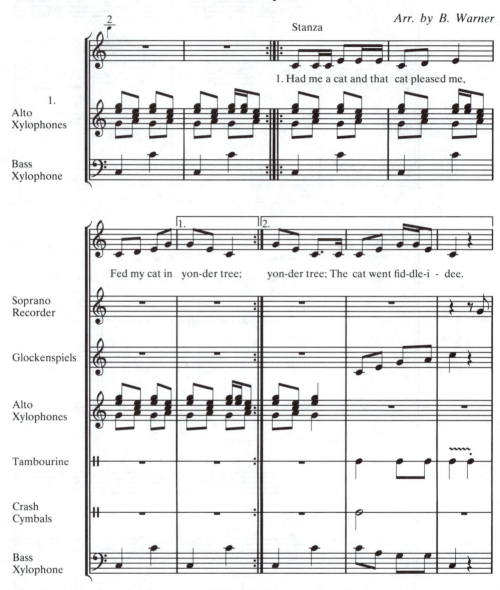

From Sharp, *English Folksongs from the Southern Appalachians*

Stanza

2. Had me a dog and the dog pleased me,

Alto
Xylophones

Bass
Xylophone

Fed   my   dog   in   yon - der   tree.   yon - der   tree.

Alto
Xylophones

Bass
Xylophone

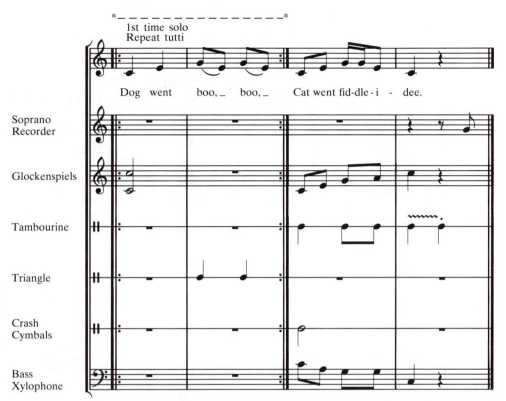

1st time solo
Repeat tutti

Dog went boo,_ boo,_ Cat went fid-dle-i - dee.

Soprano
Recorder

Glockenspiels

Tambourine

Triangle

Crash
Cymbals

Bass
Xylophone

Dance attacca

I Heard the Angels Singing
(Do-mode on F)

Arr. by B. Warner

Soprano
Glockenspiel

Soprano
Metallophone

Alto
Metallophone

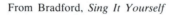

One morn - ing   soon,___   One morn - ing   soon,___

Soprano
Glockenspiel

Soprano
Metallophone

Alto
Metallophone

Cello or
Bass Metallophone

From Bradford, *Sing It Yourself*

Run, Chillen, Run!
(Do-mode on C)

Arr. By B. Warner

From Crawford Seeger, *American Folksongs for Children*

Stanza

This child fan, and this child flew, This child lost his

SX

AX

BX

Sun - day shoe! Run, chil-len run, the pat-ter roll-er catch you,

SX

AX

WB

BX

run, chil-len run,   it's   al - most   day!

The Old Sow
(Do-mode on F)

Arr. by B. Warner

From Bradford, *Sing It Yourself*

My Paddle's Keen and Bright
(La-mode on D)

Arr. by B. Warner

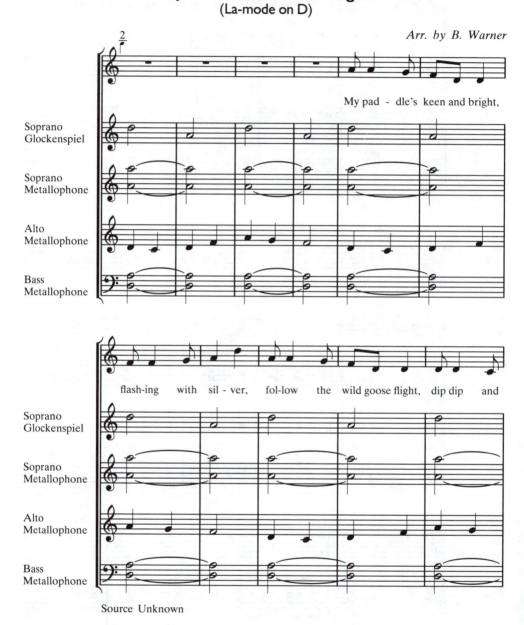

My pad - dle's keen and bright,

flash-ing   with   sil - ver,   fol-low   the   wild goose flight,   dip dip   and

Soprano Glockenspiel

Soprano Metallophone

Alto Metallophone

Bass Metallophone

Source Unknown

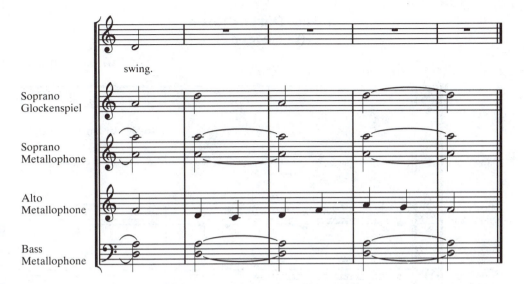

Rosie, Darling Rosie
(La-mode on E)

Arr. by B. Warner

From Bradford, *Sing It Yourself*

Lord Thomas and Fair Ellender
(La-mode on E)

Arr. by B. Warner

Come rid-dle us all, our

dear, good moth-er, come rid-dle us all — as one, _____ Wheth-er

I shall mar-ry fair El - len-der, — or bring the brown — girl

From Sharp, *English Folksongs of the Southern Appalachians*

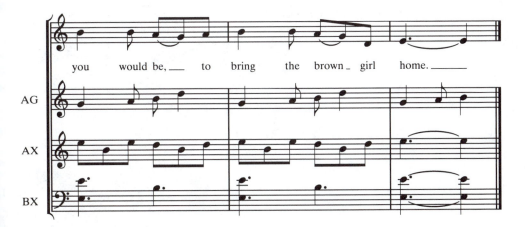

Goin' roun' the Mountain
(La-mode on E)

Arr. by B. Warner

Glockenspiels

Hand Drum

Alto and/or
Bass Xylophone

Goin' roun' the moun-tain   two by   two, _   Goin' roun' the moun-tain

two   by   two, __   Goin' roun'   the   moun-tain

From Bradford, *Sing It Yourself*

Go to Sleep
(La-mode on D)

Arr. by B. Warner

Go   to sleep,   Go_to sleep - y,

Go   to sleep-y lit-tle   ba   -   by.   Hush li'l ba - by and

Soprano
Metallophone

Alto
Metallophone

Bass
Metallophone

From Library of Congress, AAFS 1324, A2 and A3

don't you cry, _ Go to sleep-y lit-tle ba - by.

Soprano
Metallophone

Alto
Metallophone

Bass
Metallophone

Soprano
Metallophone

Alto
Metallophone

The Tree in the Wood

(originally So-mode on C, but arranged as Do-mode on F)

Arr. by B. Warner

From Sharp, *English Folksongs from the Southern Appalachians*

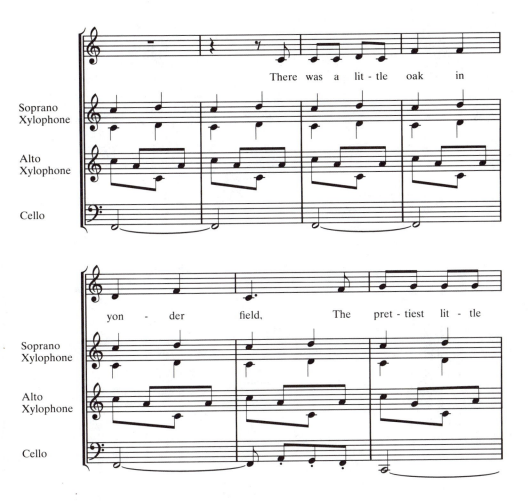

Soprano
Xylophone

Alto
Xylophone

Cello

There was a lit - tle oak in

Soprano
Xylophone

Alto
Xylophone

Cello

yon - der field, The pret - tiest lit - tle

*The section between the crosses (+ - - - - +) becomes longer with every verse.

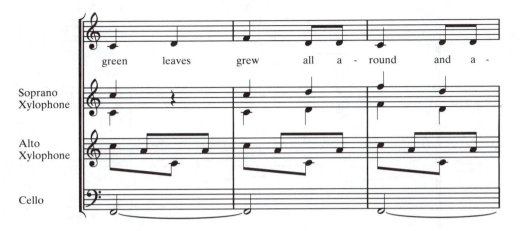

green leaves grew all a - round and a -

Soprano
Xylophone

Alto
Xylophone

Cello

round, and the green leaves grew all a -

Soprano
Xylophone

Alto
Xylophone

Cello

INDEX

SONGS AND VERSES